JIGSAW PUZZLES

JIGSAW PUZZLES

An Illustrated History and Price Guide

ANNE D. WILLIAMS

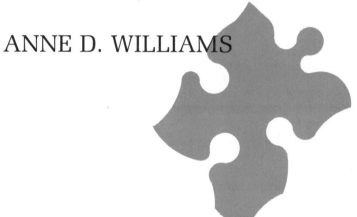

Photographs by
Harry L. Rinker

Wallace-Homestead Book Company
Radnor, Pennsylvania

Published in Radnor, Pennsylvania by Wallace-Homestead,
a division of Chilton Book Company

Designed by Anthony Jacobson

Manufactured in the United States of America

Front Cover: clockwise from top, *Clown with Dog* (see Fig. 8-30);
Tally-Ho Scroll Puzzle (Fig. 12-12); *Fields* (Fig. 13-15);
Baby Ruth (Fig. 14-17); *A Dream* (Fig. 10-32). Back Cover: Photograph
for "Author puzzle" by Allan Detrich.

Prices listed are intended only as guidelines. They do not represent
an offer to buy or to sell. Neither the author nor the publisher
assumes any liability for losses related to the use of prices
in this book.

The author is engaged in continuing research on the history of jigsaw
puzzles and their makers, and welcomes additions, corrections, and
comments from readers. Please send them to: Anne D. Williams, Dept.
of Economics, Bates College, Lewiston, ME 04240.

Library of Congress Cataloging in Publication Data
Williams, Anne D. (Anne Douglas), 1943–
    Jigsaw puzzles : an illustrated history and price guide / Anne D.
Williams ; photographs by Harry L. Rinker.
        p. cm.
    Includes bibliographical references and indexes.
    ISBN 0-87069-537-1
    1. Jigsaw puzzles—History. I. Title.
GV1507.J5W55   1990
793.73—dc20   89-51558
                                                    CIP

1 2 3 4 5 6 7 8 9 0   9 8 7 6 5 4 3 2 1 0

For my mother,
Frances McLean Williams

CONTENTS

CONTENTS

CONTENTS

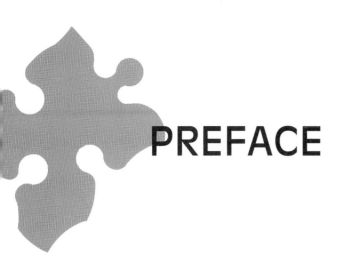

PREFACE

MY FASCINATION with jigsaw puzzles is rooted in my early experiences. Puzzles were both solitary challenges and family affairs. No holiday gathering was complete without a wooden puzzle spread out on the cardtable for everyone to work on (or at least kibitz). Nor were the festivities really over until days later, when the last piece had been plucked from its hiding place in the rug and triumphantly fitted into place.

Although the scarcity of new wooden puzzles in the 1960s put a temporary crimp in this family tradition, I eventually learned that cutting puzzles with a jigsaw was an accessible craft. After making a few of my own, I began to appreciate the skill, imagination, and patience of the earlier cutters. And with the discovery that old puzzles turn up at quite reasonable prices in flea markets, I soon was hooked as a collector.

But then there was the problem of identifying my finds. There was no reference work on the American jigsaw puzzle. Ten years ago, when I knew of several dozen American puzzle manufacturers, I thought it would be useful to compile a comprehensive history of all such companies. Today, with a list of about fifteen hundred different puzzle brands, I have realized that the task may never end. For example, the puzzle craze of the Great Depression spawned hundreds, if not thousands, of puzzle companies of all sizes. I have been fortunate to be able to interview some individuals who were in the puzzle business at that time. But records and memories of many of the smaller firms are long gone; it will be difficult to find all the pieces to complete this historical puzzle.

This book is just a first step in writing down the history of American jigsaw puzzles and their makers. There are surely many omissions that need to be rectified. I would be most grateful for any additional information that readers can supply. Comments should be sent to: Anne D. Williams, Department of Economics, Bates College, Lewiston, ME 04240.

ACKNOWLEDGMENTS

I HAVE ALREADY had a great deal of help from other collectors, dealers, scholars, and puzzle makers. Although it is impossible to list them all, I would like to acknowledge some of the most important contributions.

First, I would like to thank the people associated with the puzzle business who have helped me delve into unpublished history by responding to my questions and supplying copies of old company catalogs and other records. Jody Hollister Colby first introduced me to the craft of puzzle cutting in the mid-1970s. Since then the individuals listed below have been specially helpful with my research on these manufacturers:

Marjorie Bouvé: Catherine L. Allen
Milton Bradley Co.: George Merritt's office, James O'Connor
James Browning: Louise Barnard, J. S. Guiles
Consolidated Paper Box Co.: Chris McCann
E. E. Fairchild: Betty and Bill Barnard
Alden L. Fretts: Lora N. Willey
Hallmark Cards, Inc.: Sally Hopkins, John Robrock
G. J. Hayter: Gerald J. Hayter, Gordon Hayter
C. I. Hood & Co.: Walter Hickey
Jaymar Specialty Co., Inc.: Ralph Kaufman

Charles P.B. Jefferys: William H. Jefferys, Jr.
Madmar Quality Co.: Miles Bickelhaupt
Par Puzzles Ltd.: the late Frank Ware
Parker Brothers Inc.: June Butcher, John J. Fox, Angie Gagnon, Eva Gagnon, Philip Orbanes
Saalfield Publishing Co.: Ann Mack
Silent Teacher: Patricia Eldredge
Springbok Editions: Robert and Katie Lewin
J. K. Straus Products Corp.: Al Berger, Matteo Luberto, Amy Straus
Carroll A. Towne: Carroll A. Towne
Tuco Work Shops: Dick Bickford, Don Scott, Roger Slattery
Viking Manufacturing Co.: Steve Guardiano
Warren Paper Products: Michael Cassidy, Warren Eggleston, Jan Shook
Western Publishing Co.: Kim McLynn, John Zierten.

Many more have supplied information that cannot fit into this book but must wait for a subsequent volume. And librarians all over the country have helped to track down obscure facts about local companies.

I have been privileged to study jigsaw puzzles from a number of large collections, including those of: the American Antiquarian Society, Lee and Stuart Bauer, Lillian Colodny, the Essex Institute, Sue

Gustafson, Linda Hannas, Kevin Holmes, David Howland, Gay Hoyt and Larry Barbour, the Library of Congress, Chris McCann, Paul Noll, Susan Nicholson, Dick Oinonen, Old Sturbridge Village, Jim Rohacs, Chuck Small, and the Smithsonian Institution. Dozens of other collectors have also kindly shared information about their puzzles. And many individuals, from close relatives to total strangers, have generously donated puzzles and other research materials that have added to my knowledge of puzzle history. I have learned much from the members of the American Game Collectors Association, as well as from several dealers who have taken a special interest in helping to build my collection. The listing of companies in the Index to American Puzzle Manufacturers owes much to all these individuals.

I owe a special debt to several other important collectors who graciously allowed their puzzles to be illustrated in this book. The collection of Herbert and Jacqueline Siegel, with its strength in nineteenth century children's puzzles, was particularly important. Other puzzles are shown from the collections of Connie Moore, John Seymour, and Gus and Marty Trowbridge. I am grateful to Wallace-Homestead Book Company for allowing me to use several illustrations from Lee Dennis's book, *Warman's Antique American Games* (Warman Publishing Co. Inc., 1986). I also wish to thank Allan Detrich for permission to use two of his slides. Finally, several contemporary puzzle manufacturers generously supplied photographic materials for Chapter 17, including: F. A. Bourke Inc., Elms Inc., FryeWeaver Puzzles, J. S. Guiles, Capt. G. G. Ely Kirk, Jaymar Specialty Co., Steve Malavolta, Random House, and Stave Puzzles Inc. The rest of the puzzles shown are all from the collections of either Harry L. Rinker or myself.

The editors at Wallace-Homestead require a separate paragraph of thanks. Consulting Editor Harry L. Rinker first encouraged me to write a book about puzzles in 1984. Later, his sharp insights have helped me deal with all aspects of this project, from broad questions to small details. Harry's zest, in his role as official photographer for the book, meant that we shot far more than the required number of photographs. In fact, he has thrown himself into this project with so much eagerness that in under a year he has amassed an excellent collection of his own, with emphasis on advertising, personality, and other die-cut puzzles. As a result, just over 25 percent of the puzzles pictured here are from his collection.

Finally, I would like to thank the friends who have been enthusiastic and supportive fellow travelers on this puzzling voyage of mine. I am specially grateful to: the long-time friends who accompanied me on so many quests for information and puzzles over the last decade; others who helped assemble puzzles when deadlines loomed; the academic colleagues who dug into their own fields to answer my questions about history, technology, and art; and the curators of the Bates College Museum of Art who proposed the 1988 exhibit, *Pieces in Place: Two Hundred Years of Jigsaw Puzzles*, and helped to make it a success.

My family has aided and abetted me from the start. From Libby and James on up to Great-Aunt Elsie, all have shared my interest and turned up new puzzles to study. I owe the largest debt to my mother, Frances McLean Williams, who has shared my passion for puzzles and has made the greatest contributions to my collection. Although failing eyesight ended her role as an active co-collector, she has since listened with enthusiasm and interest to my tales of the puzzle world. She and my late father, Elwood Williams III, have been my greatest supporters.

JIGSAW PUZZLES

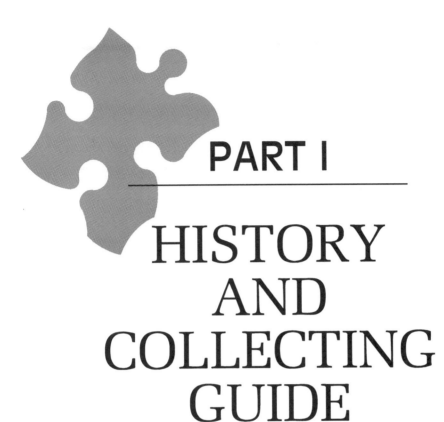

PART I

HISTORY AND COLLECTING GUIDE

1

JIGSAW PUZZLES:
A BRIEF HISTORY

WHAT IS THE FASCINATION of a jigsaw puzzle? Puzzles are an important part of childhood, from the preschooler's simple five-piece Mickey Mouse puzzle to the older child's map of the United States cut into fifty pieces. But then it ends—or does it? For many the intrigue of the puzzle continues into adulthood. Why?

The struggle to bring order and beauty out of the chaos of hundreds of disconnected pieces motivates virtually all puzzlers. Global problems like international politics or domestic ones like household budgeting may offer more of a challenge; however, puzzles have the advantage that they can be solved, admired, and then put back in the box on the owner's terms. Puzzling is a flexible sport, amenable to both solitary pursuit and social activity. Groups of puzzlers can be as cooperative or competitive as they like, either helping each other find pieces or racing to see who can put their sections together fastest.

Collectors, of course, view puzzles not just as an enjoyable activity, but as a window on the past. Puzzles over the last two centuries have depicted current events, literature, fashion, entertainment, and daily life. Revolutions and slavery, the creation and space travel, movies and comic strips, work and sports, Rembrandt and Rockwell, sarsaparilla and soap—all of these subjects decorate jigsaw puzzles.

The puzzles themselves also embody the advances in technology and craftsmanship that have occurred over time. The delicate hand-colored engravings of the earliest puzzles yielded to the brilliant chromolithography of the late nineteenth century, and then to the modern color lithography of today. The simple cuts of the first puzzles reflected the primitive saws that were used. As machinery changed over the centuries, from power saws to steel rule dies to computer-controlled water jets, cutting designs became more intricate and imaginative. Cheaper materials and better tools also made possible mass production, in contrast with the limited editions of the earliest years.

This chapter surveys the history of the pictorial jigsaw puzzle, looking in turn at: puzzles for children, puzzles for adults, advertising puzzles, and novelty puzzles. Chapter 2 gives detailed histories of thirty-one of the most important puzzle manufacturers. Chapters 3 and 4 discuss issues of importance to puzzle collectors, including identification, storage, and values. Chapter 5 explains how to use the twelve topical chapters in Part II, which include over 700 pictures and detailed descriptions of puzzles sold in the United States through 1970. Although most collecting interest focuses on puzzles made before 1970, Chapter 17 shows some interesting contemporary products that collectors are buying today.

▪ European Origins

Dissected puzzles, consisting of pieces that can be assembled into a specified shape, date back as far as Archimedes in ancient Greece.[1] But the true pictorial jigsaw puzzle—a picture glued to thin wood or cardboard and cut into small pieces—originated in eighteenth-century Europe.

John Spilsbury, a young London map maker, appears to have invented the jigsaw puzzle around 1760, and marketed his wares as educational tools "to facilitate the teaching of Geography."[2] His dissected maps had an immediate success with upper class parents, who were concerned with the intellectual progress of their progeny (Fig. 1–1). He soon extended his line of map puzzles to include distant regions like Africa, the Americas, and Jamaica, as well as Britain and the world. Although Spilsbury's premature death in 1769 cut short his triumph, dissected puzzles proved to be much more than a passing fad.

By 1800 almost twenty other London map makers and publishers had jumped on the puzzle bandwagon, including two prominent publishers of children's books and games, the Darton and Wallis families. The early examples of their work are sober and didactic, clearly designed for instruction rather than for amusement. In addition to maps, most firms added biblical, moral and historical subjects to their puzzle lessons. For example, in order to complete Wallis's *Key to the New Testament* (Fig. 1–2) children had to know the order of the Bible chapters.

These early puzzles were luxury products, costing as much as a pound, more than the average laborer's weekly earnings. Manufacturers used fine hardwoods—mahogany, walnut, and oak—for puzzles and boxes. The prints were engraved in black and white, then tinted by hand with watercolors. Typically, only the edge pieces interlocked, to save time in the laborious process of cutting the pieces one at a time with hand-held fret saws. (A fret saw looks like a coping saw with a very

Fig. 1-1. Spilsbury's *Europe Divided Into Its Kingdoms* is the oldest surviving jigsaw puzzle, circa 1766. It is 17¾" x 19½", 55 hand-colored and hand-cut mahogany pieces. The wood box is 11" x 12".

Fig. 1-2. *Key to the New Testament*. J. Wallis Sen. and J. Wallis Jun., London, England. Circa 1810. 11¼" x 7¼", 32 hand-colored and hand-cut mahogany pieces. Wood box, 8¼" x 6½", is illustrated in Chapter 7.

fine blade.) The puzzles generally had fewer than 50 pieces, and were intended only for children. Because the plain labels gave only the title of the puzzle, a guide picture was usually enclosed in the box.

The nineteenth century brought many changes in the young puzzle industry. First, the subject matter became lighter. Although maps and histories continued to be a staple of production, publishers also dissected more playful subjects, including nursery rhymes and fairy tales. Vivid puzzle illustrations began to portray current events, from Queen Victoria's Coronation to the great fire at the Tower of London. Children could put together the exciting adventures of William Tell, rather than being limited to dull depictions of lives of the prophets.

At the same time, changes in production methods brought down the price of puzzles and made them more accessible to consumers. Manufacturers shifted away from hardwoods to the less expensive softwoods. Lithography soon replaced the more time-consuming process of engraving. Hand-coloring continued until 1860 or later, but was streamlined and made cheaper when firms set up assembly lines of young children with stencils and paint pots. Puzzle makers also devoted more efforts to marketing; they replaced the simple typeset labels of the eighteenth century with large, colorful lithographed labels, often showing a portion of the assembled puzzle.

The 1800s also saw the growth of the jigsaw puzzle in other countries. France, Germany, and the Netherlands became major producers of puzzles during this period. The European puzzles differed from the English ones in that they had interlocking pieces throughout (Fig. 1–3). European companies often sold their puzzles in sets, with three or four puzzles in a box. Boxes were large enough so that the assembled puzzles could lie flat, in contrast with the English boxes where the puzzle had to be broken up in order to fit into the box.

With the jigsaw puzzle firmly established in children's play, nineteenth century manufacturers began to develop new variations on the theme. *Sigward the Little Castle-Tacker* (sic), was made out of thick wood, so the assembled puzzle of a castle could be stood up, ready to attack and knock down (Fig. 1–4). Other puzzles, consisting of identical rectangular pieces, were reversible; they formed a picture puzzle on one side and served as alphabet blocks on the other.

Cube puzzles, made out of uniform wood cubes, appeared around 1825. The

TIREZ SI VOUS L'OSEZ C'EST LE DRAPEAU DE LA FRANCE!

Fig. 1-3. This puzzle from the French Revolution of 1848 shows the fully interlocking style of European cutters. 6" x 8½", 12 hand-colored and hand-cut wood pieces. From a set of three puzzles entitled *Don't Shoot, It's My Brother* by Codoni of Paris, illustrated in Chapter 6.

Fig. 1-4. *Sigward the Little Castle-Tacker* (sic), a German puzzle that doubles as a construction toy. Circa 1850. 10″ x 12″, 22 hand-colored and hand-cut wood pieces. Wood box, 9½″ x 10¾″.

six different sides of the cubes each contributed to a different picture. These can be very difficult to assemble, especially when the six pictures are similar, because the shape of the piece gives no clues for assembly. Metamorphosis puzzles were cleverly designed to make even more different pictures. Favorite themes included comic characters, whose heads, bodies, and legs could be rearranged to form hundreds of absurd and sometimes grotesque combinations.

▪ Early Children's Puzzles in the U.S.

American consumers were buying imported puzzles, primarily from England, early in the 1800s. By the mid-nineteenth century some English makers were producing United States map puzzles explicitly for the American market. Germany was the second most important supplier of puzzles to the new nation before 1860. German puzzles are typically labeled in three or more languages, reflecting Germany's growing dominance worldwide in the toy market. Imports from France were more limited, judging from the number of puzzles that survive in this country today.

Domestic production of jigsaw puzzles began in the United States at mid-century. In 1849 Samuel McCleary and John Pierce of New York patented their method of die-cutting map puzzles. (Their cumbersome technique, involving a separate die for each piece, was not very successful and soon disappeared.) Following in Spilsbury's footsteps, they marketed their *Geographical Analysis of the State of New York* as an educational game. The box contained extensive testimonials from Governor Hamilton Fish and prominent educators of the day, such as the president of Union College and Emma Willard, founder of the Troy (N.Y.) Female Academy.

A few other American firms published jigsaw puzzles in the decade before the Civil War, including Samuel L. Hill of Brooklyn, W. and S. B. Ives of Salem, Mass., Charles Magnus and McLoughlin Brothers of New York, V. S. W. Parkhurst of Providence, and Thomas Wagner of Philadelphia. Their puzzles were very similar to the contemporary English ones; most were sawed from wood, used hand-colored lithographs, and were packaged in wood boxes.

Puzzle production soared in the United States after the Civil War. McLoughlin Brothers, the most important U.S. producer of puzzles in the nineteenth century, had been established earlier but ex-

Fig. 1-5. The *B.B.B.B. Puzzle,* by Wallie Dorr of New York, celebrated the opening of the Brooklyn Bridge. Copyright 1889. Frame tray puzzle, 5¾" x 17¾", 30 hand-cut wood pieces. Cardboard box, 6" x 18". (Courtesy of the Siegels)

panded rapidly after 1870. The quarter-century betweeen 1860 and 1885 brought the arrival of McLoughlin's three biggest and longest-lived competitors in the game and puzzle business, Milton Bradley (Springfield, Mass.), Parker Brothers (Salem, Mass.), and Selchow & Righter (New York, N.Y.). (Chapter 2 provides detailed histories of these four firms, along with other major producers in the United States.)

The industrial revolution was in full swing in post-Civil War America, and the growing puzzle industry took advantage of it. Puzzle makers turned to the relatively new process of color lithography with enthusiasm, and hired artists who used the new techniques to produce stunning and exciting puzzle pictures. Although maps, nursery rhymes, and fairy tales continued as popular subjects, there was a proliferation of puzzles that glorified the country's new technical achievements, especially in transportation (Fig. 1–5). Trains, ships, battle cruisers, bicycles, balloons, bridges, etc., all appeared in vibrant color on puzzles during the last quarter of the nineteenth century.

Like all manufactured toys, puzzles were more widely distributed during this period. Rising incomes, rapidly growing urban populations, and improved distribution of products meant that more families had access to jigsaw puzzles. At the same time, companies were able to keep costs down through more efficient production techniques. The nineteenth-century American firms used power scroll or band saws, rather than the hand-held fret

saws employed to cut the first English puzzles. Many also saved labor costs by stacking their puzzles, and cutting two or more at a time. (Nail holes in the corners and a loose fit are reliable signs that a puzzle was stack-cut.)

In another cost-saving move, American companies began to replace wood with less-expensive materials. Some companies, like Milton Bradley, continued to offer deluxe editions of some puzzles, making them of wood and packaging them in sturdy wood boxes. But most of the children's puzzles made after 1880 used heavy cardboard instead of wood, since cardboard was both cheaper and easier to cut. Some of the simpler "sliced" cardboard puzzles were cut with a guillotine-like knife

Fig. 1-6. One of a dozen puzzles included in *Sliced Nations* by Selchow & Righter, New York. Patented 1875. 7½" x 7¼", 6 sliced cardboard pieces. Cardboard box, 9" x 8".

or perhaps even with a primitive straight die (Fig. 1–6).

As domestic manufacturers advanced, the role of imported puzzles diminished. Nevertheless, Germany sent substantial numbers of puzzles to the United States until the outbreak of World War I. Many of these were small puzzles, under 25 pieces, intended for very young children. American consumers also bought many of the six-sided cube puzzles from Germany. English puzzles were less common in the United States during the last quarter of the nineteenth century, although the firms of Spear and Tuck were important exporters of puzzles after 1900. Most of the imports were unlabeled as to manufacturer; beginning in 1893, however, they were required by law to identify the country of origin.

▪ Children's Puzzles between the World Wars

The outbreak of World War I in 1914 brought a temporary halt to most imports from Europe, and provided a great stimulus to domestic manufacturing, especially in the toy industry. Since 1920, the vast majority of children's puzzles sold in the United States have been produced by American companies. Imports have been limited primarily to a small number of wooden puzzles, which could be produced less expensively abroad because of lower labor costs there.

The 1920s and 1930s brought some fundamental changes in the puzzle industry. Milton Bradley absorbed the venerable firm of McLoughlin Brothers in 1920, marking the end of the latter's brilliant lithography and its dominance in puzzles and games. Bradley and Parker Brothers continued as major players in the puzzle business, with Selchow & Righter also active periodically. The years between World Wars I and II also saw the rise of some important new makers of children's puzzles, including Consolidated Paper Box (Somerville, Mass.), Madmar Quality Co. (Utica, N.Y.), Saalfield Publishing Co. (Akron, Ohio), and Whitman (a division of Western Publishing Co. of Racine, Wis.). (See Chapter 2 for detailed histories of these companies.)

The subject matter of jigsaw puzzles began to change during this period. Although the classic maps, nursery rhymes,

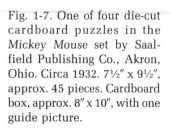

Fig. 1-7. One of four die-cut cardboard puzzles in the *Mickey Mouse* set by Saalfield Publishing Co., Akron, Ohio. Circa 1932. 7½″ x 9½″, approx. 45 pieces. Cardboard box, approx. 8″ x 10″, with one guide picture.

and fairy tales still inspired many puzzles, designers increasingly turned to the licensing of popular copyrighted characters to capture children's attention. The new media of movies, cartoons, and radio provided a novel and modern popular culture that riveted and delighted children (and adults too). There was some hint of this trend even around 1900 when McLoughlin Brothers issued puzzles depicting the Yellow Kid, Outcault's pioneering comic strip character, and Palmer Cox's delightful Brownies.

By the early 1930s Mickey Mouse and his friends had made their debut on the jigsaw puzzle (Fig. 1–7) as had dozens of other comic characters ranging from Blondie to the Katzenjammer Kids. Many of the puzzles of this period were advertising premiums, touted on the radio and given away with toothpaste, soap, cereals, etc. They featured favorites like Amos 'n Andy, The Goldbergs, and Radio Orphan Annie. (See the section on advertising puzzles, below.) New children's books were not ignored. Johnny Gruelle's Raggedy Ann and Harrison Cady's illustrations of the Thornton Burgess characters also appeared on puzzles.

In addition to changing subject matter, the techniques of puzzle production changed dramatically after World War I when die-cut cardboard puzzles largely supplanted traditional hand-cut ones. Although a few dies had been used to cut puzzles at the end of the 1800s, they were quite simple and were limited to noninterlocking pieces. By the 1920s, modern steel rule dies which could be formed into intricate interlocking designs had appeared, and had been adopted by most

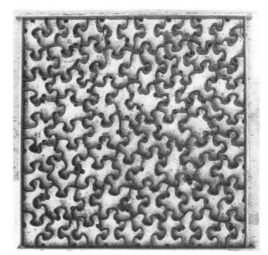

Fig. 1-8. This steel rule die, embedded in a wood block, was used for stamping out small (7″ square) cardboard puzzles.

producers of children's puzzles. A die itself looked like a large cookie cutter, with steel rules bent to cut every piece of the puzzle (Fig. 1–8). Dies brought great cost savings since they were used in presses to stamp out an entire puzzle at once. A few workers with a press could turn out hundreds or even thousands of puzzles per day in contrast with the tedious traditional process of using saws to cut each piece individually. Although the initial construction of a die was very expensive, once made it could cut 100,000 or more puzzles before wearing out.

The use of cardboard also cut costs. At the end of the nineteenth century many manufacturers had substituted thick cardboard for wood. By the 1920s they shifted to still thinner cardboard (1/16″ to 1/8″ thick), which was both cheaper and easier to cut with the new dies.

▪ Children's Puzzles after World War II

Milton Bradley, Consolidated Paper Box, Madmar, Parker Brothers, Saalfield, and Whitman continued as major producers of children's puzzles after World War II. Several other companies that were founded before 1945 also rose to prominence in children's puzzles during or after the war, including Jaymar Specialty Co. (Brooklyn,

N.Y.), Joseph K. Straus (Brooklyn, N.Y.), and Warren Paper Products (Lafayette, Ind.).

The children's puzzles of the 1950s and 1960s continued the trends established earlier. Most manufacturers cut their puzzles with dies, rather than saws. The exceptions were Madmar, Straus, and G. J. Hayter, the English firm whose Victory puzzles were imported in great numbers beginning around 1950. Some of the other makers like Milton Bradley and Parker Brothers continued to produce the ever-popular map puzzles in sturdy wood versions, even though the rest of their products were cardboard.

Licensing became even more important with the spread of television in the 1950s. Howdy Doody, Hopalong Cassidy, Superman, Huckleberry Hound, and the Beverly Hillbillies were just a few of the television characters with puzzle spinoffs. Virtually every Disney movie had puzzles associated with it, from *Sleeping Beauty* to *101 Dalmatians* to *Mary Poppins*. Puzzles given away as advertising premiums however, continued only sporadically; they never again reached their heyday of the early 1930s.

Today's children's puzzles have come a long way from Spilsbury's first dissected maps. Yet puzzles retain their educational mission to some extent even today. Puzzle maps encourage youngsters to learn the

Fig. 1-9. The Gilman *Little Clock Builder* has movable hands, shows arabic numerals on one side and roman numerals on the other. 10½" diameter, 20 hand-cut plywood pieces. First patented in 1918, this puzzle was later copied by several other companies.

countries, their states, and their capitals, just as they did over two hundred years ago. Over the years puzzle lessons have expanded into new areas, like learning how to tell time with a puzzle showing the face of a clock (Fig. 1–9). And of course, puzzles also continue to help young children develop the basic skills of coordination, color and pattern recognition, and spatial relationships.

▪ The First Puzzles for Adults

Throughout the eighteenth and nineteenth centuries, puzzles were intended only for children. The change came at the turn of this century when larger puzzles (75 pieces or more) for adults were developed. The stimulus for this type of puzzle making went back to the Philadelphia Centennial Exposition of 1876, when the power scroll saw (later known as a jigsaw) was introduced to the general public.[3] The ensuing flurry of Victorian fretwork was fueled by the foot-powered treadle saw (Fig. 1–10),

which was relatively inexpensive and sold widely.

It seems to have been the home craftsperson, rather than established puzzle manufacturers, who extended the puzzle from a child's toy to the large complex pictures designed to challenge adults. The Rev. Charles P. B. Jefferys (1862–1900) of Philadelphia is the earliest documented maker of adult puzzles. Figure 1–11 shows one of the many puzzles he cut for family and friends at the time of the 1898 Span-

Fig. 1-10. The *New Rogers* treadle scroll saw, made by C. B. Rogers & Co., Norwich, Conn. In 1880 it sold for $3.

Fig. 1-11. *A Yellow War Correspondent* was made by Charles Jefferys, Philadelphia, Pa., in 1898. 12½" x 9", 84 hand-cut mahogany pieces. Wood box, 5½" x 8½".

ish-American War, using contemporary political cartoons.

Puzzles emerged commercially as a popular pastime for adults in Boston around 1906–07. By 1908 the wooden adult puzzle, known as the "Whatami," had become a full-blown craze, spreading to other major eastern cities and replacing diabolo as the amusement of the day. Several contemporary articles and short stories described the inexorable progression of the puzzle addict: from the skeptic who initially ridiculed puzzles as silly and childish, to the perplexed puzzler who ignored meals while chanting "just one more piece"; to the bleary-eyed victor who finally triumphed in the wee hours of the morning. A cartoon of Taft and Bryan competing for pieces of a large puzzle map of America appeared in the 1908 presidential campaign.

Puzzles for adults were an immediate hit in high society. The E. I. Horsman Co.

advertised its Perplexyu puzzles as being "all the rage at Newport," and several companies named their products "society" puzzles. Peak sales came on Saturdays when retailers and factories were "besieged by customers about to take weekend trips to the country, who clamor for puzzles to take with them in order to add to the gayety at their destinations."[4]

Unlike children's puzzles, which usually had specially-designed pictures, adult puzzles used commercially available lithographs or magazine prints. These puzzles thus represent the popular art of the day. Subjects were diverse, ranging from Japanese prints to fine art masterpieces. The artists of the golden age of illustration—Maxfield Parrish, the Leyendeckers, Howard Chandler Christy, etc.—are abundantly represented on the puzzles of this period (Fig. 1–12).

The early adult puzzles, though small, were very difficult. Cuts were made ex-

Fig. 1-12. Valdemar T. Hammer, an amateur cutter in Branford, Conn., used a Howard Chandler Christy print for this puzzle around 1909. 11″ x 16″, 265 hand-cut wood pieces.

actly on the color lines; if two adjacent pieces had different colors, there was no clue that they fit together. Puzzle pieces did not interlock, another feature that contributed to their difficulty. A common complaint was that a playful pet or rambunctious child or careless maid had bumped the card table and scattered pieces whose assembly represented hours of work. (Patent records of the period are replete with inventions of special trays for assembling puzzles which claimed to prevent such tragedies.) Finally, in contrast with children's puzzles, adult puzzles were sold without any guide pictures on the box. In some cases deliberately vague or misleading titles deprived the puzzler of any clues and kept the true subject a mystery until the last piece was fitted into place.

Adult puzzles from the first decade of the twentieth century generally used solid wood, often fine mahogany. Cigar boxes were a readily available source of wood for amateur cutters; some puzzles of the period have a picture on one side and the cigar box label on the other. Around the time of World War I the newly developed plywood began to replace solid wood for puzzles. Plywood made superior puzzles that were less susceptible to breakage or warping of the pieces. Most companies packaged their adult puzzles in cardboard boxes, though wood boxes were occasionally used.

The first makers of adult puzzles worked locally and on a small scale. One Boston youth was said to have put himself through college with his Whatami puzzles. In New York, Margaret Richardson began her Perplexity puzzles in March 1908 by cutting three or four puzzles per week. But as the passion for puzzles took hold, the volume of her production soared. Established manufacturers like Parker Brothers and Milton Bradley jumped into the fray, advertising wood puzzles for adults nationally during the 1908 Christmas season. The toy industry trade magazine noted with satisfaction that demand was expected to remain strong for a long time: "one great attraction about these puzzles is that once solved its owner yearns for another one to conquer."[5]

Parker Brothers quickly established its Pastime brand as a best-seller. During 1909, the peak of the craze, the company even ceased to make other games. All of its resources, including over 200 workers, were devoted to production of its jigsaw puzzles. Parker also appears to have originated the idea for cutting pieces into recognizable shapes—dogs, stars, butterflys, letters, etc. Within a few years, Pastime puzzles were clearly distinguishable from

Fig. 1-13. This detail illustrates the best of the intricate cutting and figure pieces developed by Parker Brothers. The full puzzle is shown in the color section.

those of other makers by abundant inclusion of these delightful figure pieces (Fig. 1–13).

Most of the early manufacturers of adult puzzles were located in New England or the middle Atlantic states. Although *Collier's National Weekly* published a feature on puzzles at the end of 1909,[6] interest was much weaker away from the East Coast. Interest in puzzles was concentrated among the middle and upper classes. The clear reason was cost. Puzzles in 1909 sold for around one cent per piece, or $5 for a 500-piece puzzle. In an era when earnings averaged $50 per month, it is obvious why puzzles did not become an entertainment for the working class.

But even the middle class could not afford repeated outlays of $5 per puzzle. Lending libraries and puzzle exchanges offered a solution to the problem. One of the earliest and longest-lived rental libraries was M. Isabel Ayer's Picture Puzzle Exchange which operated in Boston from around 1908 to 1940. She offered puzzles for sale or to loan. She also would cut puzzles to order and carried a full line of supplies for the amateur cutter. A drawback of borrowing or exchanging puzzles was the perpetual problem of missing pieces. Libraries tried to guard against such problems with special labels urging care by borrowers, such as this verse:

> *Please don't lose a piece of puzzle.*
> *So just keep the dog in muzzle.*
> *Trouser cuff and Morris chair*
> *Are a menace—Please use care.*

Although the first puzzle mania tapered off by 1910, puzzles emerged as an acceptable and enjoyable recreation for adults. Demand continued at lower but steady levels over the next two decades, supplied by Parker Brothers nationally and at the local level by firms like Boston's Picture Puzzle Exchange.

▪ The Depression Puzzle Craze

The Great Depression of the 1930s ushered in the biggest jigsaw puzzle craze in the country's history. Some psychologists hypothesized that puzzles offered a welcome escape from the tragic realities of the times, or perhaps an opportunity to conquer a small puzzle in an era when most problems were insoluble. Economists noted the high unemployment rate which gave many people more free time for leisure activities. Others pointed out that fads in games and toys followed 20-year cycles, so the puzzle mania of 1932–33 was slightly overdue.

MASS PRODUCTION WITH DIE-CUTTING

The Depression puzzle craze was more democratic than the 1908–09 one, with price being a major factor. Die-cutting, which was used in children's puzzles in the 1920s, was adopted for the larger and more intricate adult puzzles in the early 1930s. The craze apparently began in the spring of 1932 with die-cut cardboard advertising puzzles, distributed free to consumers in order to promote products.[7] (See below for an extensive discussion of advertising puzzles.) Lithographers and other businesses then started to produce puzzles for sale, seizing the opportunity to revive their faltering businesses. Within a few months, cardboard puzzles were selling nationally at newsstands for only 25 cents each.

The weekly puzzle was the marketing gimmick that fueled the fad (Fig. 1–14). University Distributing Company's Jig of the Week was one of the first examples, appearing in early October 1932. Friends rushed to the newsstands to buy the newest design, issued every Wednesday, and then competed to see who could assemble the puzzle most quickly. By January 1933 there were several hundred firms making puzzles. They bombarded consumers with weekly series like the Weekly Jig, Picture Puzzle Weekly, Every Week Puzzle, Jiggers Weekly, Movie Cut-Ups, Once-A-Week Puzzle, and B-Witching Weekly. One news company even hawked its weekly puzzles on commuter trains in the New York City area.[8] Within a few months prices had fallen as low as 10 cents per puzzle.

It is difficult to prove which firm was responsible for starting the craze. Einson-Freeman (Long Island City, N.Y.), Tuco Work Shops (Lockport, N.Y.), University

Fig. 1-14. A 14½″ x 9¼″ advertising poster for a weekly puzzle, *Love Birds*, by artist R. Atkinson Fox.

Distributing Co. (Cambridge, Mass.), and Viking Manufacturing Co. (Boston, Mass.) were all active during the fall of 1932, and have credible claims as instigators of the fad. (See Chapter 2 for details of their histories.) Certainly all were major producers. By early 1933 it was reported that Einson-Freeman had hired over 400 new employees to produce three million puzzles per week.[9] And in April the S.-M. News Co., which distributed the Jig of the Week nationally, estimated that newsstands were selling six million puzzles weekly.[10]

Quality differed among the many producers. Lithography varied from being quite good to being rather muddy. Some puzzles interlocked throughout, and a few even had figure pieces built into the cutting dies. The quality of the cardboard also varied. Tuco's thick (3/16″) pieces appealed to puzzlers familiar with wood pieces, but most companies used thinner cardboard.

Interestingly, the puzzles of 1932–33 were sold without guide pictures on the box. Some makers, who perhaps felt that all novice puzzlers needed help, included a small guide picture inside the box. But it was not until around 1935 that most makers of die-cut adult puzzles adopted the practice of printing the guide picture on the box, enabling prospective purchasers to inspect the scene before deciding which puzzle to buy.

The craze was short-lived, only seven months, although total sales during that period reached an incredible 100 million.[11] The bank holiday, when banks were closed for over a week in March 1933, along with total saturation of the market combined to burst the puzzle bubble. By May, the Jig of the Week had disappeared. Demand for puzzles fell to normal levels. And most of the new puzzle companies withered away.

REVIVAL OF HAND-CRAFTED WOOD PUZZLES

What of the traditional hand-cut wood puzzle during this period? Interest in wood puzzles had picked up steadily as the Depression deepened. In January 1931 Parker Brothers issued its largest Pastime puzzle catalog to date. At the same time, thousands of one-person businesses emerged as unemployed workers began to cut and sell puzzles locally to supplement their incomes. The slump in industrial and home construction meant that architects, machinists, cabinet makers, etc. had little work; but with their skills and tools it was easy for them to enter the puzzle business. Even those with no previous training began to make puzzles, using instructions published in magazines like *Popular Science Monthly*. However, in contrast with the 1909 craze, when many women cut puzzles, most of the Depression-era cutters were men.

Department stores like Macy's and Bamberger's marketed wood puzzles under their own brand names. Gimbel's commissioned a puzzle of over 50,000 pieces for display in its New York store. Both

Fig. 1-15. Charles W. Russell of Auburn, Mass. made this puzzle, *Quality and Service*, from a puzzle lending library poster in the 1930s. 19" x 14", 538 hand-cut plywood pieces, including figure pieces. Cardboard box, 9½" x 7½".

department and drug stores all over the country installed electric jigsaws, and hired cutters to make puzzles from photos brought in by customers. They drew large crowds who went on to buy both puzzles and saws.

As the wood puzzles were considerably more expensive than the die-cut ones, the 1930s brought the revival of the puzzle lending library. Many were operated by the small local makers who rented puzzles out for 5 cents per day or 25 cents per week (Fig. 1–15). In some areas borrowers could have their puzzles delivered, either by the cutters themselves or by milkmen who added puzzles to the products handled on their routes.

Unlike the adult puzzles sold in the 1908–09 craze, most of the Depression-era wooden puzzles had interlocking pieces. Many of the cutters imitated the Pastime style of cutting and filled their puzzles with figure pieces. Others, looking for higher volume, used the same type of strip-cutting found in most of the cardboard puzzles. The puzzle was first cut into horizontal interlocking strips, after which the vertical cuts were made, as in (Fig. 1–16.

The puzzles of the 1930s, whether die-cut or hand-cut, reflected a certain yearning for the exotic and foreign. Few could afford to travel in those depression years, but putting together a *Scene in Venice* (Fig. 1–17) or *The Orient's Magic Spell* provided a temporary escape from the woes of real life. It is interesting to note that most puzzle manufacturers used commercially available prints; sometimes the smaller makers of wood puzzles used pictures from magazines or calendars. As a result, dozens of firms might make puzzles from the same print. Certain scenes of the American Revolution, Dutch flower markets, and English fox hunts turn up over and over again. There is a difference between the die-cut and hand-cut puzzles in this respect, however. The University Distributing Co., for example, issued fewer than three dozen different Jig of the Week puzzles, although each one might have sold hundreds of thousands of copies. A small-scale local manufacturer of wooden puzzles might have sold only about 500 puzzles during the same period, but each puzzle would show a different scene.

Fig. 1-16. *Posies*, an Old Colony puzzle by Edward Little of Ansonia, Conn., illustrates the use of strip-cutting. 1930s. 12″ x 9″, 207 hand-cut plywood pieces. Cardboard box, 4½″ x 7¼″.

LUXURY PUZZLES: PAR

Frank Ware and John Henriques, founders of the famous Par Company Ltd., began their company like many other puzzle makers in the Depression. Neither had

Fig. 1-17. Carroll Towne's *Scene in Venice* is an excellent example of Depression-era craftsmanship. 11¾″ x 16″, 449 hand-cut plywood pieces, including figure pieces. Cardboard box, 5¼″ x 9¼″.

a job, and they cut their first puzzle with a coping saw at the dining room table in early 1932. Although most of the cutters of that period returned to their regular jobs as the economy improved, Ware and Henriques continued to increase the quality and quantity of their puzzle production.

Par specialized in personalized puzzles for its customers and routinely included names, anniversary dates, etc. among the intricate pieces. Within a few years they were established in a Manhattan penthouse, turning out puzzles for a growing list of celebrities, including movie stars, royalty, and industrial barons. Ware and Henriques also delighted in teasing their clients, with tricks like irregular edges, color-line cutting, fake corners, and deceptive titles. Par's great success made them one of the longest-lived producers of wood puzzles for adults, second only to Parker Brothers.

▪ Adult Puzzles since the Depression

The sales of six million puzzles a week during the peak of the 1932–33 craze have not been matched since in the United States. Nevertheless, demand for adult puzzles continued at a respectable pace after the Depression. There was a modest surge of interest in puzzles during World War II, when wartime scarcity cut into other amusements and patriotic themes appealed to puzzlers (Fig. 1–18).

During the 1950s, puzzles faced increasingly stiff competition from television and other diversions. The lull in interest in jigsaw puzzles came to an abrupt end in 1964 when a new firm, Springbok Editions of New York, burst on the scene with several innovations. Using high quality lithography and masterpieces of fine art, they caught the public's attention with their circular and octagonal puzzles. They challenged the puzzler who was bored with scenes of covered bridges and seaside sunsets, and also attracted new devotees to the jigsaw puzzle. Within a few months they had sold over 100,000 copies of an abstract modern painting by Jackson Pollock, billed as "the world's most difficult jigsaw puzzle."

Springbok's success stimulated the other makers of die-cut puzzles, with the result that there were continuous improvements in quality after 1965. Today's puzzles have much crisper lithography and more vibrant colors than those of earlier days. Most companies also have moved towards using somewhat thicker cardboard than before, resulting in sturdier pieces that are easier to handle.

Unlike the die-cut puzzles, wooden puzzles did not fare so well after the 1930s. Rising labor costs led to higher prices, because the wooden puzzles still had to be cut one piece at a time. With cardboard puzzles readily available, consumers be-

Fig. 1-18. During World War II many puzzles had patriotic themes, such as this *Guardians of Liberty* by an unknown maker. 11¾" x 9", 183 hand-cut plywood pieces.

gan to balk at the price increases and domestic production of wood puzzles declined. Parker Brothers shut down its Pastime puzzle department around 1959 when it could no longer compete with the die-cut puzzles. The other commercial makers of wood puzzles in the U.S.— Madmar, Par and Straus—all followed suit within fifteen years.

Wood puzzles did not completely disappear in the United States, however. Some department stores continued to import wooden puzzles from Europe (especially the Victory and Gold Box puzzles made by Hayter and then Spear), and to sell them at fairly reasonable prices.

The last fifteen years also have seen the rise of a few specialty puzzle firms, seeking to fill the void left when Par's founder retired in 1974. The first and most famous of these is Stave Puzzles of Norwich, Vermont. Owner Steve Richardson got into the puzzle business in 1974 when a former Par customer was looking for alternative sources of luxury puzzles. Stave not only continued the Par tradition of personalized work, but has set new standards of quality in luxury wood puzzles. The firm hires artists to design pictures spe-cially tailored for puzzles, and the cutting designs interact with the graphics to increase the trickiness of the puzzle.

Stave puzzles command top of the line prices, $2 and up per piece, and over $2000 for some extravagant limited-edition, 500-piece creations. These astronomical prices have fostered competition as others have sought to cash in on this specialty market. The 1980s have brought several new firms, most producing puzzles around $1 per piece, not cheap but considerably below Stave. The work of companies like J. S. Guiles, Capt. Kirk, Elms, and F. A. Bourke is described in Chapter 17 in some detail. One of the most innovative technologically is J. C. Ayer & Co., which is using computer-controlled water jets to automate the cutting of wood puzzles.

The last fifteen years also have seen the emergence of hand-crafted wooden puzzles that double as sculptures for permanent display. Some artists, like Greg FryeWeaver and Steve Malavolta, use layering with several different woods to create the design element in a puzzle with hundreds of pieces. Others like Carol Leith of Monkey Puzzle specialize in painted puzzles with just a few striking pieces.

▪ Advertising Puzzles

The advertising puzzle is a publicist's dream. What else could induce consumers to spend hours poring over pieces and fitting together the issuing company's name and products? The first advertising puzzles, The Silent Teacher series, appeared in the late 1870s. These wood puzzles were primarily educational; they were reversible with a map on one side. The other side usually displayed an advertising poster either for Sherwin Williams paints (Fig. 1–19) or for White Sewing Machines and Bicycles. They were published in great numbers by several companies in New York state, as is detailed in Chapter 2.

The C. I. Hood Co., of Lowell, Mass., was one of the first companies to issue advertising puzzles uncluttered with lessons for children. Its *Rainy Day and Balloon Puzzle*, issued in 1891, was strictly a promotional piece, sent free to customers who sent in three wrappers from Hood's patent medicines. Hood's produced this and several other later puzzles in huge quantities, using a simple die to mass produce cardboard puzzles. A few other die-cut advertising puzzles appeared between 1890 and 1910 for products as diverse as bread, pianos, toothbrushes, and socks.

The heyday of the advertising puzzle came during the Great Depression in 1932–33. In fact, the advertising puzzle is said to have started the puzzle mania of those years. Puzzles appeared in great numbers, promoting virtually every type of product: gasoline, toilet paper, candy, soap, flashlights, and carpets. Some had a significant impact. Contemporary reports claimed that

Fig. 1-19. The Silent Teacher puzzles usually had advertisements on the reverse of traditional dissected maps. This one, manufactured in the 1880s by Rev. E. J. Clemens of Clayville, N.Y. shows New York state and a Sherwin Williams ad. 15¼″ x 12½″, 64 hand-cut wood pieces. The cardboard box, 7¼″ x 9¼″, is illustrated in Chapter 2.

Frances Tipton Hunter's charming picture of a boy brushing his puppy's teeth (Fig. 1–20) increased sales of toothbrushes by 400 percent when distributed as a puzzle.[12]

Many puzzles were issued by sponsors of popular radio programs. Sohio's puzzle series featured the adventures of Gene, Glenn, Jake and Lena, the radio personalities who broadcast nightly on WTAM and WLW. Cocomalt distributed two "Flying Family" puzzles in conjunction with its sponsorship of a radio program about the Hutchinson family's travels. Children who drank Cocomalt every day for a month became "Flight Commanders" and received additional premiums when their parents signed and mailed in the weight chart enclosed with the puzzle.

The advertising puzzles of the 1930s varied in size, from 30 or 50-piece puzzles for children to 250-piece ones aimed at adults. Virtually all were made from thin cardboard, using the relatively new die-cutting process. Most had interlocking pieces at least for the borders; many interlocked throughout; and some even contained figure pieces. The vast majority were packaged in paper envelopes for easy and inexpensive mailing, although a few came in boxes. In designing their advertising puzzles, companies often used the serv-

Fig. 1-20. Advertising puzzle for the Prophylactic Brush Co., Florence, Mass. Circa 1933. 10¾″ x 13¾″, 50 die-cut cardboard pieces. Paper envelope, 11″ x 14″, with guide diagram.

ices of famous contemporary illustrators, from Dr. Seuss to Tony Sarg.

Production of advertising puzzles has never since reached the heights of 1932–33. But companies have continued to issue them in modest quantities up to the present day. Chapter 14 describes advertising puzzles of all periods in detail.

▪ Novelty Puzzles

Over the last 140 years, since jigsaw puzzles were first produced in the United States, many companies have sought ways to improve and even transform the basic puzzle. And consumers too, sometimes jaded by the old standby, have welcomed some novelty to jazz it up.

Puzzle competitions have been a perennial idea, with the first contest sets appearing during the 1908–09 craze. Parker Brothers was one of the first companies to provide instructions on how to use a number of puzzles at parties in a speed contest. Puzzles also have been designed as integral parts of more complicated games, involving elements of chance or strategy as players competed to finish their puzzles first.

Message puzzles date back to the beginning of this century. Tuck, an English manufacturer of both postcards and puzzles, began marketing mailable postcard puzzles in this country in 1909. In the same year Parker Brothers produced a small heart-shaped valentine puzzle. Christmas card puzzles, and other greetings soon followed, along with letter puzzles — blank puzzles that could be written on before the sender broke them up and mailed them.

Books have also been associated with puzzles in many different ways. Mystery puzzles were specially popular during the 1930s. The picture on the puzzle would show the solution to the murder, whose story was provided in a small booklet. Although a written solution was usually included, it would be disguised through a device like backward printing or invisible ink, to discourage readers from peeking ahead until after they had completed the puzzle.

Children's books have often done double duty as puzzles. During the 1950s, Whitman published many Little Golden Books with jigsaw puzzles inside the back cover. The Platt and Munk *Junior Bank Book* in the 1920s contained slots for coins and glued paper pieces to stick over the slots when they were filled. In the process of accumulating $5 a child would complete four different picture puzzles (Fig. 1–21).

Another extension has combined the jigsaw puzzle with a different type of puzzle. Crossword puzzles cut into pieces were popular during the 1930s. In recent years there have been a number of treasure hunt games, where the completed puzzle formed a cryptogram which had to be decoded to win the prize offered by the manufacturer.

Fig. 1-21. Platt & Munk published the *Junior Bank Book and Picture Puzzle* in the 1920s to encourage children to save. When the book was filled with coins, the gummed paper pieces made four 5¼″ x 6¼″ puzzles. The cover is illustrated in Chapter 16.

Finally, there have even been a number of edible puzzles produced over the years, made out of chocolate or candy. Their highly ephemeral nature means that very few have survived for study by today's puzzle historians! Chapter 16 describes these and other novelty puzzles in more detail.

---

1. Jerry Slocum and Jack Botermans, *Puzzles Old and New*, Seattle: University of Washington Press, 1986, p. 13

2. Linda Hannas has documented Spilsbury's role as inventor of the jigsaw puzzle in *The English Jigsaw Puzzle: 1760 to 1890* (London: Wayland, 1972), based on her study of contemporary city directories and trade cards. Betsy and Geert Bekkering have recently challenged Spilsbury's place as the first puzzle maker in their book *Stukje Voor Stukje* (Amsterdam: Van Soeren, 1988). They note that some early Dutch puzzles used maps printed by Covens & Mortier of Amsterdam around 1725. There is, however, no direct evidence that Covens & Mortier ever cut puzzles, or even that the puzzles were cut before 1760. The Dutch puzzle makers may have worked after Spilsbury and used old maps for puzzles. The Bekkerings counter this argument by saying that outdated maps would not have been acceptable to educated consumers. They thus conclude that the early Dutch map puzzles were probably dissected as well as printed before Spilsbury's time.

3. Julius Wilcox in "Fret-Sawing and Wood-Carving," *Harper's New Monthly Magazine*, Vol. 56, No. 334, March 1878, pp. 533–540, describes the impact of the Philadelphia exhibits on sales of treadle scroll saws.

4. "Stick To It, and You May Solve a Puzzle Picture," *New York Times*, July 26, 1908, pt. 5, p. 11.

5. "Picture Puzzles," *Playthings*, November 1908, p. 34.

6. George Fitch, "Picture Puzzles," *Collier's National Weekly*, November 20, 1909, p.23.

7. "Jig-Saw Jag," *Business Week*, January 18, 1933, p. 8.

8. "Jig Saws," *Playthings*, February 1933, p. 40.

9. "Three Million Puzzles Weekly," *Queensborough*, Vol. 19, No. 2, February 1933, p. 51.

10. "Reports Indicate Extent of Jigsaw Craze," *Toy World*, April 1933, p. 60.

11. "The Lure of Puzzle Inventing," *Popular Mechanics*, January 1935, p. 128A.

12. "Some Facts on Jigsawcracy," *Playthings*, April 1933, p. 170.

2 MAJOR JIGSAW PUZZLE MANUFACTURERS: 1850–1970

HUNDREDS OF COMPANIES have produced puzzles in the United States over the last 150 years. This chapter describes some of the most important companies in some detail. For a comprehensive list of all the firms that were known to exist through 1970, consult the index of manufacturers, which also gives some brief information about each company's location, dates, and type of product.

The businesses described below are presented in alphabetical order by company name. In cases where puzzles did not have the company name on the box (such as Perfect puzzles, made by Consolidated Paper Box), cross-references are included to help the reader. This chapter also includes three English companies: Hayter, Spear, and Tuck. Because their products were imported into the United States in great numbers over many years, they are widely available to American collectors today.

The information comes from a variety of sources, which are noted in the introduction and the bibliography. Some of the historically prominent companies—for example, Milton Bradley and Parker Brothers—are still in business. Interviews and searches of company archives have turned up some rich material. Other companies, like McLoughlin Brothers and Par, were in business for such a long time that a fair amount of published material exists about some of them.

Interviews with former puzzle makers and their descendents have produced extensive information about a few of the smaller companies, particularly the wooden puzzle makers who flourished for a few years during the Great Depression. Some of these companies are included in this chapter, not so much because they were major producers, but because they are typical of the hundreds of companies that operated at that time. Documenting the histories of all these firms, mostly one-person operations, is a huge research task that has only just begun.

Finally, this chapter includes a few of the major producers about which little is known today, such as Consolidated Paper Box and the Leisure Hour Puzzle Co. Undoubtedly future research will turn up some of the details of these companies' histories. Today, however, our knowledge is limited to what we can learn by studying the products that have survived from these companies.

▪ Marjorie Bouvé
Brookline, Mass.

Marjorie Bouvé (1879–1970) is most famous for founding in 1913 the Boston School of Physical Education, now known as the Bouvé-Boston School of Northeastern University. In earlier years, while living with her family in Brookline, she also had a jigsaw puzzle business. She cut her Ye Squirlijig brand puzzles and sold them to other members of Boston's high society during the 1908–10 craze. She used beautiful solid mahogany wood, chose colorful pictures, and packaged the puzzles in brown cardboard boxes. Ye Squirlijig puzzles are quite difficult, since they are noninterlocking and cut on color lines. Although Bouvé puzzles once numbered in the thousands, they are uncommon today.

▪ Milton Bradley Co.
Springfield, Mass.

Milton Bradley arrived in Springfield in 1856 at age 20. After a few years as a draftsman, he set up as the first lithographer in Springfield in 1860. He produced his first game, *The Checkered Game of Life* in that year; although it was quite successful, he viewed games as only a sideline at that time. In fact, the company might still be just dabbling in games if Abraham Lincoln had not grown a beard!

At the time of the 1860 election, Bradley had produced a lithograph of the next president, based on a photograph showing a beardless Lincoln. The pictures sold well initially, leading Bradley to run off vast quantities of the print in anticipation of still greater demand when the new president took office. But shortly thereafter, when Lincoln grew a beard, no one wanted the out-of-date pictures. Bradley's investment in all those prints lost its value, leading him to think more positively about producing games instead of commercial lithographs.

During the Civil War, Bradley first worked as a draftsman on the design for military equipment. In 1861, however, he got back into the game business, producing a small travel kit of *Games for Soldiers* containing nine games including checkers, backgammon, and his own *Checkered Game of Life*. It was a great success during the war, and the company has been devoted to the game business ever since.

Milton Bradley added dissected maps and puzzles to the company catalog in the late 1860s. An early best seller was *The Smashed Up Locomotive: Mechanical Puzzle for Boys*, which showed an engine and tender and identified all the parts (Fig. 2–1).

Milton Bradley himself was strongly influenced by the work of Froebel, a German educator who studied the role of directed play in child development. Thus, the company produced many games and other products for use in kindergartens and schools. The numerous dissected maps in the company's nineteenth century catalogs reflect this preoccupation with the educational value of games.

The company has produced hundreds of different children's puzzles during its 130-year history. The early children's puzzles were cut with band saws, primarily from thick cardboard, although some map puzzles were cut from wood for greater durability. After about 1920 the company used dies to cut the children's puzzles. The large format puzzle sets of the 1900–1935 period are perhaps the most attractive. One striking puzzle, *The Twilight Express*, is a direct descendent of earlier railroad puzzles; it consists of six separate

Fig. 2-1. Milton Bradley sold many editions of the *Smashed Up Locomotive* puzzle between 1870 and 1900. This one is probably later than the one illustrated in Chapter 11. 10½" x 27¾", 61 sliced and die-cut cardboard pieces. Cardboard box, 6" x 8". (Courtesy of the Siegels)

puzzles of an engine and various cars which can be combined to form a train over nine feet long.

Milton Bradley also has been one of the longest operating producers of puzzles for adults. During the 1908–10 craze the company produced wooden Perfection puzzles and the less expensive cardboard Bradley's Picture Puzzles. They also manufactured several brands of hand-cut plywood puzzles during the depression years. The top of the line was the Premier puzzle, which incorporated many figure pieces into the interlocking cut. Others included the Piedmont, Beach, and Chevy Chase puzzles. At peak production in the 1930s they had 32 saws in use. But prohibitive costs meant that hand-cut puzzles were abandoned in the early 1940s when James Shea was brought in from outside to manage the company.

Milton Bradley introduced many brands of die-cut puzzles for adults during the Depression. The 1936–37 catalog lists the Buckingham, Etonian, Sheffield, and Strand puzzle lines. Many other brands soon followed. The most famous is the Big Ben series which was introduced in 1942 and is still in production today, with a dozen new pictures issued each year.

Many individual Milton Bradley puzzles are difficult to date precisely, because the company kept them in production for decades. The four-digit serial numbers that appear on boxes after about 1900 mean little; when one puzzle went out of production, its number would be assigned to a new one. Among the nineteenth-century puzzles, some were produced not only in regular editions with cardboard boxes, but also in deluxe editions packaged in wooden boxes; these are highly prized today.

Milton Bradley has had many links to other firms in the industry. In 1920 it acquired McLoughlin Brothers (see below), and maintained it as a separate operating unit until 1944 when the McLoughlin name was dropped. In 1943 Milton Bradley sold its book publishing department to Platt and Munk. Playskool, which makes pre-school puzzles, became a subsidiary of Milton Bradley in 1968. In 1984 Hasbro Industries of Pawtucket, Rhode Island, acquired Milton Bradley and continues to operate it as an independent unit.

Because of Milton Bradley's long history, collectors today can find examples of the company's puzzles easily, especially the die-cut adult puzzles made during this century. Pre-1900 puzzles are rather scarce, except for map puzzles which are relatively common.

• James Browning
East Orange and West Caldwell, N.J.

James Browning, a carpenter and builder by trade, was born around 1887. He took up cutting puzzles after World War II as a semi-retirement occupation. He used two brand names, U-Nit for more expensive mahogany-backed puzzles and Leisur Hour (sic) for those made out of plain bass plywood. Both came in plain white cardboard boxes. When Parker Brothers shut down their Pastime line in the late 1950s, Browning bought many of the prints they had on hand. He generally followed the Pastime cutting style, but with less color line cutting and more abstract geometrical figure pieces.

Browning sold his puzzles primarily through F.A.O. Schwartz in New York. He also operated a rental library from his home for some time. His output was about 400–500 puzzles per year during the 1950s and 1960s, with the result that his puzzles are relatively abundant today, particularly in the east.

▪ Consolidated Paper Box Co. Somerville, Mass.

Led by C.W. Babcock & Son, four Boston area box manufacturers merged in 1931 to form the Consolidated Paper Box Co. The new firm added jigsaw puzzles to its product line during the 1932–33 craze. Within a few years the company was using Perfect Picture Puzzles as a brand name. The company usually marketed children's puzzles in boxed sets of two to six puzzles (Fig. 2–2). Puzzles for adults, originally packaged in small boxes (7″ x 5″), were being sold in larger ones (10″ x 7″) by the end of World War II. Consolidated may have been the first producer of adult puzzles to include a small guide picture on the box. Except for its first Idle Hour and New Art

series puzzles, all its boxes have guide pictures. The Perfect puzzles continued in production until around 1960.

Consolidated probably produced several other brands of puzzles during its history. The Big Star and Big 10 puzzles of the early 1930s are so similar to Perfect puzzles that they can reliably be attributed to Consolidated. The company also produced boxes for some other companies; the Consolidated name appears as the box manufacturer on some of the Jig of the Week series puzzles, produced by the University Distributing Co. (see below).

Perfect puzzles are abundant and widely available to collectors.

Fig. 2-2. This *Parade* puzzle has been found in several different children's puzzle sets made by Consolidated Paper Box Co. during the 1930s. 7″ x 9½″, 24 die-cut cardboard pieces.

• Einson-Freeman Co., Inc. Long Island City, N.Y.

According to a 1935 article in *Popular Mechanics*, Einson-Freeman was responsible for starting the puzzle craze early in 1932, with a die-cut advertising puzzle that boosted a client's sales by 400 percent (see the Prophylactic Brush puzzle in Fig. 1–20). Whether or not this attribution is correct, Einson-Freeman was for a while a major player in the puzzle competition during the Great Depression. And its success in the puzzle business induced it to continue to produce paper advertising premiums throughout the rest of the 1930s and the 1940s.

The Queensborough Chamber of Commerce magazine (February 1933) reported that Einson-Freeman shifted from manufacturing window display advertising into puzzle production in August 1932. Some of the first puzzles were advertising premiums produced for nationally advertised brands such as Prophylactic Brush, Pepsodent, Listerine, Kolynos, Squibb, McKesson & Robbins, Sapolin, Dif, Westinghouse, and others. During the next six months the company added over 400 employees, reaching production levels of 3 million puzzles per week by early 1933.

Einson-Freeman also manufactured its own line of jigsaw puzzles, most notably the Every Week puzzle series, which sold for 15 cents through American News Co. and its branches. Some of the less frequent series included: the Currier and Ives DeLuxe puzzles; Radio Stars puzzles featuring Eddie Cantor (Fig. 2–3), Rudy Vallee, and

Fig. 2-3. Box for a Radio Star puzzle published by Einson-Freeman in 1933. The puzzle is illustrated in Chapter 13.

Kate Smith; Crime Club puzzles (short detective stories by Edgar Wallace with solutions found in the accompanying puzzles); and Problem puzzles (the box showed four scenes of a problem with the solution to be found in the puzzle).

The Every Week puzzles from number 10 on are quite common today. (Numbers 1 through 9 have not yet come to light, and it appears that the series began with number 10.) The advertising puzzles are seen frequently, but usually do not show the Einson-Freeman name. Other Einson-Freeman puzzles are less common, but still available.

• E. E. Fairchild Corp. Rochester, N.Y.

Disentangling the complex history of the E. E. Fairchild Corp. is tricky since it involves four different companies in the toy industry. Its origins go back to 1900 when Harry O. Alderman and Elmer E. Fairchild founded a new firm in Rochester, New York. Their Alderman-Fairchild Co. produced paper boxes, primarily specialty candy boxes for the nearby Fanny Farmer factory. They soon expanded into paper novelties, and by the 1920s had a moderately large line of games. When the Alderman-Fairchild Co. dissolved around 1926, two companies with similar products emerged.

All-Fair Inc., located in nearby Churchville, continued to produce games in the late 1920s, using the All-Fair Toys & Games brand name. One of its most famous alumni is Herman G. Fisher who was All-Fair's vice-president and general manager in the late 1920s. After trying unsuccessfully to buy the company in 1930, Fisher moved on to establish the Fisher-Price Co. in East Aurora, New York. Fisher-Price specialized in toys for preschool children and in the last decade has produced some frame-tray puzzles.

By the early 1930s E. E. Fairchild Corp. was both a box maker in Rochester and the manufacturer of All-Fair games and puzzles at the Churchville factory. (It is unclear whether All-Fair Inc. simply adopted the Fairchild name then, or whether E. E. Fairchild was a separate company that bought out All-Fair.) During the 1930s E. E. Fairchild Corp. made its first die-cut puzzles, including brands such as All-Fair, Fairco, Finesse, Genesee, and Master. After World War II, Fairchild became a major producer of inexpensive puzzles for adults, and established a large plant in Ranson, West Virginia. Its popular series included the Circle-Cut, Ful-Lock, Sta-Lock, and Tru-Lock series, as well as the Shape puzzles with irregular edges.

In 1974, fire destroyed Fairchild's Ranson, West Virginia plant, with the ultimate result that the Fairchild family sold out in 1975. The new owner, Schaeffer Ross Co. of Webster, New York, continued to produce puzzles under the Fairchild name for three years, and then sold the puzzle line to Selchow & Righter.

Because of their long production history, Fairchild puzzles are widely available to collectors today.

▪ Alden L. Fretts
Pittsfield and West Springfield, Mass.

The Yankee Cut-Ups puzzles, cut in 1932–33 by Alden L. Fretts (1897–1980), exemplify some of the best of the Depression-era workmanship by small scale makers of wood puzzles. A young draftsman who lost his job in the Depression, Fretts then worked as a door-to-door salesman and also cut puzzles with a foot-powered treadle saw. He displayed and sold them in a shoe repair shop in Springfield, Mass., and rented puzzles at the price of 28 cents for three days. His wife Gladys helped by sanding the pieces after they were cut, and by assembling each rental puzzle when it was returned to make sure that no puzzles had been lost.

Fretts' puzzles are cut from bass plywood and interlock so tightly that an as-

Fig. 2-4. Plywood pattern pieces used by Alden L. Fretts for his puzzles. His signature piece, Pal, appears in the upper right.

sembled puzzle can be picked up by one corner without any pieces falling out. Most of his puzzles include a number of figure pieces (Fig. 2–4). His signature piece, a dog named Pal, usually appears in the lower right corner. He probably cut several hundred puzzles during the depression years, but surviving ones are not so common today.

▪ Hallmark Cards, Inc. Kansas City, Missouri

Joyce C. Hall (1891–1982) moved to Kansas City as a teenager in 1910 and began selling postcards, stationery, gifts, and books. He was soon joined by his two brothers; as the firm of Hall Brothers Inc., they introduced their own line of greeting cards in 1915. Although they began to use the Hallmark brand name in the 1920s, the company officially changed its name to Hallmark Cards Inc. only in 1954.

Hallmark is best known in the puzzle world for the Springbok puzzles that it began making in 1967. But it also made some earlier ventures into die-cut puzzles, mostly puzzles that had a twist. In the 1930s they sold several brands of puzzles including Cross-Word Jumbles, a very difficult series of double-sided puzzles. One side depicted an art masterpiece; the other showed a completed crossword puzzle. The puzzle was cut into rectangular pieces from the crossword side; and the puzzler was supposed to assemble the pieces based on the crossword puzzle clues, since the shapes of the pieces were not distinctive.

The company introduced jigsaw puzzle greeting cards around 1940 and continued to manufacture them for decades. The sender was instructed to sign the card, take the pieces apart, and mail them in the small pouch or box that was supplied.

In 1967 Hallmark acquired Springbok Editions Ltd. (see below), and entered the puzzle industry on a large scale. Since then the company has turned out hundreds of different designs for adult puzzles, both traditional puzzles and novelties such as mystery puzzles and a psychological puzzle game, *Your Secret Self.*

Hallmark's Springbok puzzles continue in production after twenty-three years, and are abundantly available to collectors. Greeting card and other puzzles produced before 1967 are quite scarce.

▪ G. J. Hayter & Co., Ltd. Bournemouth, England

As a young boy, Gerald J. Hayter was intrigued by a wooden jigsaw puzzle distributed in a political campaign by one of the candidates. As a result he took up puzzle cutting as a hobby, which he continued into adulthood. During a brief stint of employment at a bank, he moonlighted by selling puzzles that he cut in the evenings. He was soon successful enough to give up banking altogether and to enter the puzzle business full-time. His firm, founded shortly after World War I, became one of the largest and longest-lived producers of wood puzzles in England.

The Hayter Company exported a substantial fraction of its production to the United States, where its Victory puzzles were sold through department and toy stores. Company catalogs show a wide variety of children's and adult puzzles, ranging in size from 5 to 2000 pieces. The children's puzzles are difficult to date precisely, since many were in continuous production from the 1930s through the 1980s.

Fig. 2-5. *The Victory Jungle Puzzle*, produced by G. J. Hayter for over fifty years, is cut on the outlines of the animals so they can be used as play figures. 13¼″ x 24″, 87 hand-cut plywood pieces. Cardboard box, 9½″ x 16½″, with guide picture. This puzzle also was produced in two smaller sizes.

Some of the perennial favorites included the *Jungle* (Fig. 2–5), *Circus*, *Farm-Yard*, and *Dogs* puzzles, all of which featured special cut-out animal pieces that also served as play figures.

All of the children's puzzles, as well as some of the adult puzzles, were supplied with a guide picture glued to the lid of the box. Transportation pictures, including ocean liners and trains, were among the most popular, judging from the catalogs. Hayter also produced the Victory Artistic Series, a luxury line of adult puzzles packaged in gold boxes with no guide picture. A company catalog explains that "the chief interest of solving a jig-saw lies in not knowing the subject which the puzzle makes, but to see the picture gradually form as the pieces are assembled." These puzzles also incorporated many figure pieces to whet the interest of the puzzler. How-

ever, they were stack cut with thick blades, resulting in a looser fit than some other companies' high quality wood puzzles.

In 1970 the company was sold to J. W. Spear & Sons, Ltd. (see below) which continued puzzle production until 1988. Spear made relatively few changes, but did phase out the Artistic brand name and introduced the Gold Box series as a replacement. Cutting on the latter was less careful, resulting in puzzles with cruder figure pieces and a looser fit than before. Spear continued Hayter's earlier practice of subcontracting for other puzzle companies; for example, Springbok Editions' line of wood puzzles was actually manufactured by Hayter in England.

Because they were imported into the United States for over fifty years, Victory puzzles are commonly available to collectors today.

▪ C. I. Hood & Co. Lowell, Mass.

After several years of apprenticeship and training, Charles I. Hood (1845–1922) became a partner in a Lowell, Massachusetts apothecary store in 1870. Within a few years he had built an empire centered around his much-touted nostrum, Hood's Sarsaparilla. Hood's advertising was imaginative and diverse, starting with calendars

in 1886. The company was the first to produce die-cut advertising puzzles, beginning in 1891 with the *Rainy Day and Balloon* puzzle. Customers received the puzzle in exchange for three trademarks from Hood's wrappers.

Hood continued to distribute premium puzzles over the next twenty years,

A WEDDING IN CATLAND.

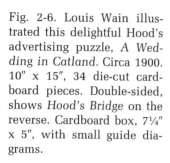

Fig. 2-6. Louis Wain illustrated this delightful Hood's advertising puzzle, *A Wedding in Catland*. Circa 1900. 10″ x 15″, 34 die-cut cardboard pieces. Double-sided, shows *Hood's Bridge* on the reverse. Cardboard box, 7¼″ x 5″, with small guide diagrams.

including the *Hood's Four-in-One Puzzle*, the *Wedding in Catland* illustrated by Louis Wain (Fig. 2–6), *Hood's Auto Race*, *Hood's Farm Puzzle*, and the *Panama Canal Puzzle*. Charles Hood's death in 1922 brought an end to the company; however, its name can still be seen on the original factory's smokestack in Lowell.

Although the company produced only a small number of titles, each puzzle was printed in great numbers. As a result, they are perhaps the easiest of the early advertising puzzles to find, with the *Rainy Day and Balloon Puzzle* being the most common.

▪ Jaymar Specialty Co., Inc.
Brooklyn, Lake Success, and New York City

Jaymar Specialty Co. got its start around 1925 with the help of Louis Marx, the "Toy King," whose firm was famous for its metal toys. Louis Marx financed his father Jacob and his sister Rose in setting up Jaymar, a new company to produce wood and paper toys. The two companies were tightly aligned for many years, with Jaymar using the Marx showroom in the New York Toy Building (at 200 Fifth Avenue) for about a decade. Even after Jaymar established a separate showroom, it was always on the same floor as the Marx space. Until the early 1950s the Marx Company handled all the selling for Jaymar.

During the 1950s, under the leadership of Max Borden and Ralph Kaufman (the current president) Jaymar became more independent of Louis Marx. The result is that Jaymar is a strong and thriving com-

pany today. It is still a family firm, closely held by the descendents of Rose Marx Borden. It maintains its showroom at 200 Fifth Avenue in Manhattan, as well as several different production facilities. In 1984 the company headquarters were relocated from the original address in Brooklyn to more modern facilities in Lake Success, N.Y. The Louis Marx Company, however, has not survived. Quaker Oats bought out Marx in 1972 and promptly began to lose money. Subsequent owners were also unsuccessful and by 1980 the Marx line was totally defunct.

Jaymar's entry into the jigsaw puzzle business in 1942 illustrates its historically close association with the Marx toy company. Because of World War II much of the Marx production line was idle then; metals were needed for the war effort and

Fig. 2-7. Subtracting A Zero, one of the Modern Fighters for Victory Series by Jaymar. 14″ x 21¾″, 306 die-cut cardboard pieces, including figure pieces. Cardboard box, 8″ x 10¼″, with small guide picture, is illustrated in Chapter 15.

were not available to toy manufacturers. So some of the Marx workers were employed making wood and paper toys for Jaymar. Bill Keller, an executive at the Marx plant in Erie, Pennsylvania, was very instrumental in developing the puzzle line, according to Ralph Kaufman. In fact, the pictures used on the Jaymar Modern Fighters For Victory puzzles were copyrighted by Louis Marx & Co. in 1942 (Fig. 2–7).

Jaymar quickly expanded its line of puzzles for adults and introduced children's puzzles right after World War II. It has been a leader in production of die-cut frame-tray and other children's puzzles. Jaymar is one of the oldest Disney licensees in the toy business, and has produced Disney theme puzzles for both children and adults. Jaymar has held licenses for many other characters over the years, ranging from Molly Goldberg and Kukla, Fran 'n Ollie to Li'l Abner and Bozo the Clown.

Jaymar's puzzle production has grown tremendously over the years. In the 1940s and early 1950s puzzles accounted for at most 15 percent of total company sales. Today the figure is closer to 50 percent, all children's puzzles. Jaymar discontinued production of puzzles for adults in 1988, deciding instead to concentrate on its highly successful children's puzzles. Other products today include toy pianos and other musical and scientific instrument toys. The current logo of "Jaymar" enclosed in an oval has been used since about 1959.

Because of the company's long history, Jaymar puzzles are abundant today. The scarcer and more valuable ones date from the 1940s, with World War II and Disney themes being the most valued collectibles.

- ## Leisur (sic) Hour (see Browning, above)

- ## Leisure Hour Puzzle Co.
  ## Melrose, Mass.

Except through its surviving puzzles, little is known about the Leisure Hour Puzzle Co. (This company's products should not be confused with the Leisur Hour puzzles made by James Browning nor with the Leisure Hour Picture Puzzle made by an unknown company.) City directories for Melrose do not record the Leisure Hour Puzzle

Co. at all. Most likely, it was a one-person operation active in the 1908–1915 period.

The company invariably used solid wood, rather than plywood, and cut the pieces along color lines, making the puzzles very difficult. The plain boxes have simple labels with the puzzle title written in by hand. The company also sold puzzles under other brand names, including L. S. & H. Picture Puzzle of Portland, Maine and The Original Thread and Needle Shop of Boston. These puzzles are still quite plentiful in New England, indicating that the firm must have produced large quantities of puzzles for some time.

▪ Madmar Quality Co. Utica, N.Y.

When Miles H. Bickelhaupt began to produce wooden toys and novelties in 1914, he called his new company Madmar, based on the name of his daughter Madeleine Mary. The firm began puzzle production around 1920 and sales grew rapidly until the peak of the Depression craze in 1933. During the 1940s and 1950s, as puzzle sales tapered off, other product lines came to dominate Madmar's business. When Bickelhaupt retired in the mid-1950s, Foster Paper Company of Utica bought the business. It continued to make Madmar puzzles on a limited basis until 1967.

Madmar made hand-cut puzzles for both children and adults, using both plywood and composition board. They also produced die-cut puzzles on a limited scale.

They used the Blue Ribbon, Interlox, and Mayfair brand names for the adult puzzles. Children's puzzles came in dozens of different series including: Raggedy Ann, Tiny Tot, Aviation, Favorite, Playmates, etc.; some used illustrations by popular artists like Johnny Gruelle, Maxfield Parrish, Harrison Cady, and Clara Burd. Madmar offered a large selection of dissected maps, both under its own label and under the labels of Montgomery Ward and other department stores.

Although most Madmar puzzles were stack cut, four at a time, the pieces had a tight fit, because cutters filed the saw blades to make them thinner. Madmar puzzles for both children and adults are easily found today.

▪ McLoughlin Brothers New York, N.Y.

McLoughlin was one of the most prominent names in American publishing history for a century. John McLoughlin began publishing children's books in New York in 1828. When he and his partner retired in 1848, his sons John Jr. and Edmond took over the business. They adopted the McLoughlin Brothers name around 1858, and began to make some important innovations.

During the 1850s the firm diversified. In addition to their staple product, books, they introduced a variety of toys, including jigsaw puzzles, blocks, games, paper dolls, and valentines. Their first jigsaw puzzles, produced around the time of the Civil War, were made from hand-colored pictures glued to wood. After the Civil War, the company moved boldly into the burgeoning field of chromolithography. In 1870 they expanded with a new Brooklyn factory, at that time the largest color printing plant in the United States. In 1887, McLoughlin bought out the Peter G. Thomson

Company, a much smaller competitor based in Cincinnati, Ohio.

The new color printing techniques contributed to McLoughlin Brothers' dominance in the production of printed goods for children for the rest of the nineteenth century. The pictures used for jigsaw puzzles are typical of the dynamic and colorful artistry of the firm. Although their earliest illustrations were shamelessly copied from European sources, in the post Civil War period they relied more on newly emerging native talent. Justin Howard, whose cartoons created Uncle Sam, illustrated numerous McLoughlin products. Other artists who supplied illustrations included Thomas Nast (known for his Santa Claus pictures in addition to his political cartoons) and Palmer Cox (creator of the Brownies).

McLoughlin Brothers got a lot of mileage out of their artwork by presenting it in a number of different formats. A set of six lithographs used to illustrate a book, often was used in a six-sided cube puzzle. The set also could be used to produce six different jigsaw puzzles, usually sold in pairs. Nevertheless, by the 1890s demand for the company's products was so high that its firm employed seventy-five artists.

The most striking McLoughlin puzzles are the large-format ones (50 pieces or more) published between 1885 and 1905. The scenes of locomotives, ships, and fire engines embody an action that is irresistible to children and adults alike (Fig. 2–8). McLoughlin puzzles also highlighted current events such as the 1892–93 Columbian Exposition in Chicago, and the Spanish-American War. The large number of these puzzles that have survived today is some indication that McLoughlin Brothers must have produced them in great quantities and distributed them widely during the late nineteenth century. In fact some of the more popular items appeared in McLoughlin Brothers catalogs for over two decades.

Distribution may have increased too

Fig. 2-8. *The Werra* is typical of McLoughlin's large puzzles of the 1885–1905 period. 23½" x 17½", 48 hand-cut pressboard pieces. Wood frame and cardboard box, 12" x 9", with guide picture.

in response to some cost-cutting moves by the company. By around 1885 the company had replaced wood with pressboard in virtually all of its jigsaw puzzles. By 1900, even the six-sided cube puzzles were hollow cardboard rather than solid wood. And the sturdy nineteenth-century boxes with wood frames had given way to boxes made entirely of cardboard.

The twentieth century, however, was unkind to the venerable firm. After the death of John McLoughlin Jr. in 1905, his sons were not able to keep up with new developments in the printing industry. The firm lost out to its competitors, and in 1920 was sold to the Milton Bradley Company of Springfield, Massachusetts. Although Milton Bradley continued to publish McLoughlin Brothers books until the mid-1940s, the era of the McLoughlin puzzle ended in 1920.

• Par Company, Ltd.
New York and North Massapequa, N.Y.

The Par Company, often described as the Rolls Royce of the puzzle business, began like many others in the depths of the Great Depression. John Henriques and Frank Ware, two young men with no job prospects, cut their first Par puzzles at the dining room table in early 1932 and displayed them in a Manhattan shop window. Unlike most of the contemporary firms, which disappeared after a few years, Par grew even stronger and more prestigious as time went on.

Their secrets were marketing and quality. Ware and Henriques were friends with some Broadway producers. With these contacts they quickly developed a clientele of the rich and famous, including such notables as Bing Crosby, Gary Cooper, Clare Booth Luce, Marlene Dietrich, and Marilyn Monroe, as well as various Vanderbilts, DuPonts, and Fords.

Par puzzles were renowned for their custom cutting and personalization. Ware and Henriques would happily cut names, dates, messages, or special figure pieces into a picture selected by the buyer. One of their most famous clients, the Duke of Windsor, always insisted that his puzzles contain pieces cut in the shapes of the family crest and his four cairn terriers; puzzles for his wife had to include the initials "W.W." patterned after her signature.

Ware and Henriques also delighted in tricking puzzlers with irregular edges and gaps within the picture (Fig. 2–9). They put no pictures on the boxes and devised titles that were intentionally deceptive; for example, a puzzle of P.T. Barnum and Jenny Lind was labeled *The Nightingale's Knight.* The "par time" supplied on the label was a constant source of frustration to clients, since it was based on the time that it took Henriques (a *very* fast puzzler) to assemble the puzzle.

Par's prices, like the quality of the puzzles, were sky high; in the mid-sixties prices ranged from $75 for the smallest size to $2000 for the top-of-the line puzzle. But Par's popularity was not limited to rich celebrities. The partners had begun by renting their puzzles out by the week, and they continued this service for three decades. Eventually, tired of coping with the problem of missing pieces, they sold off

Fig. 2-9. The Par puzzle, *Stepping Out,* is particularly tricky because wood has been removed to accent the pieces shaped like band players. 1940s. 15½" x 19½", 549 hand-cut mahogany plywood pieces, including figure pieces and irregular edge. Cardboard box, 7½" x 9¾".

the rental collection at a fraction of their regular prices. The rental puzzles, of course, are not personalized and generally have less imaginative cutting than those that were produced for special orders.

Par puzzles are easily recognizable. The plain black boxes with green labels were so sturdy that most have survived. Even if the box is gone, the fine mahogany plywood, the intricate figure pieces, and the seahorse signature piece are distinctive.

Par puzzles continued in production for almost fifty years. The partners cherished their independence and the creative possibilities of their chosen craft. But in 1974 Ware retired and turned the business over to his long-time assistant, Arthur Gallagher. (Henriques had died in 1972.) Gallagher operated Par from Long Island for a few years, until he too retired around 1980. At that point Par vitually disappeared from the scene, although Gallagher's former assistant, John Madden, still cuts about a dozen puzzles per year on a part-time basis.

Although thousands of Par puzzles were made over the years, they rarely turn up at antique shows or flea markets. Par puzzles were so expensive to start with that their original owners treasure them and pass them down within their families. The puzzles that do appear for sale are snatched up quickly, especially the special-order ones with irregular edges and personalized cutting designs.

• Parker Brothers, Inc. Salem, Mass.

Pastime Puzzles

George S. Parker produced his first game, *Banking*, in 1883 at the age of sixteen. His immediate success led him to expand rapidly, and his first children's puzzles appeared in his 1887 catalog. His company continued as a major producer of children's puzzles well into the 1960s.

Parker's children's puzzles, although very attractive and highly collectible, are not the company's claim to fame in the puzzle field. Parker's renown derives instead from their Pastime line, excellent wood puzzles for adults produced for half a century. July 1908 ads in *Playthings* show that Parker was the first major company to get involved in the puzzle craze of the time. In 1909 the company stopped making games and devoted all its resources to puzzle production. At their peak, they employed 225 operators of jigsaws, all of them women, to cut puzzles. Puzzle production also mushroomed during the early 1930s, with the Depression puzzle craze.

Pastime puzzles are instantly recognizable by the color line cutting and the marvelous figure pieces, cut to resemble birds, animals, letters, people, and many imaginative and delightful geometric shapes (Fig. 2–10). The figure pieces were introduced around 1910, patented in 1917, and copyrighted in 1932. Although the company developed a book of patterns for cutters to follow, the best workers designed their own more elaborate figure pieces. Their pride in their work is reflected in the fact that each puzzle box has an inside label to identify the individuals who cut and finished it and the date. Pastime puzzles were sold in boxes with no guide pictures. The boxes were usually white, although colored boxes were sometimes used before 1920.

Parker Brothers did custom work for some clients, using the most talented puzzle cutters to fill these special orders. Miss Josephine Flood bought numerous intricately cut Pastimes during the 1930s and 1940s, to sell and rent out from her Picture Puzzle Mart on New York's Park Avenue. Department stores like Macy's and Bamberger's sold similar puzzles in wooden boxes; these were probably also cut by Par-

Fig. 2-10. *End of a Perfect Day—Happy Skaters* is a typical Pastime puzzle with many figure pieces. 1920. 10" x 15", 200 hand-cut plywood pieces. Cardboard box, 4½" x 9".

ker Brothers. Another special Pastime item was the contest set, consisting of a boxed set of four to twelve small puzzles, for use as party games.

While the Pastime puzzles were the top of the line item, Parker also aimed at the lower end of the market with other wooden puzzles, including the Climax, Jig-A-Jig, and Jig Wood puzzles. These were all noninterlocking with no figure pieces. Paramount puzzles, sold under the Salem Puzzle Company name, were actually made by Parker Brothers; although similar to the Pastime puzzles, they were not of the same high quality, and were perhaps produced by apprentices. None of these brands had the longevity of the Pastimes.

Parker produced wooden puzzles for adults in great numbers over the years. The company issued separate catalogs for the Pastime puzzles, each containing a hundred or more titles and illustrating some of the subjects. Puzzle production dwindled after World War II, when rising labor costs forced price increases and cutbacks in demand. The company ultimately shut down the Pastime puzzle department in the late 1950s. They then shifted to producing some die-cut puzzles for adults, but those too were phased out in the late 1970s.

Because of their long production history, Parker Brothers puzzles are easily found today. Standard Pastime puzzles are quite common; special editions like the Flood puzzles and the multi-puzzle contest sets are harder to find. Among the children's puzzles, only those made before Parker Brothers incorporated in 1901 are scarce.

▪ Perfect Picture Puzzles (*see* Consolidated Paper Box Co., above)

▪ Picture Puzzle Exchange Boston, Mass.

M. Isabel Ayer operated the Fountain Pen Store in the Old South Building, Boston, at the beginning of this century. When the first puzzle craze struck, she quickly expanded her business. Her listing in the 1909 city directory advertises: "Puzzles for sale and to loan; pictures, wood, saw blades, boxes, labels, etc., to make puzzles." She also cut puzzles to order for customers who brought in their own pictures. She operated at various addresses in Boston (on Tremont, Exeter, Bromfield, and Province streets) until the early 1940s.

She made hand-cut puzzles for adults, using solid wood in the early years and later plywood. The puzzles are quite difficult, noninterlocking and cut on color lines. The cardboard boxes are dark green, on which a small embossed wreath pattern can be discerned. Because she sold puzzles for over thirty years, Ayer's puzzles are now relatively common throughout New England.

▪ Margaret Richardson
New York, N.Y., and Dennis, Mass.

Margaret H. (Mrs. Hayden) Richardson started making her Perplexity puzzles as a one-person operation in March 1908 at the beginning of the first great craze for adult puzzles. Three months later the *New York Times* reported that she was employing twelve workers who were turning out over one thousand puzzles per month. Although most of the puzzles were sold through Brentano's Fifth Avenue store, she also took private orders, particularly from society people who bought puzzles for weekend house parties.

Perplexity puzzles are noninterlocking and cut along color lines from solid wood, making even the smallest puzzles very difficult to complete (Fig. 2–11). The plain white boxes show a perplexed man studying a puzzle piece.

Richardson must have continued in the puzzle business for some time, judging from the fact that Perplexity puzzles turn up fairly frequently today. Some puzzles have a Cape Cod address on the label, and perhaps are later than the New York ones.

Fig. 2-11. The narrow jagged pieces in *The Gleaners* are typical of Margaret Richardson's Perplexity puzzles. 12" x 15½", 406 hand-cut wood pieces. Cardboard box, 6¼" x 6¼".

Fig. 2-12. The *Tillie the Toiler* puzzle set is one of many comic character puzzles that Saalfield sold in the Depression. Each of the four puzzles is 8″ x 9¾″, approx. 50 die-cut cardboard pieces. Cardboard box, 8¼″ x 10″, with one guide picture.

▪ Saalfield Publishing Co. Akron, Ohio

Arthur J. Saalfield founded the Saalfield Publishing Co. in 1900. By 1909 the company had incorporated and begun to move into the field of children's books, where it was an industry leader for over half a century. Saalfield also published a number of related products including die-cut puzzles, games, and activity sets.

Saalfield's biggest production of puzzles came during the 1930s and 1940s. The company began making its Interlox series of adult puzzles during the Depression years, along with an extensive line of children's puzzles. It also was particularly successful with its boxed sets of comic character puzzles, including such favorites as Mickey Mouse, Bringing Up Father, Just Kids, and Tillie the Toiler (Fig. 2–12). During World War II the company added topical puzzles such as *Liberators of the World*, depicting FDR and Churchill, and the Victory Series of war scenes.

Between World War II and the company's bankruptcy in 1974, puzzle production concentrated on simple frame tray puzzles for children. Saalfield puzzles are quite abundant today and are easily found by collectors.

▪ Selchow & Righter Co. New York and Bay Shore, N.Y.

E. G. Selchow, originally a box maker in New York, got into the puzzle and game business in 1870. He had supplied boxes to Albert Swift, a manufacturer of games. When Swift got into financial trouble, Selchow as one of the creditors was able to take over the business. He kept John Righter, Swift's talented clerk, to help run the business. By 1880 Righter had become a full partner, and the company's name was changed to Selchow & Righter.

Over the next century or so, the company became most famous for three best-sellers: *Parcheesi*, *Scrabble*, and *Trivial Pursuit*. Puzzles, though less renowned, also constituted an important part of the

Selchow and Righter line during its history. The firm began to manufacture simple strip puzzles — *Sliced Birds, Sliced Animals*, etc. — during its first decade, issuing them at first under the name of E. G. Selchow. Although some of the pictures were blatantly plagiarized from John James Audubon's drawings, the company got the courts to agree in 1895 that another maker of sliced puzzles was violating Selchow & Righter's trademark. In addition to sliced puzzles, Selchow & Righter produced some standard children's puzzles during the nineteenth century.

During the first quarter of the twentieth century, Selchow and Righter was primarily a jobber, selling other companies' products to retailers. The company then shifted to manufacturing and began to develop new products. In 1933, in addition to reintroducing sliced puzzles, Selchow & Righter produced a varied line of puzzles for children and adults. They used the Pandora and Rak-A-Brane brand names,

and produced both die-cut cardboard and hand-cut wood puzzles. Although most of these were dropped soon after the Depression puzzle craze ended, the sliced puzzles continued in the product line until the mid-1950s. The company also briefly brought back adult puzzles, including a Vista brand, during the 1970s.

Selchow & Righter continued as a family business until 1986, when it was purchased by Coleco, a toy manufacturer. Coleco discontinued the Selchow & Righter name in 1988, shortly before filing for bankruptcy. In 1989 Hasbro bought most of Coleco's assets and transferred the remaining Selchow & Righter products to its Milton Bradley division.

Sliced puzzles are easily found today. Originally sold in sets of a dozen or so, they are now being broken up and sold as individual puzzles without the box. Other Selchow & Righter puzzles are less common but still available.

▪ Silent Teacher

The Silent Teacher, one of the most popular series of wood puzzles in the last quarter of the nineteenth century, served the dual purposes of both education and advertising. The front of each puzzle featured a map cut along political boundary lines: the world, the United States, or an individual state. The reverse often displayed advertising for one of two Cleveland companies: Sherwin Williams paints or White sewing machines and bicycles. (A few of the puzzles, however, had a second map or plain paper on the reverse.)

These are considered to be the first advertising puzzles, in the sense that they promoted Sherwin Williams and White products. However, the puzzle manufacturers were based in New York state and sold the puzzles independently through a network of agents; so we can only speculate on the relationship between the manufacturers and the advertisers. The puzzle

manufacturers might have been able to charge Sherwin Williams and White for the advertising space; alternatively, they might have used the posters as a convenient and cheaply available backing for the map puzzles. The Sherwin Williams archivist reports that these particular posters were used only for the puzzles and not for other company publicity, lending some support to the first hypothesis. There is also evidence that White gave away jigsaw puzzles as premiums to customers who bought sewing machines; this fact suggests that White may have either commissioned certain puzzles, or bought up large quantities for their own use.

The various companies involved in the production of the Silent Teacher series were probably related to each other, but the passage of a century has obscured the connections. The earliest version may be the one published in a wood box by G. N.

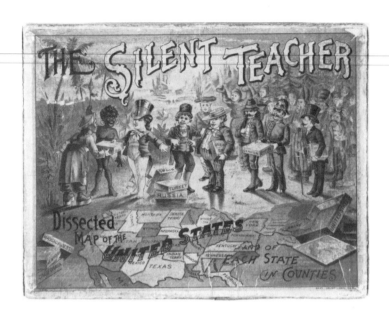

Fig. 2-13. The box for the Silent Teacher puzzles sold by E. J. Clemens. The puzzle is illustrated in Chapter 1.

Tackabury, a map maker of Canastota, New York. The first dated edition was produced in a plain green cardboard box by the Union Sectional Map Co., of Norwich, New York; the 1877 copyright is credited to E. J. Clemens, W. L. Scott, and L. C. Hayes.

During the 1880s the Rev. E. J. Clemens of Clayville, New York, seemed to be operating the business alone. He adopted a colorful label showing people of all nations buying dissected maps of their countries from an American salesman (Fig. 2–13). An inside label discussed at great length the educational merits of the puzzles and other games available from his Object Lesson Publishing Company. Still later, he took more credit for the puzzles and changed the label to read "Clemens' Silent Teacher." During the 1890s the business passed to C. E. Hartman of Utica, N.Y., who contin-

ued to use the "Clemens' Silent Teacher" name. Production may even have continued for a few years during the twentieth century.

Silent Teacher puzzles usually can be identified even if the original box has not survived. Virtually all the puzzles are double-sided. The map side may bear either the Clemens or the Hartman name, although the early editions used maps by commercial map makers like the Coltons. All the puzzles used bright green paper to cover the edges; the overlap on both sides serves to frame the lithographs. Finally, if the reverse contains advertising, the pictures of Sherwin Williams or White products are distinctive evidence they are from the Silent Teacher series.

These puzzles are fairly common today in the East and the Midwest where the vast majority of them were originally sold.

• J. W. Spear & Sons, Ltd. Enfield, England

The J. W. Spear & Sons company has been a prominent international producer of puzzles, games, paper dolls, and constructional toys for over a century. The com-

pany, which began as a pencil manufacturer in England in 1878, opened a factory in Nuremburg, Germany in 1886. It published many of its products in several different languages, and exported them throughout Europe and to the United States.

Spear apparently produced jigsaw puzzles during two distinct periods. Most of its early children's puzzles date from the 1890–1935 period. They typically were published in sets, with three or four puzzles lying flat in a box. The boxes sometimes identified the company only as "J.W.S. & S., Bavaria." Puzzles were hand-cut from thick cardboard rather than wood.

More recently Spear got into the production of both children's and adult wooden puzzles when it acquired the G. J. Hayter Co. in 1970. (See Hayter, above.) However, it ended production of the Victory and Gold Box series in 1988 and sold its puzzle making equipment to another English company, Michael Stanfield Ltd. Collectors in the United States today turn up Spear puzzles from both periods on a regular basis.

▪ Springbok Editions, Inc. New York, N.Y.

Springbok Editions puzzles generally are credited with having caused the resurgence in interest in jigsaw puzzles that began in the mid-1960s. Despite its brief existence as an independent company from 1963 to 1967, Springbok created tremendous excitement during those years.

Owners Katie and Bob Lewin had been intrigued by circular jigsaw puzzles produced in England by John Waddington Ltd. In the early 1960s, with some technical assistance from Waddington, they founded Springbok Editions to produce similar die-cut puzzles for adults in the U.S. The novelty of the circular puzzles, sold in circular boxes, in itself had a strong market impact. But another innovative move by the company was just as important, their focus on fine art. Although jigsaw puzzles had

sometimes used art masterpieces as subjects, by 1960 most adult puzzles featured standard photos of covered bridges, snow-capped mountains and other scenic beauties.

Springbok had an immediate success in 1964 when it introduced such titles as *The Adoration of the Magi* by Fra Filippo Lippi and Jackson Pollock's *Convergence* (billed as "the world's most difficult jigsaw puzzle"), reproduced with high-quality color lithography from the originals. The latter sold well over 100,000 copies within a few months (Fig. 2–14).

Museums were delighted to cooperate in this endeavor; the Albright-Knox Gallery in Buffalo reported that visitors began to arrive at the museum asking specifically where they could find the infamous Pol-

Fig. 2-14. *Convergence* by Jackson Pollock made a very difficult puzzle because the colors change unpredictably from one piece to the next. 11½" x 19½", 340 die-cut cardboard pieces. Cardboard box, 6" x 14", with guide picture.

lock painting, over which they had already struggled for so many hours. Mrs. Lewin commented: "You understand a Jackson Pollock better after you have made the puzzle." Springbok even commissioned some original art for its puzzles, including works by Salvador Dali as well as noted wildlife illustrators like Roger Tory Peterson.

Springbok was also the first to cater to the hard-core puzzlers, the ones who used to do puzzles upside down because they found the picture side too easy. Springbok challenged them with solid color puzzles including *Red Riding Hood's Hood* (all red), *Close-up of the Three Bears* (all brown), and *Snow White without the Dwarfs* (all white). Assemblages of objects, ranging from hats to antique cars, were another puzzle feature introduced by Springbok to increase the difficulty of puzzles.

Although the vast majority of Springbok's puzzles were die-cut, the company also marketed some wooden puzzles. The company subcontracted the actual cutting of the wooden puzzles to G. J. Hayter in England (see above).

The rapid success and growth of Springbok puzzles took the Lewins by surprise. They were involved in other companies at the time and felt it would be hard to give Springbok the resources needed for continued success in competition with established puzzle companies. At the same time Hallmark Cards was looking to enter the puzzle business on a large scale, and began to court Springbok. The sale was consummated in 1967, and Springbok became a division of Hallmark. Because of their immense popularity from 1963–67, Springbok Editions puzzles are still quite easy for collectors to acquire.

▪ Joseph K. Straus Products Corp. Brooklyn, N.Y.

Joseph K. Straus was one of the largest American producers of wood jigsaw puzzles in the post-World War II years. Joseph Straus spent his career working for the Ullman Co., which had made some jigsaw puzzles, in addition to their regular line of prints and picture frames. In 1933 he rented space from Ullman and set up his own puzzle business, along with his wife. They had an immediate hit with a puzzle depicting FDR, and continued to make wooden puzzles for about forty years.

The company became known for its basic no-frills wood puzzles, sold at an affordable price (two cents per piece in the mid-1960s.) Cutting techniques were streamlined with stack-cutting often used to keep costs down. Most puzzles featured a standard strip-cut pattern, with no figure pieces. Children's puzzles were often sold in sets of two or three. Map puzzles were a perennial favorite in the children's puzzle line.

Straus packaged its earliest puzzles in plain orange boxes with no picture on the box. During the late 1940s and the 1950s the company used plain blue, tan, or mottled boxes with a small guide picture on the cover. A few years after the company's 1957 incorporation, it adopted a blue and white box with a puzzle design on the cover and the guide picture on the bottom of the box.

In addition to its standard puzzle line, Straus also created some more elaborate items. Sculptured puzzles, cut in two layers, gave a three-dimensional effect. The company sold some puzzles with simple figure pieces under their own Regal label and also under the F.A.O. Schwarz Special Cut label. Straus did some special orders, including a limited edition *Lindbergh Tapestry* jigsaw puzzle distributed by *American Heritage* in 1970 (Fig. 2–15).

Straus developed their own puzzle club as a marketing tool. They sold by mail,

Fig. 2-15. Straus made only 3000 copies of *The Lindbergh Tapestry* for distribution by *American Heritage* as a premium. 10½" x 29¾", 500 handcut plywood pieces. Cardboard box, 7" x 10½". Contains guide picture.

shipping a different puzzle each month to club members. The company also distributed puzzles widely through department stores in the East and Midwest.

The firm closed in 1974 when the original family members retired. Straus puzzles, after being in production for over forty years are quite easy for today's collectors to find.

▪ Carroll A. Towne
Auburndale, Mass.

Cal Towne's experience with jigsaw puzzles is typical of many during the Depression. After graduating from the University of Massachusetts in 1928, he married and embarked on a career. But the stock market crash in 1929 cost him his job as a landscape architect and hard times ensued. Encouraged by a fiercely loyal wife who loved jigsaw puzzles, he bought a saw for $29.50. Together they began a business of renting and selling puzzles.

Towne's initials suggested the brand name, Cut by CAT, and each puzzle included his cat-shaped signature piece. His puzzles are imaginatively cut, with many figure pieces and deceptive color line cutting. They are packaged in plain boxes with no guide picture. His wife Emily did all the sanding, checking and packaging. She also staved off the tax collectors, who came to collect on the proceeds of the rental operation, by reading them the riot act about harassing hard-working but poor and struggling young couples!

Towne's puzzle enterprise came to an end around 1933 when the cheaper die-cut cardboard puzzles flooded the market. He later put his puzzle-making talents to use in his career as a planner for the Tennessee Valley Authority; his interchangeable jigsaw maps facilitated the quick preparation of charts to show the geographical distributions of various population characteristics.

Since Towne was only in the puzzle business for a couple of years, examples of his work are hard to find today.

▪ Raphael Tuck & Sons
London, England

Raphael Tuck & Sons, one of the biggest and most renowned producers of postcards worldwide, was also an important puzzle manufacturer in England. Founded in London in 1866 as a small retailer of prints and frames, the firm began to publish its own greeting cards in 1871. By the turn of the century it was a major publisher of postcards and prints as well as of printed goods for children, including puzzles, paper dolls and books. The company established a New York office in the 1890s

Fig. 2-16. Tuck's Labrador Zag-Zaw series had polar themes in the prints, cutting designs, and boxes. This puzzle shows St. Anthony, Headquarters of Grenfell Mission. 7½" x 16", 195 hand-cut plywood pieces. Cardboard box, 5½" x 8½".

to handle American sales; by 1900 they had to move to larger quarters on Fifth Avenue.

Nineteenth-century puzzle production was limited to wooden children's puzzles, often sold as sets in wooden boxes with an accompanying book. By World War I, the firm began to use die-cutting for some of the children's puzzle line.

When the first craze for adult puzzles struck in 1908, the company responded in two ways. First, it created picture-puzzle postcards. A flat mailing packet with space for a message enclosed a die-cut puzzle made from a Tuck postcard; an uncut version of the same card graced the front of the packet, so that it resembled a standard postcard when mailed. Tuck cleverly marketed these puzzle cards in boxes of six. The package promoted their use for party games, where guests could compete in a race to assemble a puzzle most quickly.

The company also ventured into wooden adult puzzles with the development of the Zag-Zaw series around 1909. Unlike the postcard puzzles, which were only produced for a few years, the Zag-Zaw puzzles were a staple of the Tuck product line until the start of World War II. A number of company catalogs have

survived, each depicting a hundred or more different pictures available and with sizes ranging from 50 to 2000 pieces.

All the Zag-Zaw puzzles incorporated figure pieces into the cutting. Although the early designs were crude, puzzles produced in the 1920s and 1930s displayed a splendid variety of figure pieces, from mice to legs to flowers. Over time there was also a transition from a noninterlocking to a fully interlocking cut. Tuck sold its Zag-Zaw puzzles in plain boxes, usually orange or dark red, with no picture to guide the puzzler.

During the 1930s Tuck produced a special series of Labrador Zag-Zaw puzzles, sales of which benefitted the International Grenfell Association (Fig. 2–16). The puzzle pictures pertained to the medical mission established by Sir Wilfred Grenfell in Labrador; the pieces shaped like seals, kayaks, and penguins also highlighted the polar theme.

Tuck went out of the puzzle business during World War II, when its plant was destroyed in the London blitz. Because Tuck puzzles were sold by major department stores in the United States for many years, however, they are fairly common for today's collectors.

■ Tuco Work Shops, Inc. Lockport, N.Y.

Tuco Work Shops produced puzzles for almost forty years, as a division of The Upson Company, a manufacturer of wallboard. The story began during the depths of the Great Depression. The construction industry was devastated, and orders for wallboard had slowed to a trickle. Company executives, searching for an alternative source of revenue, turned to jigsaw puzzles. They developed their own steel dies and began producing puzzles from $\frac{3}{16}$" wallboard in the fall of 1932. The puzzle name, Tuco, was derived from The Upson Company's initials.

Tuco puzzles were first marketed only through Kresge's stores. But as the demand for puzzles grew in 1933, Tuco used other outlets. Roger Slattery, manager of the Tuco Work Shops from 1932 to 1970, reports that within a year Tuco was shipping as many as 50,000 puzzles daily. Retail stores would send their own trucks to the Lockport plant in order to assure a supply for their customers.

The puzzle craze of 1932–33 diminished after about a year. The Upson Company, however, continued to produce Tuco puzzles until 1971. Tuco puzzles were noted for several characteristics. Wallboard, the material used to make Tuco puzzles, was thicker than the cardboard used by other manufacturers; so Tuco puzzles came closer to the weight and feel of the more expensive hand-cut wood puzzles. Because of this thick material, Tuco's steel rule dies had to be stronger, and thus less intricate, than those of the competitors. As a result, Tuco puzzles were noninterlocking until the mid-1950s, when the company began to use thinner board (Fig. 2–17).

Finally, Tuco marketed its puzzles without pictures on the boxes throughout the 1930s. The first puzzles in the Art Picture Puzzle series, depicting famous masterpieces, had plain orange boxes. Within a few months multicolored puzzle pieces decorated many Tuco boxes. Tuco introduced the Deluxe series, with small pictures on the boxes around 1940. Some Tuco products, such as Dubl-Thik puzzles, did not use the Tuco name and were marketed independently.

In 1971 the Upson Company sold off the Tuco Work Shop division to Munro Games in Buffalo, New York. Tuco puzzles

Fig. 2-17. Throughout the 1930s and 1940s Tuco puzzles had thick noninterlocking strip-cut pieces, as shown in this example, *A Merry Chase*. 11" x 15", 204 pressboard pieces. Cardboard box, 8¾" x 6½".

did not prosper under Munro ownership, and the puzzle line was resold several times. The Tuco name finally disappeared around 1983. The Tuco manufacturing equipment, however, was reconditioned in the 1980s and is still being used by Buffalo Games Inc. of Buffalo, New York to produce jigsaw puzzles.

Tuco puzzles are widely available to collectors today. The most desirable are those from the 1930s and 1940s, especially thematic puzzles, such as those of World War II, and puzzles by popular artists like Hintermeister.

▪ U-Nit (*see* James Browning, above)

▪ University Distributing Co. Boston and Cambridge, Mass.

Information about the University Distributing Co. today comes only from the products that have survived. The company is best known for its Jig of the Week series, produced for seven months during the height of the 1932–33 puzzle craze (Fig. 2–18). Distributed by S.-M. News Company, a new 300-piece puzzle appeared on the newsstands every Wednesday at the bargain price of 25 cents. While most of the puzzles were rectangular, the company experimented with irregular edges on occasion. University Distributing also marketed two smaller lines, the Jig 400 and the monthly Jig De Luxe puzzles.

University Distributing also sold Jig

Wood puzzles, an inexpensive brand of wood puzzles for adults. Parker Brothers was simultaneously advertising their own Jig Wood puzzles (in identical boxes) in 1933. It is not clear which company actually produced the puzzles. It is even possible that still another company manufactured the Jig Wood puzzles and licensed them to both Parker Brothers and University Distributing.

Jig of the Week puzzles, particularly numbers 13 through 24, are widely available today. Early and late puzzles in this series, as well as the other University Distributing brands, are less common.

Fig. 2-18. This 10½″ x 14″ poster advertises *The Fortune Teller*, Jig of the Week Puzzle no. 29.

• Viking Manufacturing Co.
Boston, Mass.

Viking Manufacturing Company was one of the largest of the many manufacturers of die-cut puzzles which blossomed brightly in 1932–33, but quickly faded away when the jigsaw craze ended. Puzzles in its Picture Puzzle Weekly series retailed for 25 cents and were distributed through newsstands by the American News Company, Inc., and its branches. Viking also produced a more expensive monthly puzzle, and some personality puzzles, including at least two *Ed Wynn Picture Puzzles.*

Two other companies producing weekly puzzles may have had some connection with Viking. The Advertising Novelty Mfg. Co. of Philadelphia, Penna.,

also produced a Picture Puzzle Weekly series, using virtually the same box design as Viking. Kindel & Graham of San Francisco published advertisements showing their Jigger Picture Puzzle Weekly in another essentially identical box.

By 1936 Viking was in bankruptcy. Court records reveal that its sales from June 1932 through April 1933 totalled $377,216. Assuming that most of Viking's sales came from the 25-cent puzzles, that figure implies production of almost 1.5 million puzzles in less than a year. It is not surprising that Viking puzzles still can be found easily today.

• Warren Paper Products Co.
Lafayette, Indiana

Like many producers of die-cut puzzles, the Warren Paper Products Company started out as a paper box manufacturer. Founded in 1921, Warren began to diversify in the 1930s when it introduced the Built-Rite line of toys. At first these included paperboard construction toys, doll houses, and models of other buildings. Consumer demand for cardboard toys continued to increase, especially during World War II when metal toys were scarce.

Warren entered the puzzle business relatively late, during the 1940s, but soon became an important producer of puzzles. Puzzles have accounted for about two-thirds of the company's sales throughout

the post-World War II era. Warren used the Built-Rite brand name for both children's and adults' puzzles until 1975. From 1976 to 1986 the Warren name alone appears on all the puzzles. This latter period also saw considerable growth in the use of licensed characters for Warren's children's puzzles.

Random House Publishing of New York acquired Warren in 1986. The company, now known as the Warren Division of Random House, continues to produce a broad line of jigsaw puzzles, games, coloring books, and preschool products.

Old Warren puzzles are widely distributed and easy for collectors to find.

• Western Publishing Co.
Racine, Wis.

Western Publishing Company had its beginnings in 1907 when E. H. Wadewitz purchased a small print shop in Racine. The company, known initially as Western Printing & Lithographing Co., established

Whitman Publishing Co. as a subsidiary in 1916 to handle its children's book business. Western expanded its line considerably over the next quarter-century, adding die-cut jigsaw puzzles and games in

Fig. 2-19. This *Fuzzy Wuzzy Flocked Pre-School Picture Puzzle* is typical of the frame tray puzzles that Whitman produced after World War II. Copyright 1961. 14½″ x 11½″, approx. 25 die-cut cardboard pieces, including figure pieces.

1923, playing cards in 1925, Big Little Books in 1932, and Little Golden Books in 1942.

Both juvenile and adult puzzles bore the Whitman name for most of the company's publishing history. Children's puzzles through the 1930s typically were boxed sets. After World War II the company also became a leader in frame tray puzzles (Fig. 2–19). They even published some Little Golden Books with a small frame tray puzzle inside the back cover. Western has used many licensed characters for its children's puzzles, ranging from Disney to western heroes to Sesame Street.

Western's most prominent lines of adult puzzles were the widely distributed Gold Seal and Guild series introduced after World War II. The company also produced numerous adult puzzles in earlier years, including the Blue Ribbon series in the 1930s and the Fighters for Freedom and Masterpiece series in the 1940s.

In 1960, the company went public and adopted the Western Publishing Co. name. However, it continued to use the Whitman Publishing Co. name on its puzzles until Mattel acquired Western in 1979. Shortly thereafter the Whitman name was phased out and replaced by the Golden line of puzzles, games, books, etc. Mattel divested Western in 1984, and the company continues to operate as an independent entity.

Western's Whitman puzzles were produced by the millions over the years and are abundantly available to collectors. Guild and Gold Seal puzzles are very common; the pre-1945 puzzles can be somewhat harder to find.

▪ Whitman (*see* Western Publishing Co., above)

3 HOW TO DEVELOP A JIGSAW PUZZLE COLLECTION

COLLECTIONS CAN RANGE from just a few objects to thousands. If you aren't careful, your collection can get out of hand. This chapter addresses some of the specific problems facing jigsaw puzzle collectors, from finding and identifying puzzles to displaying and caring for them.

▪ Choosing a Focus

A few collectors can afford to buy anything they like. But most of us have limited resources—time, space, and funds — and early on must establish some criteria for further acquisitions. Puzzle collectors come in many shapes and sizes, each motivated by a different set of collecting goals. There are four broad groups of collectors: the players, the spectators, the savers, and the augmenters.

PLAYERS

Some people turn into puzzle collectors because they are accumulators who enjoy working puzzles. When they discover that the closets are full of puzzles, they refuse to follow the normal course of holding a yard sale or donating the surplus to a charity sale. Instead, they rework all their puzzles, decide that the old ones are really better than the new ones, and start looking for more. The realization that many old puzzles are cheaper than new ones fuels their search, and, voilà! An accumulation has been transformed into a collection.

These collectors look for puzzles that are fun to put together. Most spurn small puzzles, under 150 pieces, because they can be completed too quickly. Some look for special challenges, such as the very large puzzles of 2000 pieces and up. They like puzzles of virtually every subject matter, ranging from traditional scenic views to movie personalities to Norman Rockwell Christmas scenes. The diehard puzzlers in this group buy most of their puzzles at thrift stores and yard sales; if they paid antique store prices, they could not get enough puzzles to satisfy their cravings.

Some of the players concentrate on the wooden puzzles for adults. They put a premium on the craftsmanship that goes into the hand-cut puzzles, enjoy the satisfying feel of wood pieces, and generally favor the puzzles with many figure pieces. They have strong opinions about noninterlocking puzzles. Most eschew them because they don't hold together; a few collectors, however, prefer the noninterlocking puzzles where cutting along the color lines adds to the difficulty.

Another subset of players specializes in the less expensive die-cut puzzles. Some favor the weekly puzzles from the 1930s with no pictures on the boxes. Others buy only certain brands of puzzles, such as Tuco or Springbok, because they like the way the puzzles are cut.

SPECTATORS

Spectators are the collectors who would prefer to buy a puzzle assembled rather than loose in the box. They are much more interested in the graphics of the puzzle than in putting it together. For them, the picture is everything; they study the artistry and design of the print, but don't care how the pieces are cut. Their tastes vary widely. Some specialize in the delicate hand-colored prints of the earliest children's puzzles. Others concentrate on prints by Parrish, Christy, Leyendecker and others from the golden age of illustration in the early 1900s. Still others favor the striking advertising puzzles of the 1930s. Indeed, there are as many possible specialties as there are artistic styles.

SAVERS

Many puzzle collectors are engaged in a search to recapture their childhood. They collect puzzles that they either once owned or wish they had owned. They emphasize character themes (Disney, superheroes, cowboys, etc.), and usually collect primarily children's puzzles with fewer than 100 pieces. For many, puzzles are part of a larger collection that includes toys, games, books, and other childhood treasures. But unlike antique toys and some games, puzzles are still largely affordable.

AUGMENTERS

Some collectors buy puzzles as complementary pieces to a larger collection. The railroadiana collector will buy locomotive puzzles; the map collector also owns dissected maps; the cat collector searches for cats on puzzles; the old time radio buff cherishes personality puzzles from the 1930s; and the Valentine collector must have a few heart-shaped puzzles. Like the spectators, the augmenters are mainly interested in the subject matter, rather than in playing with their puzzles.

In many cases the four categories of collectors vie for the same puzzles at auctions and shows. The *Cunard Liner Aquitania* (Fig. 3−1) will appeal to most of the players, spectators, and savers, as well as to collectors of ocean liner memorabilia. In other areas the puzzle market can be quite segmented. The first Jig of the Week puzzle is a real prize for a collector of weekly puzzles, but of little value to the others.

Fig. 3-1. The *Cunard Liner Aquitania*, made in the 1930s by the Chad Valley Co. of Harborne, England, was sold on board ship for the amusement of passengers on long voyages and cruises. It is 15″ × 22″, 320 hand-cut plywood pieces. Cardboard box, 6½″ × 9¾″.

Obviously, there is no "right" way to collect puzzles. You must decide for yourself where your interests lie. Your pocketbook may play a role too. Collecting nineteenth century children's puzzles will be hard on your wallet; but twentieth century examples are much more reasonably priced. One general rule about other antiques and collectibles also applies to puzzles: buy the best that you can afford within your collecting focus. The top quality objects are the most likely to increase in value.

▪ Finding Puzzles

Once you have decided what type of puzzles to collect, the next problem is finding them. Puzzles are available through all the normal sources for antiques and collectibles: yard sales, thrift stores, flea markets, antique shops and malls, shows, auctions, estate sales, and classified ads. You can consult the local antiques newspaper for details about sources in any given area. But it is important to note some of the differences between the various sources.

Yard sales, thrift stores, and local flea markets have the lowest prices, but require the most time. If you don't have time to visit them on a regular basis, go to an antique shop or mall. The dealers have already picked through the flea markets and selected the good stuff for their shops; naturally, they have increased the prices in the process in order to repay their efforts.

Another alternative is to attend a large regional antique show. The fields of Brimfield, Mass., for example, host thousands of antique and collectibles dealers for over a week during every May, July, and September. The disadvantage of outdoor shows like Brimfield is that dealers are sometimes reluctant to display goods like puzzles, which can be ruined by rain, faded by the sun, or blown into pieces in a high wind. The large indoor shows, such as the annual March "Atlantique City" show in New Jersey, tend to be more productive for puzzles.

Specialized shows are one of the best ways for a collector to locate dealers who

---

Some Sources for Puzzle Collectors

Publications with Regular Coverage of Toys, Games, Puzzles

Antique Toy World, P.O. Box 34509, Chicago, IL 60634.
Collectors Showcase, P.O. Box 837, Tulsa, OK 74101.
The Inside Collector, P.O. Box 98, Elmont Branch, Elmont, NY 11003
Toy Shop, 700 E. State St., Iola, WI 54990.

Auction Houses that Regularly Sell Toys, Games, Puzzles

Noel Barrett, Box 1001, Carversville, PA 18913.
Christie's, 502 Park Avenue, New York, NY 10022.
Hake's Americana & Collectibles, P.O. Box 1444, York, PA 17405 (mail/phone auction).
Ted Maurer, 1931 N. Charlotte St., Pottstown, PA 19464.
New England Auction Gallery, P.O. Box 2273, West Peabody, MA 01960 (mail/phone auction).
Richard W. Oliver, Plaza One, U.S. Route 1, Kennebunk, ME 04043.
Richard Opfer, 1919 Greenspring Dr., Timonium, MD 21093.
Lloyd Ralston, 173 Post Road, Fairfield, CT 06430.
Skinner, Inc., Route 117, Bolton, MA 01451.
Smith House Toy Sales, P.O. Box 336, Eliot, ME 03903.
Sotheby's, 1334 York Avenue, New York, NY 10021.
Richard Withington, RR2, Box 440, Hillsboro, NH 03244.

handle puzzles. Most regions now have frequent antique toy shows, which are good sources for puzzles. Other collectibles shows that are worthwhile for the puzzle collector are paper, advertising, and ephemera shows, where puzzles are quite common.

Specialized auctions are another source for the puzzle collector. Large auction houses like Sotheby's and Christie's have collectibles departments, and feature toys in at least one auction per year, often in the month before Christmas. Some smaller auctioneers routinely handle toys and related items. The last decade also has seen the emergence of several mail-order auc-

tions that specialize in toys and similar collectibles.

Advanced collectors do much of their buying by mail, both in mail/phone auctions and through classified advertising. Many national antiques newspapers and magazines carry extensive advertising. There are also a number of publications that specialize in toys, collectibles, paper, and ephemera. In addition to responding to ads in these publications, many collectors also place their own want ads in them. The accompanying box lists both auction houses and national publications that are of interest to puzzle collectors.

▪ Understanding the Importance of Condition

Condition is of prime importance in buying jigsaw puzzles. A single missing piece can ruin an otherwise great puzzle. And unfortunately, because of the way puzzles are used and stored, lost pieces are a common occurence. Another frequent problem is loss of the original box, which makes it difficult to identify a puzzle correctly. Some condition problems are not immediately apparent. Even a puzzle that appears to be complete in the original box may be lacking an insert or explanatory booklet. In the case of children's puzzles a set of three

may look fine until examination of another example reveals that the box should contain four rather than three puzzles.

Puzzles, like other toys and games, were generally played with by their original owners. So some slight wear and minor defects in condition are almost inevitable. But you need to be wary about more serious defects. Broken, chipped or missing tabs can seriously detract from a puzzle's appearance, as can blank areas where the picture has lifted off from the backing (Fig. 3–2).

Fig. 3-2. This Pastime puzzle suffers from so many defects —missing pieces, missing tabs, and missing paper—that it is hardly worth repairing.

Fig. 3-3. *The Auto Race*, a Hood's advertising puzzle c. 1909, scarce puzzle that is worth buying despite several missing pieces. (Price discounted heavily because of needed repairs.) Produced in several variations around the time of the Lowell, Mass. auto races in 1908–10. The double-sided puzzle shows an owl on the reverse. 10″ × 15″, 100 die-cut cardboard pieces. Cardboard box, 7″ × 5″, with small guide diagrams. (Courtesy of the Siegels)

A puzzle or box can appear dingy just because of the accumulation of years of dust during storage in an attic. While dirt stains can sometimes be cleaned, the brown stains caused by foxing (discoloration from the acid content in the paper) can not. Foxing is a potential problem with most items printed after 1850 because of the high acid content of papers made from wood. Earlier prints on rag paper hardly deteriorate at all, even on wood-backed puzzles.

A puzzle that has been stored in a damp basement is subject to a number of problems. Mildew can damage both puzzles and boxes. Moisture can cause the picture to separate from the puzzle. In wood puzzles the pieces may warp, or layers of plywood may come unglued. Silverfish and other bugs can find fodder in the glue or paper of a puzzle. And small woodworms occasionally tunnel through pieces of wood puzzles and their boxes.

Although many of these defects can be corrected (see below), repairs are a second-best solution. It is better to avoid puzzles in poor condition in the first place, by inspecting them carefully before you buy. Of course, some highly desirable puzzles are worth buying even with condition defects, because they appear for sale so rarely (Fig. 3–3). But for a puzzle with ten or more missing pieces, virtually all of the remaining value is in the box, not in the puzzle itself.

▪ Inspecting a Puzzle

The only way to be sure of condition is to see the puzzle assembled. Dealers in top quality items usually take the time to put a puzzle together, mount it on a board, and wrap it in clear plastic, so that you can examine it carefully. But the average dealer who handles many run-of-the-mill items often can not take the time to do this. Some dealers guarantee their puzzles; if you aren't satisfied you can return purchases for a full refund. But in most cases it's *caveat emptor*, let the buyer beware. And a good rule of thumb is that only about one-half of all puzzles are complete. What's a collector to do if the puzzle is loose in the box?

The first thing to do is ask the dealer if the puzzle is complete. If the answer is "yes," ask the dealer if he put it together himself. If the answer is "yes," and you know the dealer, then you are pretty safe. If you don't know the dealer, or if he says,

"No, but the lady who sold it to me assured me it was complete," then you should proceed with caution.

You should examine the puzzle for any notations about condition. Many original owners made a practice of indicating lost pieces, either on the box or on a slip of paper inside. "All here, March 1933" written on the box lid will gladden the heart of the collector, but then there's the problem of whether any pieces have been lost in the intervening years. The condition of the box gives a clue. Crushed and broken boxes are unlikely to contain complete puzzles. Conversely, if the box is undamaged and carefully tied up with old string, there's a good chance it hasn't been touched since the note was written.

Manufacturers of older wood puzzles were quite meticulous in labeling them. When the label says a puzzle had 117 pieces, it usually did. If you have some time, you can count the pieces to see if there are still 117. Of course, even if there are, you can't be sure all 117 pieces belong to *this* puzzle. If you have a *lot* of time and the dealer is cooperative, you can even put the puzzle together on the spot. (Dealers at crowded shows tend to frown on this practice, for obvious reasons.)

Finally, it is sometimes worth buying puzzles as a lot, rather than individually. The reason is that as a group the puzzles may all be complete, but some of the pieces have been mixed up between the boxes. This happens when the original owner finds a piece on the floor, isn't sure which puzzle it came from, and puts it back into a randomly selected box. Sometimes a group of puzzles is accompanied by a box labeled "extra pieces"; obviously, it is risky to buy one puzzle from the group rather than the entire lot.

The best insurance you can have is to buy puzzles from a dealer who enjoys them and puts them together before selling them. Although such dealers are uncommon, if you find one you should cultivate her. She'll be interested in your collection and in helping you develop it. She'll be reliable in reporting on condition and cooperative in adjusting prices for the rare item that is incorrectly described. You have to cooperate too—by buying ordinary puzzles as well as the best ones, and by recognizing that a lost piece just might be your fault, rather than the dealer's.

With some care you can avoid many of the puzzles that have missing pieces, but you will inevitably acquire some defective ones. Then the question becomes "To repair? or not to repair?"

▪ Making Repairs

Although they are anathema in some collecting fields, most repairs are perfectly acceptable and even desirable in jigsaw puzzles, as long as they are clearly marked. Modern standards of conservation emphasize reversibility. Making a replacement piece for a jigsaw puzzle is perfectly reversible; if the original piece turns up later, the replacement can be discarded (Fig. 3–4).

The major constraint for most collectors is financial. Replacing a missing piece is very time-consuming and therefore costly. Restoration by a professional paper conservator may well be worthwhile for a rare and valuable nineteenth-century puzzle. But it is questionable for a commonplace die-cut puzzle of the 1930s.

Many collectors learn to do their own repairs. An X-Acto knife is all that is needed to cut new pieces for a cardboard puzzle. Replacing wooden pieces is more difficult and generally requires the use of a scroll saw (also called a jigsaw). Once the piece is cut, it can be painted or covered with colored paper to match the surrounding ones. If there is a guide picture that is the same size as the puzzle, you can make a

Fig. 3-4. A professional conservator worked on this charming 1924 Pastime puzzle, *The Guardian*. She has painted the five replacement pieces so skillfully that they hardly can be detected. 9¾″ × 12″, 164 hand-cut plywood pieces, including figure pieces. Cardboard box, 8¼″ × 5¼″.

color photocopy to decorate the replacement piece. But you should never cut up the guide picture itself to make a new piece. The final step is to identify the replace-

ment piece by signing and dating it on the back.

In the case of die-cut puzzles, it is occasionally possible to combine two incomplete puzzles to make a whole one. Don't count on it however. A given company often cut the same picture with several different dies. Or the die was bent during the course of production, so that the cuts on early puzzles don't exactly match those later in the run. Or worse, you buy two copies of the identical puzzle and discover that they are both missing exactly the same piece!

Damaged boxes usually need one of two types of restoration: cleaning or reconstruction. Collectors can do simple cleaning at home, especially for the glossy labels that adorn children's puzzles. A gentle application of a lukewarm solution of soap and water with a sponge or cotton pad can do much to remove years of accumulated grime. (Be careful to test an inconspicuous corner of the label first, as some color printing will run.)

For the box itself use a soft dry brush to brush off dirt. Do not use soap and water on cardboard boxes, as that will weaken them. Rebuilding boxes that have structural damage is best left to an expert; even small repairs with tape can ultimately damage the box if not properly done.

• Displaying and Storing Puzzles

Most collectors like to frame their best puzzles and hang them for display. The danger here is that exposure to light will fade puzzles over time. One strategy is to frame a number of items and rotate them, being careful not to have an individual puzzle on display for more than a year. Be careful to use acid-free mats in framing. And you should *never* (repeat *never*) glue the puzzle pieces to a backing. Plastic box frames (such as those made by Dax) offer a convenient alternative that allows for easy rotation of puzzles.

With limited display space, collectors

must usually store the majority of their puzzles in their boxes on shelves. Protect the puzzles before putting them away, as improper storage can lead to damage. Insert sheets of acid-free paper between puzzles that lie flat in a boxed set, to deter foxing. A box that is already fragile or damaged should be enclosed within a new sturdy box, preferably one that is acid-free. Puzzle boxes should not be stacked more than about five deep; otherwise the weight will eventually crush the boxes on the bottom. Putting a plastic bag around each box will protect the label. The bag should be left unsealed, however, to prevent a buildup of mustiness. Store the puzzles in a dry area that does not vary much in temperature. Avoid damp basements and hot attics, both of which are hazardous to the boxes and their contents.

The disadvantages of storing puzzles loose in their boxes becomes apparent when you want to show them to another collector, or someone wants to photograph them for a book. There are some solutions, other than framing, for keeping the puzzles assembled so that you can readily enjoy them. A very satisfying, but rather expensive one is to invest in some map cases, with large shallow drawers. These are ideal for holding assembled puzzles.

Alternatively, you can cut a sheet of mat board (or the thicker foam-core board for wood puzzles) to the dimensions of each puzzle. Enclose the puzzle on the board in a plastic bag (or wrap larger puzzles with plastic wrap). Tape the bag securely so that the pieces can not shift around. Attach a label to identify the puzzle and describe the box that accompanies it. These puzzle packets can then be stacked in any convenient place, and transported easily. They should, however, be unwrapped periodically to check on condition.

▪ Cataloging Your Collection

Most collectors start to photograph and catalog their puzzles after they have acquired a few dozen. Since most puzzles must be kept loose in boxes, an illustrated inventory allows you to admire and study your treasures without reassembling them.

When you acquire any puzzle, you should give it a unique collection number. This might be chronological, starting with 1 and going up as you add to your collection. Or, if you collect several different types of puzzles, you might distinguish them by using A-1, A-2, etc. for your advertising puzzles, and C-1, C-2, etc. for children's puzzles, and so on. Write the collection number inconspicuously in pencil on the bottom of the puzzle box. If the puzzle is kept assembled separately from the box, put a slip of paper giving your collection number with the puzzle. Keep a chronological list of all your puzzles in the order of acquisition.

For easy photography without any special equipment, assemble the puzzle on a sheet of mat board, carry it outside on a clear day, and take the photograph under natural light. Place the puzzle on the ground and make sure that the lens of your camera is parallel to the ground; if you take the picture on an angle, the puzzle will be distorted into a trapezoid shape rather than a rectangle. You may want to wait until you have a dozen puzzles to photograph and can shoot an entire roll of film at once. Do not take the puzzles apart until after the film is developed. (Personal experience proves that taking the puzzles apart virtually guarantees that the film will be ruined.) A Polaroid is helpful for taking an occasional photograph.

A loose-leaf notebook is one of the best ways to hold a catalog because it allows you to insert new items into a logical order. Use a separate page for each puzzle. For the puzzle itself include information about the manufacturer, series or brand, title, dimensions, material, date of production, number of pieces, and condition. You may include other information, such as the name of the artist and lithographer who did the print, and details about the cutting design. You also should describe the box, label, and any inserts, along with their condition. Include your purchasing information, such as date of acquisition, price paid, and the dealer's name. Note any repairs that have been made to the puzzle or its box. Attach a photograph of the assembled puzzle, plus a photograph or photocopy of the label.

After you have cataloged a few puzzles, you may want to develop your own

Slide no. _____ Catalog no. _____

Negative no. _____

Manufacturer _____

Address _____

Series _____ Serial no. _____

Title _____

Date cut _____ Evidence _____

PUZZLE Dimens: H _____ W _____ Pieces _____ Diecut? _____ Handcut? _____ Other? ___

    Material: Solid wood? _____ Plywood? _____ Cardboard? _____ Other? _____

    Condition: Replaced? _____ Missing? _____ Other Damage? _____

    Cutting Design: Interlocking? _____ Color Lines? _____ Figures? _____ Stripcut? _____

    Print: Manufacturer _____ Artist _____ Date _____

    Handcolored? _____

BOX/TRAY/ENVELOPE Dimens: H _____ W _____ D _____ Condition _____

    Material _____ Color _____ Picture? _____ How sealed? _____

INSERTS? _____

SOURCE _____ Date _____ Price _____

COMMENTS _____

Fig. 3-5. This sample cataloging form for jigsaw puzzles takes up about half a sheet of 8½″ × 11″ paper. The remaining space can hold a picture of the puzzle and a copy of the label.

cataloging form (Fig. 3–5). Make a neat handwritten or typed copy, giving the categories of information you want and leaving blank spaces to be filled in for each item. Your local photocopying store can run off multiple copies at a modest charge.

Your catalog will come in handy for insurance purposes if your collection is ever lost due to fire, flood, or theft. Of course, if your house is damaged, there is also a strong possibility that your catalog will be destroyed. You can protect your records by photocopying your catalog sheets and storing them somewhere else, perhaps at your office or at the home of a relative.

• Identifying Unknown Puzzles

Cataloging is more difficult for a puzzle without the original box. Sometimes the puzzle is so distinctive that you can identify the manufacturer precisely. The figural pieces in Pastime puzzles are instantly recognizable, as are the seahorse signature piece and mahogany plywood of Par puzzles. Or you may be able to identify the puzzle when you see an identical example in another collection. (Caution is necessary, however, since the same print was often used by many different manufacturers.) But even in less obvious cases, a brief study of the puzzle can enable you to classify it in terms of period and type.

The first question to ask is: How was the puzzle made? Was it hand-cut, one piece at a time with a saw? Or were all the pieces stamped out at once with a die? The material gives some clues, as almost all wooden puzzles are cut with saws. Since the cutting removes some wood between

Fig. 3-6. The noninterlocking pieces and the cutting along color lines mark this as an adult puzzle cut between 1908 and 1915. The puzzle, *The Inquisitive Peasant*, was made by Godfrey Pyle, the then teenage son of artist Howard Pyle, around 1909. 14½″ × 10″, 275 hand-cut wood pieces. Wood box, 6½″ × 4¼″.

the pieces, there is usually a noticeable kerf, i.e. a slight gap between the pieces. Cardboard puzzles may be either hand-cut or die-cut. Although die-cutting was used as early as 1890, it did not become common until the 1920s. With die-cut puzzles there is no kerf because they are cut by pressure. The edges of pieces typically are slightly rounded on the picture side but are sharp on the back of the puzzle.

With wooden puzzles the type of wood used indicates age. During the nineteenth century only solid wood was used. After 1920 virtually all wooden puzzles were made with plywood (thin layers of wood laminated together). From 1900 to 1920 both solid wood and plywood are found, with solid wood predominating until World War I.

Cutting styles are also distinctive. Nineteenth century American puzzles often had interlocking edge pieces, but rarely interlocked throughout; and many puzzles had no interlocking pieces at all. Adult puzzles made during the 1908–15 period also had mainly non-interlocking pieces, often cut exactly on the color lines (Fig. 3–6). After 1940, except for a few brands like Tuco, most puzzles tended to interlock throughout. Figure pieces did not appear in puzzles until about 1910.

The picture can offer some clues about age. Before 1860 most prints were hand-tinted with watercolors. But after the Civil War color lithography became the norm in the United States. Photographs first appeared on puzzles only around 1915, and did not really become common until around World War II. Although the name of the artist and the lithographer are often printed on the picture, it is unusual that either of these actually manufactured the puzzle. Except for the large makers of children's puzzles, most puzzle companies bought their prints from lithography houses.

The graphic design and subject matter of the picture also give a rough indication of the origin of the print. Styles in illustration have changed regularly and dramatically since Victorian times. But an old print does not necessarily mean an old puzzle. Reproductions of nineteenth-century Currier and Ives prints are still being used on jigsaw puzzles today. The large lithographers, such as Goes of Chicago or Hoover of Philadelphia, kept some prints, both originals and reproductions, in stock for years. Furthermore, an individual puzzle manufacturer might keep a print on hand for years before using it.

Identification can be a problem even when the original box has survived. Some puzzle manufacturers did not put their names or the year on their products. A few of the smaller and less active makers of wood puzzles used whatever boxes were available, usually candy boxes. In these cases, study of the box or label can still yield some information. Although wood

Fig. 3-7. Although fakes have not been much of a problem for puzzle collectors, some reproductions of Victorian items have been passed off as antiques to unsuspecting buyers. This set of puzzle cubes was actually sold by Shackman of New York City in the 1970s. Careful examination reveals that both the prints and the wooden box are new. 8″ × 9½″, 30 hand-cut wood cubes. Wood box, 9″ × 10½″, with one guide picture on lid. Contains six guide pictures.

boxes were common in the nineteenth century, twentieth-century boxes are almost all cardboard. Typography on labels, which was quite ornate in the nineteenth century, has become much simpler. Boxes for adult puzzles did not show the puzzle picture until about 1935 for die-cut puzzles, and 1945 for hand-cut puzzles. Finally, some puzzle boxes have hand-written inscriptions giving the dates when the puzzle was assembled.

Reproductions and fakes have not been a big problem so far for puzzle collectors. The prices of most original hand-cut wood puzzles are still considerably below what it would cost to reproduce them today. A few reproductions have been made, usually die-cut from cardboard, and are almost always clearly marked on the box. Recent children's cube puzzles pose the greatest danger to collectors (Fig. 3−7). They are generally unmarked as to manufacturer, often use traditional designs, and are easy for the novice to confuse with the original puzzles.

▪ Learning More about Your Puzzles

If you want to find out more about your puzzles, there are several sources available to you beyond this book. First, you can compare your puzzles with those in other collections. The best publicly accessible collections are in museums that have good collections of toys and other children's items. In addition, both large and small museums periodically display childhood treasures, particularly at Christmas, and usually include a few puzzles in the exhibition. Note that a museum can sometimes show you puzzles that are not currently on display; however, limited curatorial staff means that you must make an appointment in advance.

Other collectors are a second source of information. The American Game Collectors Association (AGCA), Box J, 4628 Barlow Drive, Bartlesville, OK 74006, includes a number of members who specialize in puzzles; furthermore, most game collectors routinely include a few puzzles in their collections. The AGCA holds an annual convention where members buy, sell, swap, attend seminars, play, and discuss games. The organization maintains an archives of information about games and the companies that made them, and also publishes much of this information in a newsletter. Because most of the major game companies also made puzzles, these are valuable sources for puzzle collectors.

If you want to delve further into the history of a particular company that made jigsaw puzzles, local libraries and historical societies are the best resource. In many cases you can search city directories or local newspapers to get more detailed information about an individual company. More general publications on toys, collectibles, and ephemera also have some coverage of jigsaw puzzles. They are listed earlier in this chapter.

4 JIGSAW PUZZLE VALUES

ANTIQUE AND COLLECTIBLE jigsaw puzzles today can be found in a range of values, from a few dollars to a few thousand dollars. What causes the price differences between a $5 Tuco puzzle from the 1930s, a $450 McLoughlin Brothers puzzle from the 1890s, and a $900 Wallis puzzle imported from England in the eighteenth century? This chapter examines the factors that influence puzzle prices in today's market.

▪ General Criteria for Puzzle Prices

In determining the value of a puzzle its four most important features are: the visual appeal of the subject matter, craftsmanship, condition, and rarity. Other salient characteristics include manufacturer, historical interest, and size. Still another set of elements has to do with the market in which the puzzle is sold.

VISUAL APPEAL AND SUBJECT MATTER

The attractiveness of a puzzle has a major influence on its value. Of course, what is perceived as attractive is subject to fluctuations in fashion. In today's market a Santa Claus puzzle is worth more than one showing a Biblical scene; and cat items sell higher than bird items. For most puzzle collectors the least desirable subjects today are the scenics (autumn foliage, thatched cottages, Venetian canals, snow capped mountains, etc.), historical subjects, and maps. The most desirable are thematic, depicting transportation subjects, comic characters, movie stars, and so on. Popular artists from the golden age of illustration (Maxfield Parrish, Jessie Willcox Smith, Norman Rockwell, Philip R. Goodwin, etc.) also attract many collectors.

The visual appeal of the box and label can be as important as that of the puzzle. Since around 1870, American children's puzzles have had colorful labels. Usually the label simply duplicates the picture on the assembled puzzle. But in some cases the graphics on the box are completely different from those inside (e.g., see Fig. 4-1). There are even some examples where the box is more important than the puzzle, such as the early *Uncle Tom's Cabin* where a unique cabin-shaped box contains a rather ordinary puzzle (Fig. 4-2).

With advertising puzzles, much of the interest derives from the original packaging. For example, the 32-page booklet accompanying Hood's *Four-in-One Puzzle* contains detailed testimonials from every

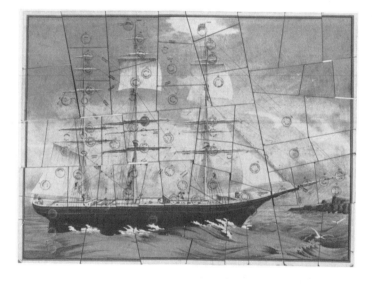

Fig. 4-1. The box for Milton Bradley's *Model Ship Puzzle* shows a much more turbulent scene than the tranquil one on the puzzle. This puzzle, in production circa 1870–90, has the names of the ship's parts on die-cut circular pieces. 16¾″ × 22½″, 106 cardboard pieces. Cardboard box, 6½″ × 8″.

state about Hood's Sarsaparilla; this patent medicine was credited with curing such varied ailments as scrofula, eczema, and old unhealed war wounds. In puzzles for adults, the appeal of the box is usually secondary to that of the puzzle.

CRAFTSMANSHIP

The hand-cut wood puzzles lead the field in craftsmanship. The best are full of intricate pieces cut to resemble animals and other familiar shapes, a feature that is unusual in the mass-produced cardboard puzzles. Top quality puzzles are made from fine hardwoods, with durable pieces more than 1/8" thick. Some of the wood puzzles, however, offer little that is superior to the die-cut ones. The pieces fit loosely because the puzzles were cut in stacks, and the monotonous strip-cutting holds no special interest.

Another factor is the craftsmanship of the printmaker. The early nineteenth-century puzzles show wide variations in the

Fig. 4-2. The roof forms the lid of this ingenious cabin-shaped box, made to hold an early *Uncle Tom's Cabin* puzzle. Unknown maker, circa 1852. 8¼″ × 11½″, 36 hand-colored and hand-cut wood pieces. Wood box, 3½″ tall, 5½″ wide, 4″ deep.

Effects of Condition Defects on Puzzle Values

All comparisons are made against a complete puzzle in very good condition, with original box or envelope also in very good or better condition, i.e., the puzzle has been used, but very carefully preserved so that signs of wear are not noticeable. That puzzle has 100 percent of the full value. In the rare case of a puzzle in mint condition (unused and in the original unopened package), it has more than 100 percent of full value as defined in this book. Puzzles with defects have a smaller percentage of the full value, as listed below.

Condition	Percent of Full Value
Missing pieces, box/envelope is very good:	
Missing one inconspicuous edge piece	60–75
Missing one conspicuous central piece	40–60
Missing 3–5 pieces distributed throughout the puzzle	15–40
Missing 10 pieces distributed throughout the puzzle	0–20
Complete puzzle, but pieces damaged; box/envelope is very good:	
Slight damage such as light foxing, a few missing small tabs or bits of paper	70–85
Extensive damage such as dingy appearance, many missing tabs or large area of paper gone	30–40
1–3 pieces have been expertly replaced and do not detract visually	75–85
Complete puzzle, very good condition; problems with box/envelope:	
Severe damage to box/envelope, such as extensive staining, crushed box, or badly torn envelope	65–75
Box or envelope is missing	50–70
Puzzle is loose in box/envelope; there is no information about puzzle condition and dealer does not guarantee completeness or condition:	15–30

care with which prints were hand-colored, ranging from the crude to the artistic. By the 1880s, advances in color lithography brought more consistency in the printing process and improvements in quality. Yet, even as late as the 1930s some prints were mass produced by cheap lithography, with murky colors and poor registration.

CONDITION

As with any antique or collectible, condition is extremely important. Damage, missing pieces, and lost boxes reduce puzzle values considerably. The accompanying box gives some general adjustments in value for frequently encountered types of damage.

Missing pieces are the most common problem for puzzles and have a major effect on value. The exact amount depends on the extent of the damage. An inconspicuous piece missing from an edge reduces value less than one from the face of a central figure. A puzzle with seven lost pieces is devalued much more than the identical puzzle with only one gone (Fig. 4-3).

The type of puzzle is also important. A single missing piece detracts much more from the appearance of a 12-piece child's puzzle than from a 300-piece adult puzzle. On the other hand, the box is usually val-

ued more in children's puzzles than in adult puzzles; even with ten missing pieces a child's puzzle with a very attractive box may retain some value.

Other damage must be assessed in terms of its impact on the puzzle's attractiveness. A single missing tab or a bit of missing paper or a minor stain, is usually not a serious problem. However, a puzzle with 20 missing tabs or extensive foxing will be heavily discounted. As in any collecting field, standards are less stringent for older items, because they are less abundant. Thus small defects that devalue a 1940s puzzle will have less impact on the value of a nineteenth-century puzzle.

A restored puzzle, whose lost pieces have been expertly replaced, is worth 15 to 25 percent less than one with all the original pieces. A missing box or envelope should subtract about 30 percent from the value of an adult puzzle, and more for children's puzzles or advertising puzzles where the package, label, and associated pamphlets are integral to the item.

The only way to be sure of condition is to see the puzzle assembled. If that is not possible, ask for a clear photo of the assembled puzzle or for the dealer's guarantee (backed by return privileges) that the puzzle is complete. Otherwise, unassembled puzzles should be priced cheaper,

Fig. 4-3. The combination of the 1933 Nash and the Chicago World's Fair background makes this an irresistible puzzle, despite the five missing pieces. But the expense of the needed repairs means that it will sell at approximately 30 percent of the value of the complete puzzle. 10¼″ × 14″, approx. 150 die-cut cardboard pieces. Envelope is not extant.

since condition, completeness, and visual appeal can not be easily ascertained. At least half of the puzzles that are loose in the box have missing pieces; puzzles that are neither assembled nor guaranteed sell at only 15 to 30 percent of full value in today's market.

RARITY

The basic laws of demand and supply apply to puzzles, just as they do in other markets. Uncommon objects tend to command higher prices. Puzzles that had high prices when they were first produced sold fewer copies originally; thus they are less abundant today and still sell at premium prices. The 15¢ to 25¢ weekly puzzles from the 1930s, however, sold millions of copies, are readily available today, and sell at modest prices of $5 to $15 each.

Scarcity alone does not always raise prices. For example, most depression-era makers of hand-cut wood puzzles operated only for a year or two. A given maker's total output would number only in the hundreds, and sales were entirely local. But because thousands of individuals went into the puzzle business at that time, many similar puzzles of that period survive today. From the standpoint of most collectors a Per-Plex puzzle from Boston is indistinguishable from a Tri-An-Mak-It puzzle from Philadelphia. Current prices are high only for those puzzles with really outstanding craftsmanship or graphics.

Age is naturally related to scarcity and has an impact on value. Pre-1900 puzzles are relatively scarce (and therefore more expensive) for two reasons. First, most nineteenth-century puzzles had individually cut pieces. This technology limited production in contrast with the mass-produced die-cut puzzles of today. Second, puzzles as playthings always have had the drawback that pieces are easily lost. Few puzzles survive intact for a hundred years or more; and those with lost pieces are often thrown away when children leave home.

MANUFACTURER AND HISTORICAL INTEREST

A few puzzles sell at premium prices because of their role in puzzle history, independent of their inherent attractiveness. Every collector would like to have an original Spilsbury dissected map, a Milton Bradley *Smashed Up Locomotive*, and a Springbok *Convergence* by Jackson Pollock. "First" has a special cachet for all collectors. Furthermore, since first editions were often produced in smaller quantities than later editions, scarcity contributes to their higher value.

Over the years some puzzle companies developed reputations for top quality, with the result that their puzzles are in great demand. Among children's puzzles, McLoughlin Brothers products command a premium because of their brilliant lithography. For adult wood puzzles, perennial best sellers are Par and Pastime puzzles because of their attractive pictures and imaginative cutting.

If the maker of the puzzle is unknown, the price is usually lower. Puzzles that were sold without any identifying information tended to be cheaper and of lower quality to start with. On the other hand, if the uncertainty about the maker is due to a missing box, a knowledgeable puzzle collector can often deduce the missing information, as is explained in Chapter 3. Of course, some of the puzzles that are now contained in candy boxes turn out to be absolutely delightful, even if there is no way to tell who made them. The point is that they would be worth more if the original box or other information about the manufacturer had also survived.

SIZE

The size factor includes both the dimensions of the puzzle and the number of pieces. For children's puzzles, the dimensions are more important. A large puzzle generally makes a more attractive display than a small one, and thus is worth more.

For adult puzzles, the number of pieces

Fig. 4-4. This Singer advertising puzzle fetched $143 when auctioned with a well-known collection of advertising material in 1989. But several toy and game dealers have sold the same puzzle at prices of $75 or under in succeeding months. Circa 1900. 7″ × 10″, 50 die-cut cardboard pieces. Paper envelope, 4″ × 6¼″, with guide diagram.

is more important than dimensions; a puzzle under 250 pieces offers little challenge to the adult puzzler, regardless of its measurements. Although pricing of adult puzzles depends on the number of pieces, it is not a lockstep relationship. A 600-piece puzzle is worth only about 50 percent more than a 300-piece puzzle, not twice as much.

TYPE OF MARKET

The assumption throughout this book is that the prices listed pertain to puzzles sold by dealers who handle many toys, games and puzzles. They are retail prices that collectors pay at shows and in shops, not the prices that dealers themselves pay. (The prices dealers pay are relevant when collectors are selling their puzzles, a topic discussed in the last section of this chapter.) Obviously there are other types of markets for collectors. Prices at yard sales, thrift stores, and local flea markets are much cheaper. The only problem is the amount

of time it takes to sift through all the material in order to come up with the few gems.

There is also a certain amount of geographical variation in puzzle prices, mainly because of supply factors. For example, wood puzzles are less expensive in New England than in the Midwest. New England was the heart of the wood puzzle industry in this country, and wood puzzles are relatively abundant there. On the other hand, die-cut puzzles made after 1930 were distributed more uniformly throughout the country, with the result that geographical differences in price are small.

Finally, puzzles are often sold in markets dominated by other collectors. For example, some advertising puzzles will command higher prices at an advertising or country store auction than they would at a general sale (Fig. 4-4). On the other hand a train puzzle at a railroadiana auction will fetch less than it would at a toy auction.

▪ State of the Market Today

This section briefly summarizes current values for several different types of puzzles. Within each category prices vary considerably, according to the general criteria listed above.

CHILDREN'S PUZZLES
PRE-WORLD WAR I

Most children's puzzles made before World War I were cut with saws from wood or thick cardboard. Early puzzles did not interlock at all. By the 1880s the big three— McLoughlin Brothers, Milton Bradley, and Parker Brothers—were using a typical scroll cut with interlocking edges and rectangular inside pieces. Most of the hand-colored puzzles were imported from Europe, although American companies also used hand-coloring before the Civil War. Wooden boxes were common before 1880, but by 1900 were almost completely supplanted by cardboard boxes. Prices are mostly in the $50 to $300 range, with higher prices for the most attractive lithographs of ships, fire engines, etc.

CHILDREN'S PUZZLES POST-WORLD WAR I

Most children's puzzles produced after World War I were die-cut from cardboard, and were sold in cardboard boxes. The label generally shows a picture of the completed puzzle. Tray puzzles became common in the 1930s and usually were sold without a box. Prices depend on pictorial appeal and generally are between $10 and $60. Character puzzles such as early Mickey Mouse, Superman, and Hopalong Cassidy puzzles can be more expensive.

HAND-CUT WOOD PUZZLES FOR ADULTS

Hand-cut wood puzzles for adults were cut with saws from 1900 on. The earliest ones were cut with noninterlocking pieces out of solid wood. Plywood replaced solid wood after 1915, and by 1925 most puzzles were completely interlocking. Boxes did not show a picture of the puzzle until the 1940s. Craftsmanship (especially figural pieces), graphics, and number of pieces are most important in determining price. Most prices are in the $10 to $75 range.

DIE-CUT CARDBOARD PUZZLES FOR ADULTS

Introduced on a large scale in 1932, die-cut cardboard puzzles for adults first featured popular subjects like hunting scenes, Venetian canals, and historical events. The early examples did not have guide pictures on the boxes, but by 1940 virtually all did. Prices are quite inexpensive, usually in the $2 to $15 range. As usual, character and personality puzzles are more expensive.

ADVERTISING AND NOVELTY PUZZLES

The first wooden advertising puzzles appeared in the 1870s. By 1890 a few companies were distributing small die-cut puzzles to promote their products. The vast majority of advertising puzzles appeared in 1932–33, usually packaged in paper envelopes and given away as premiums. Most advertising puzzles are in the $5 to $75 range.

Novelty puzzles include puzzle postcards, puzzle games, mystery puzzles, puzzle books, edible puzzles, etc., and have been produced at various times since 1900. Most prices range between $5 and $50.

• An Assessment of the Trends

Puzzle prices have been rising steadily in the late 1980s and into the 1990s. Some puzzle prices have increased 50 percent in five years as the demand for them has grown. To some extent the new interest in puzzles represents a spillover from the antique toy field. When mechanical banks are selling for $250,000, the appeal of a $500 puzzle becomes stronger. But most of the increased demand represents a growing appreciation for the puzzle itself. Collectors today recognize the attractiveness of the graphics and the craftsmanship of the older puzzles, characteristics that are hard to match with contemporary products. Recent years also have seen the development of a new focus on the general area of paper toys such as puzzles and games. Much more is known today than in the past about American production of these items.

Although all puzzle prices have increased in the past decade, the rise has been largest for character and personality puzzles. Disneyana, superhero memorabilia, cowboy items, and movie/TV memorabilia are examples of some of the most popular collecting areas today (Fig. 4-5). And dedicated character and personality collectors are snapping up puzzles along with other collectibles.

Children's puzzles also have appreciated steadily in recent years. Mc-Loughlin Brothers puzzles have done specially well, regardless of the subjects. The prices of puzzles by smaller makers have depended more on the subject matter, with transportation themes being among the most valuable.

Among adult puzzles, prices of wood puzzles have roughly tripled in the last decade. But the best of the wooden puzzles, such as the Pastimes, still seem undervalued relative to the craftsmanship that they embody. The relative abundance of the Pastimes, given that they were produced for half a century, has helped keep their prices down.

Prices of die-cut puzzles for adults are mixed. The Depression-era weekly puzzles have advanced in price, as have the World War II puzzles on military themes. But prices of post-1950 cardboard puzzles have hardly changed at all, except for the character puzzles mentioned above. It appears that the scenic puzzles put out in huge numbers by Bradley, Whitman, Fairchild, and others will continue to be in-

Fig. 4-5. Hopalong Cassidy puzzles have more than doubled in value in the last five years. This *Television Puzzles* set, produced in 1950 by Milton Bradley, contained four die-cut cardboard puzzles, each 7½″ × 9″, approx. 25 pieces. The 12″ square box also contained a cardboard television-like frame, 11½″ square.

expensive and widely available. Exceptions are the Springbok puzzles from the 1960s, with their high quality lithography and innovative subjects, which are beginning to appreciate.

The puzzle market is still developing and attracting new collectors and dealers. As the market matures, the geographical variation in prices should diminish. More dealers will sell their puzzles assembled, rather than loose in the box. This will mean fewer bargains for the risk-takers who buy the cheaper unassembled puzzles, but will mean more assurance of quality for serious collectors.

▪ Selling Your Puzzles

Virtually every puzzle collector is faced, at one time or another, with the problem of how to price puzzles for sale. The most common situation occurs when you upgrade your collection. You want to sell the lesser quality examples and use the pro-

ceeds to buy better ones. Or you may decide to specialize in one area of puzzle collecting, and sell off other types of puzzles. Or you may be moving and have to prune your collection considerably to fit into your new space. Noncollectors too have to dispose of puzzles, for example when helping a frail and elderly parent move to new quarters.

The basic rule of selling is that you will almost never receive full retail value, and you will often receive *much* less. ("Retail value" is used here as shorthand for the prices discussed throughout the rest of this book.) In part the price you get depends largely on how much time and effort you can put into getting it. Sometimes there are few alternatives. If a relative has died in a distant city, and you as executor must sell the house and its contents within a few weeks, getting good prices for a small puzzle collection is probably one of the least of your worries; you'll want to dispose of them as quickly as possible. At the other extreme, if you are selling several duplicate puzzles in your collection, you may well be in a position to hold onto them for a year in order to locate the right buyer.

Selling to a dealer is quick and easy to arrange, but will rarely yield more than 30 to 40 percent of the retail price. You should seek out a dealer who specializes in puzzles and other playthings; he can pay a higher price than the general dealer who is not in touch with the puzzle market. Chapter 3 gives some information on how to locate specialized dealers.

A collector will pay more than a dealer, perhaps 65 to 85 percent of the retail price. And sometimes the piece you want to sell is exactly what the collector has been pining for, in which case she'll pay you 100 percent of retail, or even more. The problem, of course, is locating the collector. If you do not already belong to a collectors group, the publications and other resources listed in Chapter 3 can help you find collectors. It also helps to study ads in the relevant publications and attend a couple of shows to get a sense of the market before selling.

Finally, you can improve the price that you get by providing an accurate description of your wares. Buyers are willing to pay more when a puzzle is assembled, or where there is a photograph of the assembled puzzle. You also can use this book to help identify your puzzle and provide descriptive information about it for potential buyers.

PART II

DETAILED DESCRIPTIONS OF PUZZLES BY TYPE

5 HOW TO USE PART II

THE PUZZLES illustrated in the following chapters represent the wide variety of jigsaw puzzles sold in the United States before 1970. Manufacturers are identified for virtually all of the puzzles shown. Most are American companies; but some popular European imports also are included because they are readily available to American collectors today.

Although this book includes over 750 photographs, it covers only a fraction of the total number of pre-1970 puzzles that can still be found today. The fraction is lower for adult puzzles than for children's puzzles since manufacturers typically produced more titles for adults than for children. (Unlike small children, adults are not content to do the same puzzle many times, and they constantly seek new subjects.) For example, a sampling of Parker Brothers' Pastime catalogs for three different years reveals over 2,000 different puzzle titles.

This chapter tells how to locate your puzzle, or one like it, in the book. It also explains how to interpret and use the values given in the Price Guide.

▪ General Organization

The puzzles described in the rest of this book are grouped by subject matter: advertising, history, entertainment characters, and personalities, and so on as listed in the table of contents. To find out about a circus puzzle, for example, you should look in Chapter 8 which covers cats, dogs, farm animals, zoos, circuses, and other animals. Some puzzles on each subject are shown in the color section as well.

But classification of subject matter can sometimes be ambiguous. Take, for example, a giveaway showing a performing circus elephant drawn by Tony Sarg, with the inscription "Merry Christmas from Montgomery Ward & Co." (Fig. 5-1). Depending on your collecting interests, you might place it in any of several fields: advertising, elephants, circus, Christmas, or famous illustrators. In this case the indexes at the back of the book can help you.

If you know the exact title of a puzzle, use the title index. If you know the maker's name but not the title, the index of manufacturers will tell you where references to the company and illustrations of its puzzles can be found. If both the title and the manufacturer are unknown, the subject index can help you find your puzzle.

Even if there is no listing for your specific puzzle, you can learn quite a bit about its value by comparing it with the ones

Fig. 5-1. Most premium puzzles, like this 1930s Montgomery Ward Christmas giveaway, are described in the chapter on advertising puzzles. 9″ × 8″, 15 die-cut cardboard pieces, including figure pieces. Paper envelope, 8¼″ × 9¼″.

that are included. For best results, use as a guide the value of another puzzle on the same topic, that was manufactured in the same way, in the same time period, and for the same audience. If for example you want to know the value of an 1890s wood child's puzzle showing dogs, you should not compare it with a die-cut adult puzzle of dogs from the 1950s. Look instead for another hand-cut early child's puzzle showing dogs or perhaps other animals.

Space constraints mean that it is impossible to show both the box and the puzzle for every item included. In many cases the box duplicates the picture of the puzzle inside, so that only one illustration is needed here. For adult puzzles without a guide picture on the box, this book generally shows the puzzles rather than the boxes. For children's puzzle sets, the photographs usually illustrate the box plus one puzzle in the set; the captions also describe the remaining puzzles in the set.

Chapter 15 differs from the others in that it covers all subject matters. It shows typical boxes, mainly for adult puzzles that were sold in series. Instead of trying to list every puzzle in each series, this chapter describes a typical puzzle for each series.

▪ Using the Price Guide

The prices given are based on some crucial assumptions. If the puzzle you are considering does not fit in with these assumptions, the price listed here will not apply and must be adjusted. Since Chapter 4 discusses these adjustments in detail, they are only summarized here.

The most important assumption is that the puzzle is *complete and in very good condition*. This means that the puzzle has the original box (or envelope), and that there are no missing pieces. Furthermore, the pieces show no significant damage. The box and label are structurally sound and clean. If the puzzle is incomplete, the box is missing, or there is damage to the puzzle or box, the price should be substantially lower.

A corollary is that the puzzle is sold assembled so its condition can be determined with certainty. Alternatively, it is sold with a description of condition, backed up by return privileges if it turns out to be different from the dealer's description.

Puzzles that are sold loose in the box and are not guaranteed as to condition have much lower values.

The prices listed are *retail* prices that a collector can expect to pay at a show or in a shop from dealers who handle many toys, games, and puzzles. They are not the prices that collectors receive when selling. Nor are they the prices that normally prevail at local flea markets, garage sales, etc.

The prices listed should be used only as a guide. At any point in time there is some variation in prices for identical objects, due to factors like geographical differences in markets. Furthermore, puzzle collecting is a relatively new field, and collecting trends will continue to develop over time. The prices in this book reflect market conditions in early 1990, conditions that will undoubtedly change in the future.

Remember that the market price of a puzzle is not necessarily the same as its value to your collection. You may find a puzzle at half the price listed here; but it would be quite reasonable for you to pass it up if you already have a similar one. On the other hand, it may also be quite reasonable for you to pay 50 percent above the listed price for a puzzle that fills a crucial niche in your collection and appears only infrequently in the market. In the final analysis you are the best judge of what enhances your collection. And if you don't enjoy your puzzles, it doesn't really matter what you have paid for them.

This book is not intended as a guide for investors. Serious investors should consult a financial advisor and concentrate their efforts on established markets, not on collectibles like jigsaw puzzles. You *may* do well financially with collectibles, but more than likely, when you sell your puzzles, you'll be lucky to recover your initial costs, adjusted for inflation. It is very difficult to get rich with collectibles like puzzles. Prices must skyrocket to offset the effects of buying at retail and selling at wholesale. If the joy of collecting and displaying your puzzles is not sufficient, you should turn to another activity or become a dealer.

Finally, the prices listed in this book do not represent an offer to buy or sell. Neither the author nor the publisher assumes any liability for losses related to the use of this book, or to any typographical or other errors contained in it.

▪ Explanation of the Captions

The captions in Chapters 6 through 17 give full descriptions of the puzzles illustrated, including the following information:

- Puzzle title and (if relevant) series. If the exact title is not known, an approximate title is supplied in brackets.
- Manufacturer and location. Brackets indicate that the manufacturer is inferred from the appearance of the object. Only the headquarters location is given, even if the box also lists the branch locations.
- Production date. Even if the exact date is unknown, the decade can usually be specified accurately. Any patent and copyright dates for the puzzle are given where known. Copyright dates for the prints are usually not listed since they do not give a clear indication of the production date.
- Puzzle dimensions, vertical first, then horizontal, rounded to the nearest quarter inch. Exact puzzle dimensions sometimes differ from those listed on the box. Wherever possible, the captions give exact dimensions. For frame tray puzzles, the dimensions include the frame.
- Number of pieces and description. The exact number of pieces sometimes differs from that listed on the box; wherever possible the captions give the exact number of pieces. They also indicate whether the puzzles contain any figure pieces or irregular edges. The material

used (wood, plywood, cardboard, pressboard, etc.) is stated, along with the manufacturing method (hand-cut, die-cut, sliced, or cut with water jets). Most of the wood and plywood used for puzzles is bass, poplar, birch, or some other light wood. If other fine woods like mahogany are used, they are noted. Except for the early hand-colored puzzles, which are noted, virtually all the puzzle pictures were printed in color.

- Box dimensions and description. Dimensions of the lid are given with vertical first, then horizontal. Depth of the box is not given as most boxes are less than three inches deep. The caption indicates the box material (cardboard or wood) and whether or not a guide picture appears on the box.

- Description of any inserts in the box, such as guide pictures, booklets, etc.

- For sets of puzzles, a list of all the puzzles in the set.

- Miscellaneous information such as: artist for the print, comments, credits to owners other than the author and the editor. Serial numbers of the puzzles are included where known; however some serial numbers pertain to an entire series, rather than to a single puzzle.

6 LESSONS FROM THE PAST: HISTORY AND GEOGRAPHY

EVER SINCE John Spilsbury's first dissected maps in the 1760s, puzzles have played an educational role. Geography lessons were soon joined by other schoolroom subjects—arithmetic, spelling, and history—all cut into pieces. The child who succeeded in completing the puzzles could not help but absorb some of the printed text in the process.

By the mid-nineteenth century, when American-made puzzles first appeared, the educational purpose had softened considerably. Map puzzles, of course, have continued to the present day with only a few modifications such as changing political boundaries, reversible designs, and fancier boxes. History lessons became more subtle over the years, however. Puzzle makers used pictures rather than extensive texts to teach their lessons, and they included current events in their curriculum. Wars and revolutions were specially popular topics, lending themselves readily to vivid and dynamic graphics.

This chapter contains sections which deal with: European history, world's fairs and expositions, U.S. history and politics, U.S. military history—American Revolution through World War II—and dissected maps.

Within each section puzzles are arranged chronologically by subject matter. The color section includes the following items in addition to those described in this chapter:

- *Betsy Ross and Her Friends*
- *Save Us From Such Friends!*
- *U.S. Navy Planes*
- *Moon Landing*

▪ European History

Fig. 6-1. *The British Sovereigns*. William Darton & Son, London, England. Circa 1830. 12¼″ × 15½″, 35 hand-colored and hand-cut wood (mahogany) pieces. Wood box, 7¾″ × 6¾″.

Fig. 6-2. *The Conquerors*. Every Week series, no. 19. Einson-Freeman Co., Inc., Long Island City, N.Y. Copyright 1933. 14½″ × 10½″, 160 die-cut cardboard pieces. Cardboard box, 7″ × 7″, with small guide diagram. Artist is Albin Henning.

Fig. 6-3. [*Metamorphic Soldiers*]. Unknown maker, France. Circa 1850. Set of four hand-cut and hand-colored wood puzzles, each 17″ × 8½″, 6 pieces. Pieces can be interchanged to form different characters. Wood box, 18½″ × 9¼″.

Fig. 6-4. *William Tell*. John Betts, London, England. Circa 1850. 10″ × 13¼″, 37 hand-colored and hand-cut wood pieces. Wood box, 8″ × 6½″. Contains 54–page story booklet and uncolored guide picture.

Fig. 6-5. *The Game of Patience*. Unknown maker, Germany. Circa 1860. Set of three hand-cut and hand-colored wood puzzles, each 8¼″ × 10½″, 54 pieces. Wood box, 9″ × 11½″. Puzzles include: 1) *The Parade* (illustrated), 2) *The Young Ladies Boarding School*, 3) *Gathering Rasperries* (sic).

Fig. 6-6. *Nelson at Trafalgar.*
Ken-Way, Greenwood, R.I.
1930s. 16¼″ × 22″, 628 hand-
cut plywood pieces. Card-
board box, 7¾″ × 10½″.

Fig. 6-7. *Napoleon on Board
the Bellerophon.* Zig-Zag
Puzzle, England. Circa 1909.
7½″ × 11¼″, 134 hand-cut
wood pieces. Cardboard box,
5¼″ × 7″.

Fig. 6-9. *Mentzschikoff*. Unknown maker, Germany. Circa 1850. 7″ × 5¾″, 30 hand-cut hand-colored wood cubes that make six different pictures. Wood box, 7¾″ × 6½″. Contains five guide pictures, with sixth on box lid. Three pictures show cavalry officers; others show village scenes.

Fig. 6-8. *Garde de Paris*. Penelope Puzzles, Leysin, Switzerland. 1960s. 14″ × 7″, 150 hand-cut plywood pieces. Cardboard box, 14½″ × 7¼″.

Fig. 6-10. *Ne Tirez Pas, C'est Mon Frere (Don't Shoot, It's My Brother)*. Codoni, Paris, France. Circa 1848. Set of three hand-cut and hand-colored wood puzzles, each 6″ × 8½″, 12 pieces. Cardboard box, 7″ × 9¼″. Puzzles include: 1) Shoot if you dare, it's the flag of France (illustrated in Chapter 1), 2) Attack on the Chateau d'Eau, 3) Louis Philippe's hasty departure from the Chateau of the Tuileries.

Fig. 6-11. *Highlander, Girl, and Tommy.* Patriotic Jig Saw Puzzle, England. Circa 1915. 13″ × 9″, 154 hand-cut plywood pieces. Cardboard box, 9½″ × 7½″.

Fig. 6-12. *TRH's Princess Elizabeth and Princess Margaret Rose.* Chad Valley Co., Ltd., Harborne, England. 1934. 14″ × 11″, 243 hand-cut plywood pieces. Cardboard book-like box, 7½″ × 6″, with small guide picture.

Fig. 6-13. *Sir Wilfred Grenfell on Board "Strathcona".* Labrador Zag-Zaw series. Raphael Tuck & Sons, Ltd., London, England. 1930s. 14″ × 9½″, 200 hand-cut plywood pieces, including figure pieces. Cardboard box, 5½″ × 8½″, autographed by Sir Wilfred Grenfell. Sold to benefit his Labrador missions.

▪ World's Fairs and Expositions

Fig. 6-14. *Centennial Exhibition Puzzle Blocks.* George H. Chinnock, New York, N.Y. Copyright 1875. Set of five hand-cut wood puzzles, each 20¾″ wide, 4 to 6″ high, approx. 30 pieces. Wood box, 11½″ × 22″. Contains four guide pictures, with fifth on box lid. Set includes: 1) Art Gallery, 2) Machinery Hall, 3) Horticultural Hall, 4) Agricultural Hall, 5) Main Building.

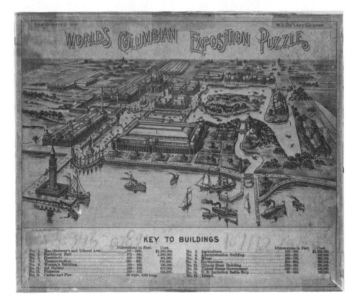

Fig. 6-15. *World's Columbian Exposition Puzzle.* W. L. DeLacy, Chicago, Ill. Copyright 1891. 14″ × 22″, 49 die-cut cardboard pieces. Cardboard box, 7″ × 8¼″, with guide picture. (Courtesy of the Siegels)

Fig. 6-16. *Souvenir de L'Exposition.* Delhaye Freres, Paris, France. 1900. Set of six hand-cut wood puzzles, each 12½″ × 16½″, 35 pieces. Wood frame and cardboard box, 13½″ × 17½″ (illustrated in color section). Puzzles include: 1) Aerial view, 2) Fireworks, 3) Aquarium, 4) Alpine scene, 5) Village scene, 6) Shipboard scene.

Fig. 6-17. *Angle-Play Picture Puzzle.* L. H. Nelson Co., Portland, Me. Copyright 1908. 8½″ × 14½″, 50 die-cut cardboard pieces. Cardboard box, 7¼″ × 7¼″. Contains rules for speed contest with puzzles. Puzzle shows Metallurgy building, probably at 1904–05 Louisiana Purchase Exposition in St. Louis.

Fig. 6-18. *Louisiana Purchase Exposition.* Unknown maker. 1904. 13½″ × 19½″, 40 handcut cardboard pieces. Box not extant.

Fig. 6-19. *New 4 in 1 World's Fair Puzzle.* Cee-Tee Novelty Co., Chicago, Ill. 1933. 7″ × 11″, 100 hand-cut plywood pieces. Cardboard box, 6¼″ × 5¼″. Scenes include: 1) Hall of Science, 2) Travel and Transportation Building, 3) Enchanted Island, 4) Sky Ride.

Fig. 6-20. *Chicago World's Fair Picture Puzzle.* Unknown maker. 1933. 11″ × 16″, 300 die-cut cardboard pieces. Cardboard box, 8″ × 6″. Puzzle shows aerial view of fair.

Fig. 6-21. *New York World's Fair.* New York World's Fair 1964–65 Corp. 1964–65. Set of two die-cut cardboard puzzles, each 6″ × 5½″, 15 pieces. Paper envelope, 6″ × 6½″.

▪ U.S. History and Politics

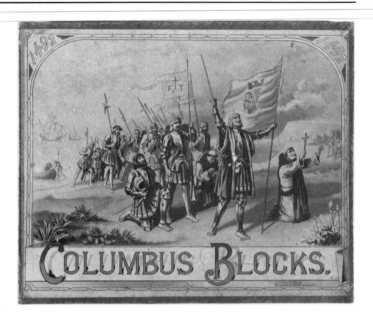

Fig. 6-22. *Columbus Blocks.* McLoughlin Brothers, New York, N.Y. Copyright 1893. 12½″ × 10″, 20 hollow cardboard cubes that make six different pictures. Wood frame and cardboard box, 11″ × 15″. Contains booklet with black and white illustrations of the six pictures, which also were used for the *Columbus Scroll Puzzles.* (Courtesy of the Siegels)

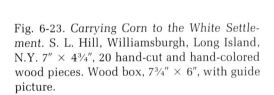

Fig. 6-23. *Carrying Corn to the White Settlement.* S. L. Hill, Williamsburgh, Long Island, N.Y. 7″ × 4¾″, 20 hand-cut and hand-colored wood pieces. Wood box, 7¾″ × 6″, with guide picture.

Fig. 6-24. *William Penn's Treaty with the Indians.* [T. S. Wagner or M. H. Traubel or Jacob Shaffer, Philadelphia, Pa.] Circa 1865. Set of five hand-cut wood puzzles, each 7½″ × 11″, 26 pieces. Wood box, 8″ × 12″, with guide picture for one puzzle. Others in set include: 1) *Pennsylvania Railroad,* 2) *Mount Vernon,* 3) *Young Donald and Lady Jane,* 4) *United States Map* (hand-colored).

Fig. 6-25. *Reading of the Declaration.* Premier series. Milton Bradley Co., Springfield, Mass. 1930s. 16″ × 21¾″, 988 hand-cut plywood pieces, including figure pieces. Cardboard box, 10½″ × 10″.

Fig. 6-26. *A Beloved President.* Pastime series. Parker Brothers, Inc., Salem, Mass. 1932. 16″ × 21½″, 557 hand-cut plywood pieces, including figure pieces. Cardboard box, 10″ × 10″.

Fig. 6-27. *Prominent Americans Comically Cut Up.* Ives, Blakeslee, & Co., New York, N.Y. Patented 1881. Set of six sliced cardboard puzzles, each 9″ × 7″, 3 pieces; can be rearranged to form humorous combination characters, illustrated in color section. Cardboard box, 9½″ × 7¼″. (Courtesy of the Siegels)

Fig. 6-28. *Vanity Fair's 1933 Inaugural.* Condé Nast Publications, Inc. 1933. 13″ × 19″, 315 die-cut cardboard pieces, including figure pieces. Cardboard box, 7″ × 10¼″, with guide diagram. Artist is M. Covarrubias.

Fig. 6-29. *Puzzle Pack: The Passing Parade.* National Association Service, Toledo, Ohio. Copyright 1943. 11″ × 9¼″, approx. 85 die-cut cardboard pieces, illustrated in color section. Cardboard packet, 11¼″ × 9½″. Contains key to world leaders shown on puzzle, along with three other verbal and graphical puzzles.

Fig. 6-30. *Spiro Agnew, Friend of the Silent Majority.* Gameophiles Unlimited, Inc., Berkeley Heights, N.J. Copyright 1970. 20″ × 16″, 500 die-cut cardboard pieces. Cardboard box, 13″ × 9¼″, with guide picture.

Fig. 6-31. *John Glenn.* Unknown maker, Japan. 1960s. 8″ × 6″, 20 die-cut cardboard pieces. Plastic envelope, 8¼″ × 6¼″.

▪ U.S. Military History

Fig. 6-32. [*Reviewing the Troops*]. [McLoughlin Brothers, New York, N.Y.] Circa 1860. 6″ × 8″, 20 hand-cut and hand-colored wood pieces. Cardboard box, 6¼″ × 8¼″. Artist is Justin Howard. (Courtesy of the Siegels)

Fig. 6-33. *Historical Puzzle Box*. Milton Bradley Co., Springfield, Mass. 1910s. Set of three hand-cut cardboard puzzles, each 12¾″ × 18″, 30 pieces. Cardboard box, approx. 13″ × 18½″, with small guide diagrams. Puzzles in set include: 1) Battle of Bunker Hill, 2) Washington crossing the Delaware, 3) Fife and drum.

Fig. 6-34. *John Paul Jones Bidding Goodbye to His Ship.* Yankee Cut-Ups series. Alden L. Fretts, West Springfield, Mass. 1933. 15¾" × 20", 550 hand-cut plywood pieces, including figure pieces. Cardboard box, 7½" × 11".

Fig. 6-35. [*Spirit of 76*]. Supplement to the Sunday Globe, Boston, Mass. Circa 1909. 8" × 6", 35 uncut paper pieces. No envelope. Many of these paper puzzles were glued to wood and cut up by amateur puzzle makers.

Fig. 6-36. *Headquarters of the Recruiting Committee*. M. Salom, Boston, Mass. Circa 1862. 11¾" × 14¾", 49 hand-colored sliced cardboard pieces. Cardboard box, 6¼" × 8¼". Contains guide picture.

Fig. 6-37. *The Glorious Finale of the War Dissected*. Charles Magnus, New York, N.Y. and Washington, D.C. 1865. 15¾" × 18½", 64 hand-colored sliced paper pieces. Cardboard box, 5" × 7".

Fig. 6-38. *Mammoth Naval Scroll Puzzle*. McLoughlin Brothers, New York, N.Y. Circa 1898. 21½" × 37", 110 hand-cut pressboard pieces, illustrated in color section. Cardboard box, 11½" × 22½". Selchow & Righter name, originally in lower right corner of box, has been overpainted. (Courtesy of the Siegels)

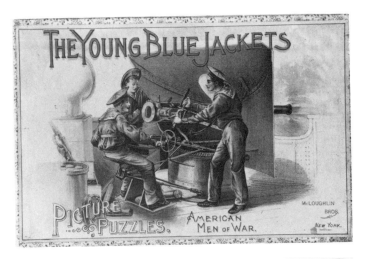

Fig. 6-39. *The Young Blue Jackets*. McLoughlin Brothers, New York, N.Y. Circa 1898. Set of two hand-cut pressboard puzzles: 1) United States Cruiser Columbia, 6″ × 10″, 18 pieces; 2) United States Cruiser San Francisco, 6½″ × 9″, 15 pieces. Cardboard box, 7″ × 10¾″. Selchow & Righter name, originally in lower right corner of box, has been overpainted. (Courtesy of the Siegels)

Fig. 6-40. *Up the Heights of San Juan*. McLoughlin Brothers, New York, N.Y. Circa 1898. Hand-cut pressboard pieces. Cardboard box, 13½″ × 18″, with guide picture.

Fig. 6-41. *General John J. Pershing.* Robert England, Hingham, Mass. 1920s. 13¾″ × 10″, 420 hand-cut plywood pieces. Cardboard box, 6¾″ × 7¾″.

Fig. 6-42. *Our Battleships Puzzle Box.* Milton Bradley Co., Springfield, Mass. Circa 1917. Set of three hand-cut pressboard puzzles, each 12½″ × 18″, 30 pieces. Cardboard box, approx. 13″ × 18¼″, with cover picture of U.S.S. Louisiana. Puzzles in set include: 1) *K-1 Submarine,* 2) *U.S.S. New York,* and 3) *U.S.S. Texas.* Serial no. 4046.

Fig. 6-43. *Liberators of the World.* Saalfield Publishing Co., Akron, Ohio. Circa 1945. 15½″ × 19¾″, 500 die-cut cardboard pieces. Cardboard box, 8½″ × 11″, with guide picture. Serial no. 1842.

Fig. 6-44. *Tank Busters and Jeeps on the Job.* Victory series. J. Pressman & Co., Inc., New York, N.Y. Circa 1943–45. 15½″ × 19½″, 365 die-cut cardboard pieces, including figure pieces. Cardboard box, 9¼″ × 11¾″, with small guide picture. Serial no. 10.

Fig. 6-45. *Rangers Landing in Africa.* Victory Series no. 318. J. S. Publishing Corp., New York, N.Y. Copyright 1944. 14″ × 15½″, approx. 320 die-cut cardboard pieces, including figure pieces. Cardboard box, 7½″ × 10″, with guide picture.

Fig. 6-46. *Army-Navy Combat Picture Puzzles.* U.S. Finishing & Mfg. Co., Chicago, Ill. 1940s. Set of eight die-cut cardboard puzzles, each 9½″ × 8″, approx. 50 pieces. Cardboard box, 8½″ × 10½″. Others in set show various fighter planes and warships.

Fig. 6-47. *Total Warfare*. Perfect Picture Puzzle. Circa 1943–45. 15½″ × 19½″, 378 die-cut cardboard pieces. Cardboard box, 9¾″ × 7½″, with guide picture.

▪ Dissected Maps

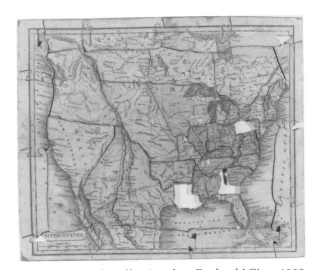

Fig. 6-48. *Improved Dissected Maps: United States*. [Edward Wallis, London, England.] Circa 1830. 9″ × 11″, 42 hand-cut and hand-colored wood pieces. Wood box, 7¼″ × 5¾″.

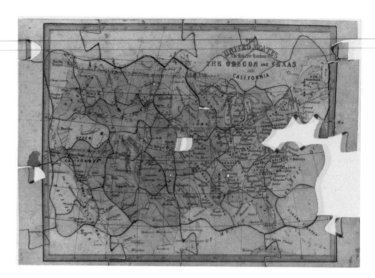

Fig. 6-49. *New Double Puzzle: United States.* Unknown maker, probably English. Circa 1848. 8½″ × 12¼″, 39 hand-cut and hand-colored wood pieces. Double-sided with *Naughty Boy and Poor Little Robin* on reverse. Wood box, 7″ × 8¾″.

Fig. 6-50. *Dissected Map of the United States.* S. Augustus Mitchell, Philadelphia, Pa., distributed by Merriam Moore, Troy, N.Y. Copyright 1854. 10½″ × 17″, 54 hand-cut and hand-colored wood pieces, cut on state lines. Cardboard book-like box, 9″ × 6½″. Contains hand-colored guide map.

Fig. 6-51. [*United States Map Cubes*]. Unknown maker, Germany. Circa 1870. 8½″ × 7″, 20 hand-colored wood cubes that make six different maps. Wood box, 10″ × 8″. Contains five guide maps, with sixth on box lid. Other sides show: 1) North America, 2) Middle Atlantic states, 3) Southeast states, 4) Midwest states, 5) South Central states.

Fig. 6-52. *Dissected Outline Map of the United States of America*. Milton Bradley & Co., Springfield, Mass. 1880s. 15½″ × 22½″, 69 hand-cut wood pieces, cut on state lines. Double-sided, shows industries on reverse. Wood box, 8″ × 9¾″. Cheaper editions of this puzzle were sold in cardboard boxes, without cutting on state lines, and without showing industries on the reverse.

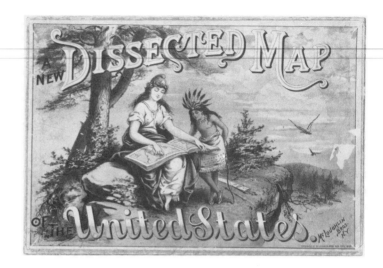

Fig. 6-53. *A New Dissected Map of the United States.* McLoughlin Brothers, New York, N.Y. 1890s. 12½″ × 18½″, 40 hand-cut pressboard pieces. Wood frame and cardboard box, 8½″ × 12¼″. Contains guide map.

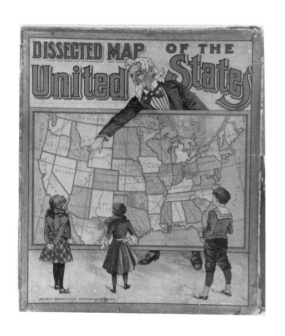

Fig. 6-54. *Dissected Map of the United States.* Milton Bradley Co., Springfield, Mass. Circa 1905. 9½″ × 14″, 30 hand-cut wood pieces. Cardboard box, 11¾″ × 10¼″.

Fig. 6-55. *United States Map.* Milton Bradley Co., Springfield, Mass. 1930s. 9½″ × 14″, approx. 55 die-cut cardboard pieces, cut on state lines. Cardboard box, 8″ × 8¾″. Serial no. 4803.

Fig. 6-56. *United States Puzzle Map.* Parker Brothers, Inc., Salem, Mass. In production circa 1915−35. 12¼″ × 20″. 53 hand-cut plywood pieces, cut on state lines. Cardboard box, 8″ × 13″. This map, copyrighted 1915, was used for the Parker Brothers map puzzles until the 1950s, but the box designs were changed over the years.

Fig. 6-57. *Moon Map Puzzle.* Selchow & Righter Co., Bay Shore, N.Y. Circa 1970. 14¼″ × 21½″, 100 die-cut cardboard pieces. Cardboard box, 8¼″ × 12¼″.

7 FAMILIAR TALES

WHEN THE FIRST MAKERS of dissected maps began to diversify, at the end of the eighteenth century, it was natural for them to adapt favorite childhood stories to jigsaw puzzles. In fact some of the largest producers of puzzles in London started out as publishers of children's books. They already had story book illustrations that could easily be glued to wood and cut up. Biblical tales were obvious topics for puzzles, continuing the educational orientation of dissected maps. Such serious subjects soon were joined by traditional nursery rhymes and fairy tales, as well as by classic fictional characters like Robinson Crusoe. By 1850, although maps and other didactic puzzles were still popular, they were vastly outnumbered by the lighter subjects.

During the twentieth century, new stories have appeared on puzzles. Favorite children's authors like Beatrix Potter, Dr. Seuss, and Johnny Gruelle have had their characters brought to life on puzzles. Adult puzzles too have featured classics of literature; Dickens' works have been specially popular because of the numerous illustrations that were done for them.

The three sections of this chapter treat: biblical stories (organized chronologically by the date of the puzzle); traditional nursery rhymes and fairy tales (organized alphabetically by title); and other stories and literature (organized alphabetically by title).

The color section includes the following items in addition to those described in this chapter:

- *David Copperfield Leaving Margate*
- *Alice in Wonderland*

▪ Biblical Stories

Fig. 7-1. *A Key to the New Testament.* John Wallis Sen. and John Wallis Jun., London, England. Circa 1810. 11¼″ × 7¼″, 32 hand-colored and hand-cut wood (mahogany) pieces. Puzzle is illustrated in Chapter 1. Wood box, 8¼″ × 6½″.

Fig. 7-2. *Scripture, Natural History & Zoology.* Edward Wallis, London, England. 1840s. 11″ × 17″, 50 hand-colored and hand-cut wood (mahogany) pieces. Book-like wood box, 8½″ × 7¼″. Hand-colored picture inside lid is similar to but not quite the same as puzzle picture which is titled *And Adam gave names to all cattle, and to the fowl of the air, and to every beast of the field.*

Fig. 7-3. *Events from Scripture.* Unknown maker, England. Circa 1850. 8½" × 12½", 37 hand-colored and hand-cut wood pieces. Wood box, 8½" × 6½". Contains hand-colored guide picture.

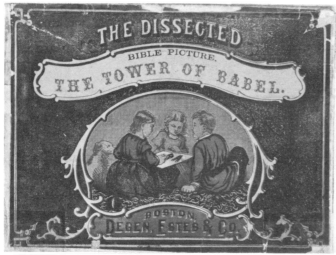

Fig. 7-4. *The Tower of Babel.* Degen, Estes & Co., Boston, Mass. 1870s. 7½" × 6", 11 hand-colored and hand-cut cardboard pieces. Cardboard box, 4¾" × 6½". (Courtesy of the Siegels)

Fig. 7-5. *The Ark Puzzle.* Seymour Lyman, New York, N.Y. Circa 1880. 13½″ × 22¼″, 25 sliced cardboard pieces, with irregular edge. Cardboard box, 6¾″ × 10″. Puzzle is illustrated in color section. (Courtesy of the Siegels)

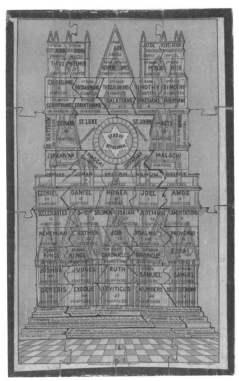

Fig. 7-7. [*Biblical Scene*]. Robert P. Stortz, Emmaus, Pa. Circa 1947. Frame tray puzzle, 11½″ × 10″, 7 hand-cut plywood pieces.

Fig. 7-6. *Temple of Knowledge.* Mrs. Alice J. Chamberlain. Circa 1890. 18¼″ × 11½″, 86 hand-cut wood pieces. Double-sided puzzle, with map of Palestine on reverse. Wood frame and cardboard box, 9½″ × 7½″.

• Traditional Nursery Rhymes and Fairy Tales

Fig. 7-8. *Aladdin and His Lamp.* Storyland series. Harett-Gilmar, Far Rockaway, N.Y. Circa 1970. 14″ × 10″, 96 die-cut cardboard pieces. Cardboard and metal cannister, 8¼″ high, 3″ diameter, with guide picture. Serial no. 422.

Fig. 7-9. *Arabian Nights Puzzle Picture.* Unknown maker, U.S. Circa 1920. 7″ × 5″, 50 die-cut cardboard pieces, including figure pieces. Cardboard box, 6″ × 8″.

Fig. 7-10. *Six Puzzle Pictures: Dame Trott and Her Cat.* McLoughlin Brothers, New York, N.Y. Circa 1880. Set of six hand-cut wood puzzles, each 7¼″ × 5½″, 20 pieces. Wood box, 10¾″ × 7¾″, with guide picture for one puzzle. Set includes: 1) *Dame Trott buys the cat,* 2) *The end of the ride,* 3) *Puss brings a fish,* 4) *The dancing lesson,* 5) *Puss making tea,* 6) *Puss in full dress.* These puzzles also were sold individually in small cardboard boxes.

Fig. 7-11. *Fairy Tale Puzzles.* Platt & Munk, New York, N.Y. Copyright 1963. Set of four die-cut cardboard frame puzzles, each 11″ × 9″, approx. 35 pieces. Cardboard box, 11½″ × 9½″, with one guide picture. Puzzles in set include: 1) *Red Riding Hood,* 2) *Sleeping Beauty,* 3) *Jack and the Beanstalk,* 4) *Mr. Samson Cat.* Artist is Tasha Tudor.

Fig. 7-12. *Four Separate Jigsaw Puzzles.* Whitman Publishing Co., Racine, Wisc. Circa 1940. Set of four die-cut cardboard puzzles, each 8½″ × 7½″, approx. 30 pieces. Cardboard box, 9″ × 7¾″. Puzzles in set include: 1) Little Miss Muffet, 2) Boy fishing, 3) Cock-A-Doodle Do, 4) Lion and boy. Serial no. 3027.

Fig. 7-13. *Funny Land.* Pandora series. Selchow & Righter Co., New York, N.Y. 1930s. Set of two die-cut cardboard puzzles, each 6¼″ × 9″, 15 pieces. Cardboard box, 6¾″ × 9½″, with guide picture for one puzzle. Puzzles show: 1) Froggy would a wooing go, 2) Owl and the pussycat (illustrated in color section).

Fig. 7-14. *The House that Jack Built*. C. C. Shepherd, New York, N.Y. Patented 1881. 15″ × 19″, 18 hand-cut wood pieces. Wood frame and cardboard box, 11″ × 12¾″. Contains 10 cardboard character pieces to place on completed puzzle.

Fig. 7-15. *Little Black Sambo*. Sifo, St. Paul, Minn. 1960s. Frame tray puzzle, 8¾″ × 11¾″, 13 hand-cut masonite pieces.

Fig. 7-16. *Little Bo-Peep/Little Red Riding Hood*. [J. W. Barfoot, London, England]. Circa 1855. 8½″ × 12¼″, 39 hand-colored and hand-cut wood pieces. Double-sided, with Little Red Riding Hood on reverse. Wood box, approx. 8½″ × 6½″.

Fig. 7-17. *Little Bo-Peep.* McLoughlin Brothers, New York, N.Y. Circa 1880. 7¼″ × 5½″, 20 hand-cut wood pieces. Cardboard box, 7″ × 5″, with guide picture.

Fig. 7-18. *Mother Goose Scroll Puzzles.* McLoughlin Brothers, New York, N.Y. Set of two hand-cut pressboard puzzles, each 12½″ × 10″, 24 pieces. Wood frame and cardboard box, 13½″ × 10¾″, with guide picture for one puzzle. Puzzles include: 1) Old King Cole, 2) Humpty-Dumpty.

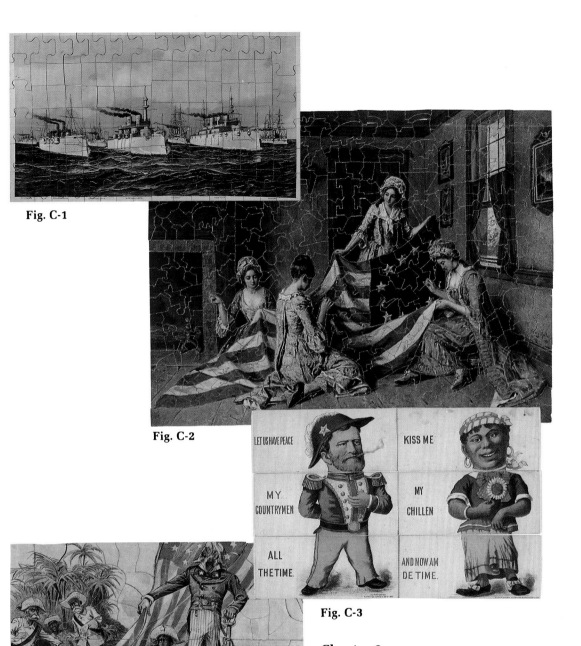

Fig. C-1

Fig. C-2

Fig. C-3

Fig. C-4

Chapter 6

Fig. C-1. *Mammoth Naval Scroll Puzzle.* McLoughlin Brothers, New York, N.Y. Circa 1898. 21½" × 37", 110 hand-cut pressboard pieces. Box is illustrated in Chapter 6. (Courtesy of the Siegels) **Fig. C-2.** *Betsy Ross and Her Friends Completing the First American Flag.* Pastime series. Parker Brothers, Inc., Salem, Mass. 1915. 14¾" × 19¾", 501 hand-cut plywood pieces, including figure pieces. Cardboard box, 10" × 10". **Fig. C-3.** *Prominent Americans Comically Cut Up.* Ives, Blakeslee, & Co., New York, N.Y. Patented 1881. Set of six sliced cardboard puzzles, each 9" × 7", 3 pieces; can be rearranged to form humorous combination characters. Figure on left is Ulysses S. Grant. Box is illustrated in Chapter 6. (Courtesy of the Siegels) **Fig. C-4.** *Save Us From Such Friends!* Charles Jefferys, Philadelphia, Penna. 1898. 10½" × 17", 187 hand-cut wood (mahogany) pieces. Wood box, 5" × 8".

Fig. C-5

THE PASSING PARADE

Fig. C-6

Fig. C-7

Chapter 6

Fig. C-5. *Souvenir de l'Exposition.* Delhaye Freres, Paris, France. 1900. Set of six hand-cut wood puzzles, each 12½″ × 16½″, 35 pieces. Wood frame and cardboard box, 13½″ × 17½″. See Chapter 6 for puzzle illustration. **Fig. C-6.** *Puzzle Pack: The Passing Parade.* National Association Service, Toledo, Ohio. Copyright 1943. 11″ × 9¼″, approximately 85 die-cut cardboard pieces. Cardboard packet is illustrated in Chapter 6. **Fig. C-7.** *U.S. Navy Planes.* Fighters for Freedom series. Whitman Publishing Co., Racine, Wisc. Circa 1943–45. 10″ × 16″, 260 die-cut cardboard pieces. Cardboard box, 5¼″ × 8¼″, with guide picture. Serial no. 3902. **Fig. C-8.** *[Moon Landing].* Victory series. G. J. Hayter & Co., Ltd., Bournemouth, England. 1969. 7½″ × 9¾″, 122 hand-cut plywood pieces. Cardboard box, 8¾″ × 11″, with guide picture.

Fig. C-8

Fig. C-9

Fig. C-10

Fig. C-11

Fig. C-12

Chapter 7

Fig. C-9. *Alice in Wonderland.* Parker Brothers, Inc., Salem, Mass. 1952. Set of four die-cut cardboard puzzles, each 6″ × 17½″, approximately 15 pieces. Cardboard box, 7″ × 18″. Sequenced puzzles each show three scenes from story.   **Fig. C-10.** *David Copperfield Leaving Margate.* Pastime series. Parker Brothers, Inc., Salem, Mass. 1933. 12″ × 17½″, 355 hand-cut plywood pieces, including figure pieces. Cardboard box, 10″ × 10″.   **Fig. C-11.** *Funny Land.* Pandora series. Selchow & Righter Co., New York, N.Y. 1930s. Set of two die-cut cardboard puzzles, each 6¼″ × 9″, 15 pieces. Box is illustrated in Chapter 7.   **Fig. C-12.** *The Ark Puzzle.* Seymour Lyman, New York, N.Y. Circa 1880. 13½″ × 22¼″, 25 sliced cardboard pieces. Box is illustrated in Chapter 7.

Fig. C-13

Fig. C-14

Fig. C-15

Fig. C-16

Chapter 8

Fig. C-13. *Circus Picture Puzzle.* Parker Brothers, Salem, Mass. 1920s. Set of two die-cut cardboard puzzles, each 7½″ × 10¼″, 15 pieces. Cardboard box, 8″ × 10½″, with guide picture for circus puzzle. Other puzzle is illustrated in Chapter 8. **Fig. C-14.** *Three Bears and Farm Scene Puzzles.* Wilder Mfg. Co., St. Louis, Mo. 1920s. 12″ × 20″, 40 hand-cut pressboard pieces. Double-sided, with farm scene on reverse. Cardboard box, 12¾″ × 20¼″, with guide picture for three bears. **Fig. C-15.** *Tom Kitten.* Frederick Warne & Co., Ltd., London, England and New York, N.Y. 1930s. 16″ × 11½″, 151 hand-cut plywood pieces, with irregular edge. Cardboard box, 8½″ × 8½″, with small guide picture. Artist is Beatrix Potter. **Fig. C-16.** *Funny Animal Puzzle Box.* Milton Bradley Co., Springfield, Mass. 1910s. Set of three hand-cut cardboard puzzles, each 9½″ × 16″, 18 pieces. Animals shown on other puzzles are: 1) elephant, bear, rabbit, goat, 2) owl, monkey. Box is illustrated in Chapter 8.

Fig. C-17

Fig. C-19

Fig. C-18

Fig. C-20

Chapter 9

Fig. C-17. *Invocation.* Glad Houser, Litchfield, Maine. 1930s. 16″ × 20″, 665 hand-cut plywood pieces, including figure pieces. Cardboard box, 6¼″ × 9¼″.   **Fig. C-18.** *The High Kick.* Figure-It-Out series. Holtzapffel & Co., London, England. Circa 1915. 14½″ × 21½″, 258 hand-cut plywood pieces, with irregular edge. Cardboard box, 5″ × 7″.   **Fig. C-19.** *[Girl with Mirror].* Unknown maker, U.S. 1930s. 12″ × 9″, 100 die-cut cardboard pieces. Paper envelope, 12½″ × 9″, with small guide diagram.   **Fig. C-20.** *Winter Sport.* Ye Squirlijig series. Marjorie Bouvé, Brookline, Mass. 1910. 10½″ × 8¾″, 99 hand-cut wood (mahogany) pieces. Cardboard box, 4¾″ × 6″.

Fig. C-21

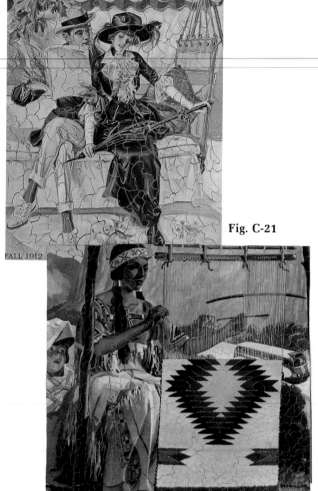

Fig. C-22

Fig. C-23

Fig. C-24

Chapter 9

Fig. C-21. *Two in a Hammock.* Frances A. Cooke, Weston, Mass. Circa 1912. 12″ × 9½″, 187 hand-cut wood pieces. Cardboard box, 3¾″ × 5¼″. Artist is Frank X. Leyendecker. **Fig. C-22.** *Rug Weaver.* Klever Kutup series. H. E. Foss, Springfield, Mass. Circa 1940. 18¾″ × 20″, 746 hand-cut plywood pieces. Cardboard box, 6¼″ × 10¼″. **Fig. C-23.** *[Basting the Turkey].* Unknown maker, U.S. Circa 1909. 11½″ × 8½″, approximately 100 hand-cut wood pieces. Box not extant. **Fig. C-24.** *Hibiscus Time in Bermuda.* Cut by Parker Brothers for Miss Josephine Flood's Picture Puzzle Mart, New York, N.Y. 1940s. 16½″ × 10½″, 266 hand-cut plywood pieces, including figure pieces and irregular edge. Cardboard box, 9¼″ × 5½″.

Fig. C-26

Fig. C-25

Fig. C-28

Fig. C-27

Chapter 9

Fig. C-25. *Day Dreams/River of Romance.* Perfect Double series. Consolidated Paper Box Co., Somerville, Mass. 1930s. 15¼″ × 10¼″, 280 die-cut cardboard pieces. Cardboard box, 7¼″ × 5″, with small guide picture for one puzzle. Artist is R. Atkinson Fox. Serial no. 102.   **Fig. C-26.** *Indian Camp Scroll Puzzle.* Picture Builders series. McLoughlin Brothers, New York, N.Y. Copyright 1894. 12¼″ × 24″, 50 hand-cut pressboard pieces. Wood frame and cardboard box, 10″ × 15″, with guide picture. (Courtesy of the Siegels)   **Fig. C-27.** *Delaware Water Gap.* See America First series, no. 58. Tichnor Brothers, Inc., Cambridge, Mass. Circa 1933. 10½″ × 13½″, 300 die-cut cardboard pieces. Cardboard box, 7″ × 9″.   **Fig. C-28.** *[The Approaching Ship].* [Parker Brothers, Salem, Mass.] 1940s. 28″ × 23″, 785 hand-cut plywood pieces, including figure pieces. Cardboard box.

Fig. C-30

Fig. C-29

Fig. C-31

Fig. C-32

Chapter 10

Fig. C-29. *Music Hath Charms.* Just-For-Fun series. H. E. Foss, Springfield, Mass. 1930s. 16″ × 10½″, 328 hand-cut plywood pieces. Cardboard box, 6¼″ × 10¼″. Artist is Norman Rockwell. **Fig. C-30.** *They'll Measure Up to the Desired Standard.* Perplexity series. E. E. Lewis, Gardiner, Maine. 1920s. 19½″ × 16¼″, 583 hand-cut plywood pieces, including figure pieces. Cardboard box, 4¼″ × 11¼″. Artist is Jessie Willcox Smith. **Fig. C-31.** *Grandfather Frog Gets a Ride.* [Madmar Quality Co., Utica, N.Y.] 1930s. Set of four die-cut cardboard puzzles, each 9″ × 12″, 12 pieces. The artist for the Raggedy Ann and Andy pictures is Johnny Gruelle. The box and another puzzle are illustrated in Chapter 10. (Courtesy of the Siegels) **Fig. C-32.** *Queen's Page.* Jig of Jigs Puzzle no. 1. Distributed by American News Co., Inc., and branches. 1930s. 12″ × 9½″, 270 die-cut cardboard pieces. Cardboard box, 7½″ × 5″. Series includes four subjects, all by Maxfield Parrish. This picture is one of Parrish's illustrations for *The Knave of Hearts.*

Fig. 7-19. *Mother Goose Scroll Puzzle.* Mc-Loughlin Brothers, New York, N.Y. Circa 1890. Hand-cut pressboard pieces. Cardboard box, 10″ × 8″.

Fig. 7-20. *Mother Goose.* Women's Educational & Industrial Union, Boston, Mass. Circa 1915. 9″ × 7″, 107 hand-cut wood pieces. Cardboard box, 3½″ × 6½″.

Fig. 7-21. *Playtime Series.* Madmar Quality Co., New York, N.Y. 1930s. Set of four die-cut cardboard puzzles, each 10″ × 8″, 12 pieces. Cardboard box, 10¼″ × 8¼″, with guide picture for one puzzle. Puzzles in set include: 1) Old King Cole, 2) Little Tommy Tucker, 3) Simple Simon, 4) Mary had a little lamb.

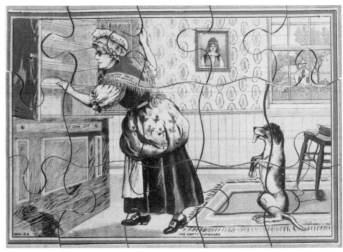

Fig. 7-22. *Old Mother Hubbard Puzzle Box.* Milton Bradley Co., Springfield, Mass. 1910s. Set of three hand-cut cardboard puzzles, each 9″ × 12½″, 15 pieces. Cardboard box, 9¼″ × 13″, with guide picture for one puzzle on lid, and three guide diagrams inside. Set includes: 1) Bare cupboard, 2) Dog feeding cat, 3) Dog riding goat. Serial no. 4214.

Fig. 7-23. *Simple Simon.* [Whitman Publishing Co., Racine, Wisc.] 1940s. Set of two die-cut cardboard puzzles, each 8½″ × 7½″, 27 pieces. Cardboard box, 9″ × 8″, with guide picture for Simple Simon. Other puzzle is Little Bo Peep.

Fig. 7-24. *Simple Simon Puzzle Box.* Milton Bradley Co., Springfield, Mass. Circa 1907. Set of three hand-cut pressboard puzzles, each 20″ × 13″, 30 pieces. Cardboard box, with guide picture for one puzzle. Set includes: 1) *Simple Simon,* 2) *Jack and the Beanstalk,* 3) *Bluebeard.* Serial no. 4159.

Fig. 7-25. *Wee Willie Winkie.* Milton Bradley Co., Springfield, Mass. 1930s. 9½″ × 7″, 30 die-cut cardboard pieces. Double-sided. Cardboard box, 10″ × 7¼″, with one guide picture. Serial no. 4341.

Fig. 7-26. *2 Picture Puzzles*. Whitman Publishing Co., Racine, Wisc. Copyright 1942. Set of two die-cut cardboard puzzles, each 7¼" × 7¼", 12 pieces, including figure pieces. Cardboard box, 7½" × 7½", with guide picture for Little Boy Blue. Other puzzle shows Little Miss Muffet.

▪ Other Stories and Literature

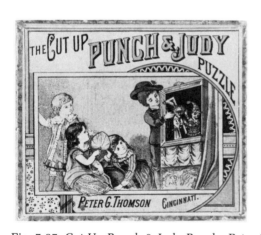

Fig. 7-27. *Cut Up Punch & Judy Puzzle*. Peter G. Thomson, Cincinnati, Ohio. 1880s. 16" × 12¼", 44 sliced cardboard pieces. Cardboard box, 5½" × 6½". Contains guide picture. (Courtesy of the Siegels)

Fig. 7-28. *Dickens Dissected Puzzle*. William A. Emerson, Fitchburg, Mass. 1880s. 10½″ × 13½″, 41 sliced cardboard pieces. Cardboard box, 4¾″ × 6″. Contains guide picture.

Fig. 7-29. *Johnny Appleseed*. Unknown maker. 7½″ × 9½″, 131 hand-cut composition board pieces. Cardboard box, 3¾″ × 5¼″.

Fig. 7-30. *Johnny's Machines.* Little Golden Picture Puzzle series no. 2. Whitman Publishing Co., Racine, Wisc. Copyright 1949. Frame puzzle, 7½″ × 6″, 8 die-cut cardboard pieces, including one figure piece. Cardboard box, 8″ × 6½″, with guide picture. Series contained six puzzles, each showing cover art for a Little Golden Book. There were four different series and a total of 24 puzzles.

Fig. 7-31. *Mr. Pecksniff Leaves for London.* Pastime series. Parker Brothers, Inc., Salem, Mass. Circa 1911. 6½″ × 11¾″, 151 hand-cut plywood pieces, including figure pieces. Cardboard box, 5¼″ × 8¼″.

Fig. 7-32. *Peter Rabbit Put-Together* Puzzle. Samuel Gabriel Sons & Co., New York, N.Y. 1920s. Set of three die-cut cardboard puzzles, each 10″ × 8½″, approx. 12 pieces. Cardboard box, 10½″ × 9″. Puzzles show: 1) Peter running from Mr. McGregor, 2) Peter meets a mouse, 3) Peter meets Miss Kitty. Serial no. T-196.

Fig. 7-33. *Sidney Carton.* Library series. Detroit Publishing Co. Circa 1920. 10″ × 8″, 165 hand-cut plywood pieces. Cardboard box, 6″ × 6″.

Fig. 7-34. *Tony Weller.* Delta series: Characters from Dickens. A. V. N. Jones & Co., Ltd., London, England. 1930s. 9½″ × 6¾″, 100 hand-cut plywood pieces. Cardboard box, 11½″ × 9″, with guide pictures on bottom of box showing the entire series of 12 puzzles.

Fig. 7-35. *Uncle Tom's Cabin.* William Spooner, London, England. Circa 1852. 8½" × 11", 31 hand-colored and hand-cut wood pieces. Wood box. Contains hand-colored guide picture.

8 ALL CREATURES GREAT AND SMALL

JIGSAW PUZZLES have featured animals of all species, from the domestic to the exotic, for over two hundred years. The antics of kittens and the ferocity of tigers have always held children spellbound, and puzzles have reflected this preoccupation. Adults have not been immune either. Quite a few adult puzzles are interspersed among the children's puzzles that are found in this chapter.

The chapter is divided into sections dealing with puzzles that show: cats, dogs, horses and farm animals, zoo and circus animals, comic animals, and Other animals and birds.

The color section includes the following items in addition to those described in this chapter:

- *Tom Kitten*
- *Three Bears and Farm Scene Puzzles*

▪ Cats

Fig. 8-1. *Home Scroll Puzzle*. McLoughlin Brothers, New York, N.Y. Copyright 1898. 10″ × 8¼″, 20 hand-cut cardboard pieces. Cardboard box, 9¼″ × 7¼″, with guide picture.

Fig. 8-3. *Cut Up Animals Spelling Slips.* McLoughlin Brothers, New York, N.Y. Circa 1900. 27 sliced cardboard pieces that make a set of puzzles. Cardboard box, 12″ × 9″.

Fig. 8-2. *Criss Cross Spelling Slips: Set Four, Kittens.* McLoughlin Brothers, New York, N.Y. Circa 1890. Set of six sliced cardboard puzzles, each 10″ × 10″, 8 pieces. Wood frame and cardboard box, 10¾″ × 9″. (Courtesy of the Siegels)

Fig. 8-4. *Pussy Cat Puzzle Box*. Milton Bradley Co., Springfield, Mass. Produced 1913–31. Set of three hand-cut cardboard puzzles, each 12¾″ × 18¼″, 30 pieces. Cardboard box, about 13″ × 18½″, with guide picture for this puzzle. Others in set show: 1) Banquet, 2) Going to school. Serial No. 4069.

Fig. 8-5. *A Fond Parent*. Jigleo Puzzle. Lee Olney, Bath, Me. Circa 1909. 7¾″ × 10¾″, 106 wood (mahogany) pieces. Cardboard box, 4″ × 5¼″.

Fig. 8-6. *Robber Kitten Picture Puzzle.* Parker Brothers, Salem, Mass. 1920s. Set of two die-cut cardboard puzzles, each 7¼″ × 10¼″, 15 pieces. Cardboard box, 8″ × 10½″, with guide picture for robber kitten.

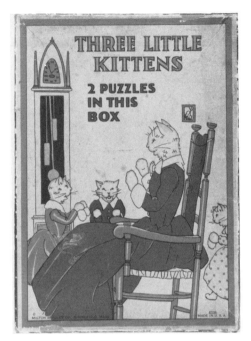

Fig. 8-7. *Three Little Kittens*. Milton Bradley Co., Springfield, Mass. 1930s. 9½″ × 7″, 30 die-cut cardboard pieces. Double-sided. Cardboard box, 10″ × 7¼″, with one guide picture. Serial no. 4338.

Fig. 8-8. *Mischievous Kittens*. Tuco Work Shops, Lockport, N.Y. Circa 1940. 11¼″ × 15¼″, 204 die-cut cardboard pieces. Cardboard box, 9″ × 6¼″, with small guide picture.

Fig. 8-9. *Heureuse Famille.* Penelope Puzzles, Switzerland. 1930s. 3½″ × 5½″, 50 hand-cut plywood pieces. Cardboard box, 4¼″ × 6″.

▪ Dogs

Fig. 8-10. *Faithful Friends.* J. W. Spear & Sons, London, England. Circa 1905. Set of three hand-cut cardboard puzzles, each 9½″ × 7″, 15 pieces. Cardboard box, 10″ × 7¾″. Contains two guide pictures, with third on box lid. Others in set include: 1) Bulldog watching chicks, 2) Girl in farmyard.

Fig. 8-11. *Dogs at Play.* R. W. Bliss, Wollaston, Mass. 1930s. 12″ × 9″, 153 hand-cut plywood pieces. Cardboard box, 5¼″ × 5¼″.

Fig. 8-12. *The Puppies Picture Puzzles.* Saalfield Publishing Co., Akron, Ohio. Copyright 1941. Set of three die-cut cardboard puzzles, each 9¼″ × 9¼″, about 30 pieces. Cardboard box, 9½″ × 9¾″. Other puzzles show: 1) cover picture, 2) puppy playing violin.

Fig. 8-13. *Boston Terrier.* Hobby Jig Saws series. Jaymar Specialty Co., New York, N.Y. Copyright 1944. 21¾″ × 13¾″, 300 die-cut cardboard pieces, including figure pieces. Cardboard box, 7″ × 10″, with small guide picture.

Fig. 8-14. *Dog Jig-Saw Puzzle.* Victory Series A.D.1. G. J. Hayter & Co, Ltd., Bournemouth, England. In production circa 1930–60. 8″ × 14¾″, 76 hand-cut plywood pieces, including 12 cut-out dogs that double as play figures. Cardboard box, 8½″ × 11″, with guide picture. This puzzle was also produced in both smaller and larger sizes.

125

▪ Horses and Farm Animals

Fig. 8-15. *Wild Horses*. Think series. Harry B. Heiser, Lancaster, Pa. Distributed by Samuel Murray, Wilbraham, Mass. 1950s. 5½″ × 8½″, 60 hand-cut 1″ thick wood pieces, which interlock in three dimensions. Cardboard box, 7½″ × 10½″, with small guide picture.

Fig. 8-16. *Thoroughbred*. C. C. Stevens, Auburn, Me. 1930s. 15″ × 10″, 373 hand-cut plywood pieces. Cardboard box, 6″ × 7¾″.

Fig. 8-17. *Old Dobbin Scroll Puzzle*. Milton Bradley Co., Springfield, Mass. 1920s. Set of two die-cut cardboard puzzles, each 7½″ × 10¼″, 15 pieces. Cardboard box, 8″ × 10½″, with guide picture for horse. Guide diagrams and poems are inside lid.

Fig. 8-18. *Farm Friends*. Zig Zag Puzzle Co., Chicago, Ill. 1933. 12″ × 10″, 200 hand-cut plywood pieces. Cardboard box, 10¼″ × 8¼″.

Fig. 8-19. *New Dissected Animal Puzzle*. Unknown German maker. Circa 1900. Set of three hand-cut wood puzzles, each 8½″ × 11½″, about 15 pieces. Cardboard box, 9″ × 12¼″. Contains three guide pictures. Puzzles are cut to the outlines of the animals which include: 1) goat, 2) duck, 3) sheep.

Fig. 8-20. [*Goats and Kittens*]. Unknown German maker. Circa 1900. 6¼″ × 8″, 20 hand-cut wood pieces. Double-sided, with picture of kittens on reverse. Cardboard box, 6½″ × 8¼″, with guide picture for kittens.

Fig. 8-21. *Wayside Watering Place*. Paramount series. Salem Puzzle Co., Salem, Mass. 10½″ × 8″, 161 hand-cut plywood pieces, including figure pieces. Cardboard box, 5″ × 7½″. Salem Puzzle Co. was owned by Parker Brothers.

Fig. 8-22. *Good Friends*. Ingleside Co., Springfield, Mass. Circa 1909. 5¾" × 7½", 79 hand-cut wood pieces. Cardboard box, 8" × 6".

Fig. 8-23. [*Rabbits*]. Joseph K. Straus, Brooklyn, N.Y. 1940s. Set of two hand-cut plywood tray puzzles, each 12" × 9", 30 pieces. Cardboard box, 10¼" × 13". Other puzzle shows girl feeding rabbits.

Fig. 8-24. *Bambino Puzzle.* Jouets Vera, Paris, France. 1950s. 7¾″ × 9½″, 12 hand cut plywood pieces. Cardboard box, 8½″ × 10″, with guide picture.

▪ Zoo and Circus Animals

Fig. 8-25. *Zoo Puzzle.* Unknown German maker. Circa 1900. Set of eight hand-cut wood puzzles, each 4½″ × 4¼″, 9 pieces. Cardboard box, 9¾″ × 9¼″. (Courtesy of the Siegels)

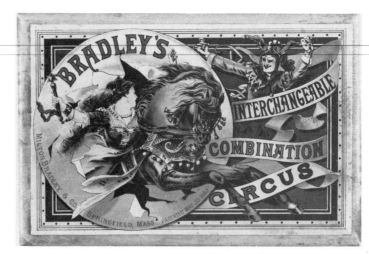

Fig. 8-26. *Bradley's Interchangeable Combination Circus.* Milton Bradley & Co., Springfield, Mass. Patented May 30, 1882. 35 sliced cardboard pieces, each 2″ × 3¼″; can be rearranged to make thousands of different scenes. Wood box, 6½″ × 9¾″. Note that Milton Bradley issued a reproduction of this puzzle in 1970; although the box is clearly marked, the puzzle pieces are not. (Courtesy of the Siegels)

Fig. 8-27. [*Circus/Alphabet Blocks*]. Unknown maker. Circa 1890. 11½″ × 20½″, 24 hand-cut wood pieces. Double-sided. Wood box, 8¾″ × 11″. One block is turned over to show the alphabet letters on the back.

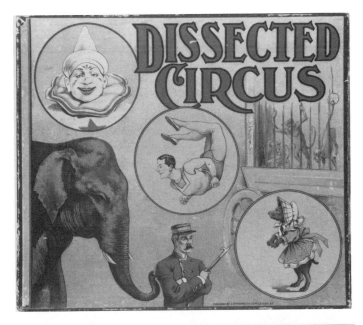

Fig. 8-28. *Dissected Circus*. J. Ottmann Lith. Co., New York, N.Y. Circa 1900. 12¾″ × 18½″, 24 sliced cardboard pieces. Cardboard box, 10¼″ × 11¾″.

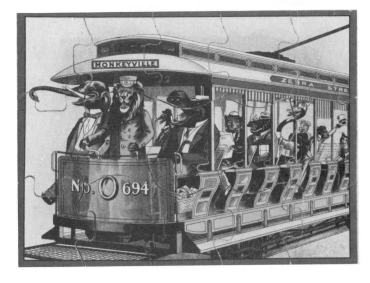

Fig. 8-29. *Circus Picture Puzzle*. Parker Brothers, Salem, Mass. 1920s. Set of two die-cut cardboard puzzles, each 7½″ × 10¼″, 15 pieces. Box, with guide picture for circus puzzle, is illustrated in color section.

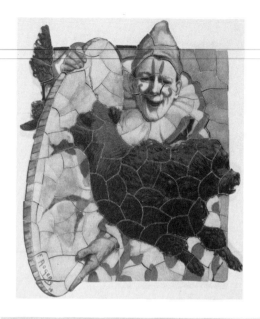

Fig. 8-30. [Clown with Dog]. Whatami Puzzle Co., Arlington, Mass. Circa 1909. 11¼″ × 9″, 114 hand-cut wood pieces. Cardboard box, 4¼″ × 4¼″.

Fig. 8-31. Big 4 Circus Puzzles: Set No. 2. Consolidated Paper Box Co., Somerville, Mass. Set of three die-cut cardboard puzzles, each 7¼″ × 9½″, 50 pieces, including figure pieces. Cardboard box, 7½″ × 10″. Puzzles in set include: 1) Chariot driver, 2) Indians on horseback, 3) Two lancers chasing clown. There were four different sets, each containing three puzzles.

Fig. 8-32. *Doo Dad Circus Game Nos. 3 and 4.* University Feature & Specialty Co. Copyright 1921. 13¾″ × 10″, 26 die-cut cardboard pieces. Double-sided, shows another circus scene on reverse. Cardboard box, 5¾″ × 6¾″.

▪ Comic Animals

Fig. 8-33. *The After-Dinner Puzzle.* Novelty Game Co., New York, N.Y. Circa 1870. 8″ × 20½″, 36 die-cut or sliced cardboard pieces. Cardboard box, 6¼″ × 9″.

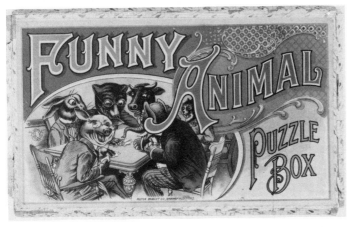

Fig. 8-34. *Funny Animal Puzzle Box.* Milton Bradley Co., Springfield, Mass. 1910s. Set of three hand-cut cardboard puzzles, each 9½″ × 16″, 18 pieces. Cardboard box, 9¾″ × 16¼″, with guide diagrams inside lid. Serial no. 4179. See color section for puzzle illustration.

Fig. 8-35. *Cleanliness.* Consolidated Paper Box Co., Somerville, Mass. 1930s. One of a set of six die-cut cardboard puzzles, each 10″ × 12″, about 35 pieces. Cardboard box, 10¼″ × 12¼″, with cellophane window. Other puzzles in set include: 1) *Manners,* 2) *Patience,* 3) *Kiddie Orchestra,* 4) *Romeo and Juliet,* 5) *Young Lovers at Full Moon* (illustrated in Chapter 9).

▪ Other Animals and Birds

Fig. 8-36. *Sliced Animals.* E. G. Selchow & Co., New York, N.Y. 1870s. Set of 15 sliced cardboard puzzles, each consisting of several pieces 1¼″ × 7″. Cardboard box, 7½″ × 8½″. Animals include: bear, buffalo, camel, cat, cow, deer, dog, fox, giraffe, goat, horse, lion, rat, sheep, zebra.

Fig. 8-37. *Cut Up Animals Scroll Puzzle.* McLoughlin Brothers, New York, N.Y. Circa 1890. Set of two hand-cut pressboard puzzles, each 12½″ × 10″, 24 pieces. Wood frame and cardboard box, 13½″ × 11″. Contains one guide picture, with other on box lid.

Fig. 8-38. *Cut Up Domestic Animals.* J. H. Singer, New York, N.Y. Circa 1910. Set of six sliced cardboard puzzles, each 5″ × 4″, 4 pieces. Cardboard box, 5½″ × 6½″, with small guide pictures.

Fig. 8-39. *Sectional Animals.* Milton Bradley Co., Springfield, Mass. In production about 1920–40 with this cover. Set of six die-cut cardboard puzzles, each 6¾″ × 9″, 8 pieces. Cardboard box, 7″ × 9½″, with key diagrams inside lid. Animals include: bear, buffalo, elephant, lion, tiger, zebra. Serial no. 4753.

Fig. 8-40. *T is For Turtle.* Artinet Series. Arteno Co., Boston, Mass. 1930s. 11½″ × 8½″, 272 hand-cut plywood pieces. Cardboard box, 3¾″ × 5¼″.

Fig. 8-41. *Sliced Birds.* E. G. Selchow & Co., New York, N.Y. 1870s. Set of 14 sliced cardboard puzzles, each consisting of several pieces 1¼″ × 6¾″. Cardboard box, 7½″ × 8½″. Puzzles include: avocet, crane, duck, eagle, finch, hawk, jay, oriole, parrot, peacock, pigeon, quail, swan, turkey.

Fig. 8-42. *The First Robin.* Mrs. Amory P. McLellan, Randolph, Me. 1930s. 10″ × 7½″, 175 hand-cut plywood pieces, including figure pieces. Cardboard box, 3½″ × 5″. Artist is H. Hintermeister.

Fig. 8-43. *Whooping Cranes Stamp.* Harry L. and E. M. Watts, Virginia Beach, Va. Circa 1960. 12¼″ × 7¾″, 226 hand-cut plywood pieces. Cardboard box, 4″ × 7¼″.

9 FACES AND PLACES

HUMAN INTEREST topics and faraway places have been staples for jigsaw puzzle makers, ever since they diversified beyond strictly educational puzzles at the end of the eighteenth century. And their customers have delighted in all sorts of subjects, from lively domestic scenes to tranquil landscapes. This chapter encompasses the range of these traditional puzzles, and includes sections on: children and families, belles and sweethearts, leisure moments, comic characters, scenes from the old west, and distant vistas.

The color section includes the following items in addition to those described in this chapter:

- *Invocation*
- *Winter Sport*
- *The High Kick*
- *[Girl With Mirror]*
- *Two in a Hammock*
- *Rug Weaver*
- *[Basting the Turkey]*
- *Hibiscus Time in Bermuda*
- *[The Approaching Ship]*
- *Day Dreams/River of Romance*
- *Delaware Water Gap*
- *Indian Camp Scroll Puzzle*

Fig. 9-1. [*Contented Baby*]. [William F. D. Prosser, Bethlehem, Pa.] 1930s. 12¾″ × 11½″, approx. 225 hand-cut plywood pieces. Wood box, 5¾″ × 9″.

Fig. 9-3. *Amusing baby*. Pastime series. Parker Brothers, Inc., Salem, Mass. 1923. 12″ × 9¾″, 202 hand-cut plywood pieces, including figure pieces. Cardboard box, 4½″ × 9″.

Fig. 9-2. [*Baby's Bath*]. Unknown maker. 10″ × 9¼″, 92 hand-cut plywood pieces, irregular edge. Box not extant.

Fig. 9-4. *The Head of the House.* Old Gallery series. A. H. Norrish Ateliers, St. Louis, Mo. 1930s. 7″ × 10½″, 119 hand-cut plywood pieces, including figure pieces. Cardboard box, 5¾″ × 8¼″.

Fig. 9-5. *Jerusalem's Bath.* Beacon Hill series. Sold at Marjorie Knapp Bookshop, Boston, Mass. 1920s. 9½″ × 7″, 115 hand-cut plywood pieces. Cardboard box, 4¼″ × 7¼″.

Fig. 9-6. *Joy Cometh in the Morning.* Pastime series. Parker Brothers, Inc., Salem, Mass. 1920. 11¼″ × 13½″, 223 hand-cut plywood pieces, including figure pieces. Cardboard box, 4½″ × 9″.

Fig. 9-7. [*Village Scenes*]. Unknown maker, Germany. Circa 1860. Set of four hand-colored sliced cardboard puzzles, each 6″ × 8″, 12 pieces. Cardboard box, 6″ × 8″. Contains three hand-colored guide pictures, with fourth on box lid. Puzzles include: 1) Mouse in the house, 2) Children at trough, 3) Home from hunting, 4) Spinning and reading.

Fig. 9-8. *The Little Ones' Puzzle Box.* Ernest Nister, London, England, and E. P. Dutton & Co., New York, N.Y. Circa 1900. Set of three hand-cut cardboard puzzles, each 7½″ × 9″, 12 pieces. Cardboard box, 7¾″ × 9½″. Contains two guide pictures, with third on lid. Set includes: 1) Beach scene (illustrated), 2) Feeding lambs (on box cover), 3) Painting scene.

Fig. 9-9. *Wash Day Picture Puzzle*. Milton Bradley Co., Springfield, Mass. 1920s. Set of two die-cut cardboard puzzles, each 10¼″ × 7½″, 15 pieces. Cardboard box, 10½″ × 8″, with one guide picture. Serial no. 4734.

Fig. 9-10. [*Dutch Children*]. Jig-A-Jig series. Parker Brothers, Inc., Salem, Mass. Circa 1909. 5¾″ × 8″, 75 hand-cut wood pieces. Cardboard box, 4″ × 5½″.

Fig. 9-11. [*The Lesson*]. Zig-Zag series. Parker Brothers, Inc., Salem, Mass. 1910s. 6″ × 8″, 33 hand-cut plywood pieces. Cardboard box, 8¼″ × 6¼″.

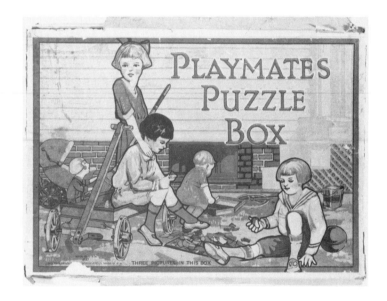

Fig. 9-12. *Playmates Puzzle Box*. Milton Bradley Co., Springfield, Mass. 1920s. Set of three die-cut cardboard puzzles, each 8¾″ × 12½″, 15 pieces. Cardboard box, 9¼″ × 13″, with one guide picture. Set includes: 1) Children with toys, 2) Three girls at service station, 3) Feeding the geese. Serial no. 4147.

Fig. 9-13. *Happyland Picture Puzzles.* Milton Bradley Co., Springfield, Mass. Copyright 1932. Set of three die-cut cardboard puzzles, each 12″ × 16″, 32 pieces. Cardboard box, 12¼″ × 16½″, with one guide picture. Set includes: 1) Hanging the laundry, 2) Grandpa's toy workshop, 3) At the beach. Serial no. 4442.

Fig. 9-14. *3 Frame-Tray Puzzles.* Whitman Publishing Co., Racine, Wisc. Copyright 1959. Set of three die-cut cardboard frame tray puzzles, each 13½″ × 10½″, about 25 pieces, including figure pieces. Cardboard box, 14¼″ × 11″. Set includes: 1) Cowboy, 2) Cowgirl, 3) Feeding the chickens.

Fig. 9-15. *United Nations Puzzles.* Leo Hart Co., Rochester, N.Y. Copyright 1944. Set of six die-cut cardboard puzzles, each 8½″ × 7″, approx. 25 pieces. Cardboard box, 9″ × 14½″, with one guide picture. Set includes: 1) England, 2) Russia, 3) China, 4) Netherlands, 5) France, 6) Mexico.

Fig. 9-16. [*Little Rich Girl*]. Pastime series. Parker Brothers, Inc., Salem, Mass. 1930s. 9½″ × 7½″, approx. 100 hand-cut plywood pieces, including figure pieces. Cardboard box.

▪ Belles and Sweethearts

Fig. 9-17. *Kentucky Belle.* Mrs. Hayden Richardson, New York, N.Y. Circa 1909. 16½″ × 24½″, 908 hand-cut wood pieces. Cardboard box, 10½″ × 9½″.

Fig. 9-18. *Portrait of a Lady*. Harriet Bates, West Medford, Mass. Circa 1930. 13″ × 9½″, 180 hand-cut plywood pieces. Cardboard box, 4¼″ × 6½″.

Fig. 9-19. *The Wood Nymphs*. H. A. Jenks, Canton, Mass. 1909. 13″ × 9¾″, 190 hand-cut plywood pieces. Cardboard box, 4½″ × 6½″.

Fig. 9-20. *An Anxious Moment*. Puzzle for Wideawakes series. E. T. Price, New Bedford, Mass. 10″ × 15″, 201 hand-cut wood pieces. Cardboard box, 5¾″ × 8¾″.

Fig. 9-21. [*Woman with Parrot*]. Unknown maker, U.S. 1930s. 8½″ × 6½″, approx. 100 hand-cut plywood pieces. Cardboard box, 5¼″ × 8¼″.

Fig. 9-22. *Old Oaken Bucket*. Louis Nelson, Springfield and Fitchburg, Mass. 1930s. 9½″ × 7½″, 106 hand-cut plywood pieces, including figure pieces. Cardboard box, 4¾″ × 7¼″.

Fig. 9-23. [*Nude*]. Unknown maker. 9½″ × 11½″, approx. 250 hand-cut pressboard pieces. Box not extant.

Fig. 9-24. *Keeping the Tryst*. Muddle series. Santway Photo-Craft Co., Inc., Watertown, N.Y. 15″ × 11″, 300 die-cut cardboard pieces. Cardboard box, 8″ × 8″.

Fig. 9-26. *Pal O'Mine*. Deluxe series. Tuco Work Shops, Inc., Lockport, N.Y. Circa 1940. 19½″ × 15″, 320 die-cut pressboard pieces. Cardboard box, 9¼″ × 7¼″, with guide picture.

Fig. 9-25. [*Bathing Beauties*]. Distributed by George W. Brelsford. 1930s. 12″ × 9¾″, 180 die-cut cardboard pieces. Glassine envelope, 14½″ × 10½″.

Fig. 9-27. *No Nudes is Bad Nudes*. Ballyhoo series. Dell Publishing Co., Inc. New York, N.Y. 15¼″ × 10½″, 333 die-cut cardboard pieces. Cardboard box, 9″ × 7″.

Fig. 9-28. *Playboy Playmate Puzzle*. American Publishing Co., Waltham, Mass. Copyright 1967. 11″ × 23½″, 297 die-cut cardboard pieces. Metal cannister, 5½″ high, 4″ diameter.

Fig. 9-29. *Romeo and Juliet at the Window*. Perplexity series. Mrs. Hayden Richardson, New York, N.Y. Circa 1909. 20½″ × 28¼″, 1171 hand-cut wood pieces. Cardboard box, 9¼″ × 9¼″.

Fig. 9-31. *What Are the Wild Waves Saying?* Huvanco, Ilford, England. Circa 1920. 10¾″ × 7½″, 141 hand-cut wood pieces. Cardboard box.

Fig. 9-30. *Embarkation.* Leisure Hour Puzzle Co., Melrose, Mass. Circa 1909. 15½″ × 10½″, 240 hand-cut wood pieces, including figure pieces. Cardboard box, 5″ × 7¼″.

Fig. 9-32. [*Young Lovers at Full Moon*]. Consolidated Paper Box Co., Somerville, Mass. 1930s. One of a set of six die-cut cardboard puzzles, each 10″ × 12″, about 35 pieces. Cardboard box, 10¼″ × 12¼″, with cellophane window. Other puzzles in set include: 1) *Cleanliness* (illustrated in Chapter 8), 2) *Manners,* 3) *Patience,* 4) *Kiddie Orchestra,* 5) *Romeo and Juliet.*

▪ Leisure Moments

Fig. 9-33. *The Lottery Shop*. Unknown maker, Germany. Circa 1860. 8″ × 10″, 45 hand-colored and hand-cut wood pieces. Wood box, 9″ × 11″, with hand-colored guide picture.

Fig. 9-34. *Come Seven*. Curley Cue Cut series. A. H. Warner & Co., Bristol, Conn. Circa 1909. 10¼″ × 8½″, 130 hand-cut wood pieces. Cardboard box, 4¾″ × 7″.

Fig. 9-35. *A Quiet Game.* U-Nit series. James Browning, W. Caldwell, N.J. Circa 1960. 10¼″ × 12¾″, 204 hand-cut mahogany plywood pieces, including figure pieces. Cardboard box, 4¾″ × 8½″.

Fig. 9-36. *Days of Real Sport.* Premier series. Milton Bradley Co., Springfield, Mass. 1930s. 9″ × 8″, 100 hand-cut plywood pieces, including figure pieces. Cardboard box, 8¼″ × 4½″. Artist is H. Hintermeister.

Fig. 9-37. *Thursday.* The Society Puzzle. Circa 1909. 11¾″ × 13¾″, 205 hand-cut wood pieces. Cardboard box, 5½″ × 4¾″.

Fig. 9-38. *Breath of Spring*. Picture Puzzle Weekly series, no. C-3. Viking Mfg. Co., Boston, Mass. Circa 1933. 14″ × 10″, 204 die-cut cardboard pieces, including figure pieces. Cardboard box, 10¼″ × 8¼″.

Fig. 9-39. *Nature's Playground*. Abercrombie & Fitch Co., New York, N.Y. 1930s. 14¾″ × 10½″, 180 hand-cut plywood pieces. Cardboard box, 6″ × 7½″. Serial no. 2354. Artist is Philip R. Goodwin.

Fig. 9-40. *A Halt by the Wayside*. Brewer Brothers, Cortland, N.Y. 1930s. 9¼″ × 14″, 200 hand-cut plywood pieces, including figure pieces. Cardboard box, 5″ × 6¼″.

Fig. 9-41. *2 Perfect Children's Puzzles.* Consolidated Paper Box Co., Somerville, Mass. 1930s. Set of two die-cut cardboard puzzles, each 10¾″ × 8¾″, 50 pieces. Cardboard box, 9¼″ × 11¼″. Set includes: 1) Tennis player, 2) Boy with dogs. Serial no. 210.

Fig. 9-42. *Dethroned.* Robert England, Hingham, Mass. 1920s. 9″ × 14″, 379 hand-cut plywood pieces. Cardboard box, 6½″ × 8½″.

Fig. 9-43. *Show Boat.* Jig-A-While Puzzle. 11¾″ × 20¾″, 258 hand-cut plywood pieces, including figure pieces. Cardboard box, 6¼″ × 8½″.

Fig. 9-44. *Twining Garlands of Roses*. Pastime series. Parker Brothers, Inc., Salem, Mass. 1916. 21″ × 28½″, 760 hand-cut plywood pieces, including figure pieces. Cardboard box, 10″ × 10″.

Fig. 9-45. *Roller Coaster*. [Fifield family cutter, Swampscott, Mass.] 1920s. 11½″ × 8¼″, 175 hand-cut plywood pieces. Cardboard box, 4¾″ × 7½″.

Fig. 9-46. *Fred's Visit to the Circus*. Porpine Puzzle Co., Melrose, Mass. Circa 1909. 10¼″ × 9½″, 195 hand-cut wood pieces. Cardboard box, 4½″ × 5¾″.

Fig. 9-47. *There's Naething Mair Precious Nor Time.* Ye Squirlijig series. Marjorie Bouvé, Brookline, Mass. 1910. 9¼″ × 16″, 197 hand-cut wood (mahogany) pieces. Cardboard box, 6″ × 9″.

▪ Comic Characters

Fig. 9-48. *The Bell & Hammer.* Unknown maker, Germany. Circa 1850. Set of seven hand-colored, hand-cut wood metamorphic puzzles, each 5″ × 4″, 6 pieces. Pieces can be interchanged to form different absurd characters. Wood box, 6½″ × 4½″.

Fig. 9-49. *Masquerade Blocks.* Charles M. Crandall, Montrose, Pa. 1870s. Set of eight hand-colored, hand-cut wood blocks, each 2″ square, that can be rearranged to form many different comic characters. Wood box, 4¾″ × 8¾″.

Fig. 9-50. [*Metamorphosis Puzzle*]. V. S. W. Parkhurst, Providence, R.I. 1850s. Set of 10 hand-colored sliced paper puzzles, each 4½″ × 2½″, 3 pieces. Pieces can be interchanged to form different amusing characters. Cardboard box, 5″ × 2¾″.

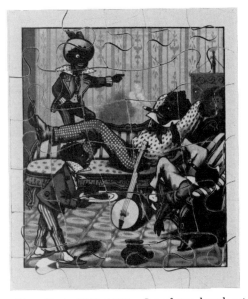

Fig. 9-51. *Chopped Up Niggers*. McLoughlin Brothers, New York, N.Y. 1880s. Set of two hand-cut wood puzzles, each 10½″ × 9″, 30 pieces. Wood frame and cardboard box, 10½″ × 8¾″, with one guide picture. (Courtesy of the Siegels)

Fig. 9-52. *Changeable Charlie.* Gaston Manufacturing Co., Cincinnati, Ohio. Copyright 1948. 6¾″ × 5¼″, 11 hand-cut wood blocks, with pictures on four sides. Pieces can be rearranged to form over 4 million different expressions. Cardboard box, 7″ × 5½″.

▪ Scenes from the Old West

Fig. 9-53. *The Alarm.* Perfect series. Consolidated Paper Box Co., Somerville, Mass. 1930s. 15½″ × 19½″, 378 die-cut cardboard pieces. Cardboard box, 9¾″ × 7¼″, with small guide picture.

Fig. 9-54. *Rescued.* Joseph K. Straus, Brooklyn, N.Y. 1940s. 19¾″ × 15¾″, 500 hand-cut plywood pieces. Cardboard box, 7¼″ × 10¾″.

Fig. 9-55. *Rodeo.* Sifo, St. Paul, Minn. Copyright 1950. Frame tray puzzle, 8″ × 10″, 36 die-cut cardboard pieces.

Fig. 9-56. *Indians Hunting Buffalo.* Every Week series. Einson-Freeman Co., Inc., Long Island City, N.Y. Copyright 1933. 10½″ × 14½″, 160 die-cut cardboard pieces. Cardboard box, 7″ × 7″, with guide diagram.

Fig. 9-57. *Cowboy Puzzles.* Platt & Munk, New York, N.Y. 1940s. Set of six die-cut cardboard puzzles, each 10¾″ × 8¾″, approx. 30 pieces, including figure pieces. Cardboard box, 11″ × 9″. Set includes: 1) Bucking bronco, 2) Horse race, 3) Horseman on bluff, 4) Children on bluff, 5) Cowboy violinist, 6) Children riding. Serial no. 145A.

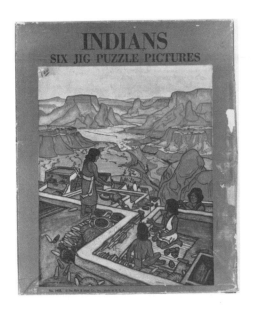

Fig. 9-58. *Indians.* Platt & Munk, New York, N.Y. 1940s. Set of six die-cut cardboard puzzles, each 10¾″ × 8¾″, approx. 40 pieces, including figure pieces. Cardboard box, 11″ × 9¼″. Set includes: 1) Navajos, 2) Pueblos, 3) Polynesians, 4) Cliff Dwellers, 5) Delawares, 6) Horsemen. Serial no. 145B.

▪ Distant Vistas

Fig. 9-59. [*European City Views*]. Unknown maker, Germany. Circa 1895. Set of six hand-cut cardboard puzzles, each 9¼″ × 13″, 40 pieces. Cardboard box, 10¼″ × 14″. Contains five guide pictures, with sixth on box lid. Set includes: 1) Vienna (illustrated), 2) Genoa, 3) Naples, 4) London, 5) Madrid, 6) Berlin.

Fig. 9-60. [*Castle*]. Unknown maker. Circa 1870. 6½″ × 8″, 20 hand-colored and hand-cut wood pieces. Box not extant.

Fig. 9-61. *St. Paul's*. Macy's, New York, N.Y. 1931. 10½″ × 12¼″, 241 hand-cut plywood pieces, including figure pieces. Wood box, 4½″ × 10½″.

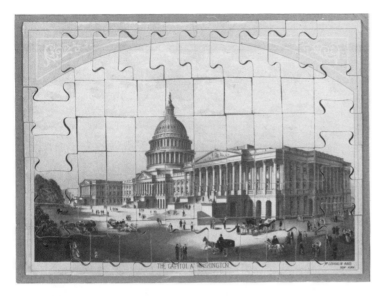

Fig. 9-62. *The Capitol at Washington.* McLoughlin Brothers, New York, N.Y. Circa 1890. 17″ × 23¼″, 60 hand-cut pressboard pieces. Double-sided, with map on reverse. Box not extant. (Courtesy of the Siegels)

Fig. 9-63. *Ye Boar's Head Inn.* Nu-Friend series. Andover Novelty Shop, Andover, Mass. 1930s. 11¾″ × 15¾″, 271 hand-cut masonite pieces. Cardboard box, 6¼″ × 6¼″.

Fig. 9-64. *Flowers of Holland*. Sparetime series. P. J. Allen, Medford, Mass. 1930s. 12″ × 9″, 215 hand-cut plywood pieces. Cardboard box, 6″ × 6″.

Fig. 9-65. [*Two Dutch Scenes*]. Tiny Tot series. Madmar Quality Co., Utica, N.Y. 1930s. Set of two hand-cut pressboard puzzles, each 6″ × 4″. Cardboard box, 8″ × 10″, with two guide pictures.

Fig. 9-66. *Sundown.* H. L. Yeaton, Conway, N.H. 1930s. 14¾″ × 11¾″, 262 hand-cut plywood pieces. Cardboard box, 6″ × 8″.

Fig. 9-67. *Snowbound.* Everybody's series. Wilkie Picture & Puzzle Co., Dayton, Ohio. Circa 1940. 16″ × 20″, 504 die-cut cardboard pieces. Cardboard box, 7¼″ × 8¾″, with small guide picture.

Fig. 9-68. *Blossom Time*. Art in Puzzles. 1930s. 8″ × 11″, 201 hand-cut plywood pieces. Cardboard box, 6¼″ × 8″. Serial no. 5273.

Fig. 9-69. *In the Land Where Dreams Come True*. De-Pend-On series. C. T. Sawyer, Fitchburg, Mass. Circa 1933. 16″ × 20″, 655 hand-cut plywood pieces. Cardboard box, 6″ × 10″.

Fig. 9-70. *High Up in the Rockies*. A. J. Crippen, Batavia, N.Y. 1940s. 9″ × 12″, 169 hand-cut plywood pieces. Cardboard box, 7¼″ × 5½″.

Fig. 9-71. *A Study in Color*. Premier series. Milton Bradley Co., Springfield, Mass. 1930s. 11¾″ × 15¾″, approx. 300 hand-cut plywood pieces, including figure pieces. Cardboard box, 9¾″ × 6″.

Fig. 9-72. *On the Zeeland Coast.* Academy series. J. Salmon, Ltd., Sevenoaks, England. Circa 1940. 10″ × 13¾″, 317 hand-cut plywood pieces. Cardboard box, 10″ × 8″, with small guide picture.

Fig. 9-73. *Getting Into Port.* Sculptured series. Joseph K. Straus Products Corp., Brooklyn, N.Y. Circa 1960. 12″ × 16″, 350 hand-cut plywood pieces, in two layers. Cardboard box, 7″ × 10¾″, with small guide picture.

Fig. 9-74. *Breaking High.* Perfect series. Consolidated Paper Box Co., Somerville, Mass. 1930s. 11¾″ × 15½″, 325 die-cut cardboard pieces, including figure pieces. Cardboard box, 8″ × 5½″, with small guide picture. Serial no. 1216.

Fig. 9-75. *In Full Sail.* Interlocking Border Jigsaw Puzzle. 1930s. 9¾″ × 8″, 100 die-cut cardboard pieces. Cardboard box, 4¼″ × 5¼″.

Fig. 9-76. *Square Sails and Eerie Shadows.* Yankee Cut-Ups series. Alden L. Fretts, West Springfield, Mass. 1933. 16½″ × 13½″, 357 hand-cut plywood pieces, including figure pieces. Cardboard box, 7¼″ × 10¼″.

10 THROUGH THE ARTIST'S EYES

ALTHOUGH SOME puzzle manufacturers maintained their own design departments, that was the exception rather than the rule. Most bought commercially available prints, selecting those that were most successful at the time. Subjects and styles have changed over the years along with popular trends in art and illustration. A study of puzzles therefore reflects and gives insight into tastes of bygone eras. Of course, some classics by Currier & Ives, Norman Rockwell, and children's illustrators like Johnny Gruelle have never gone out of fashion as puzzle subjects. Fine art masterpieces, on the other hand, have had mixed success on puzzles, and were most popular in the 1930s and late 1960s.

The puzzles in this chapter are presented *alphabetically by the artist*. The color section includes the following items in addition to those described in this chapter:

- *Music Hath Charms*
- *Queen's Page*
- *They'll Measure Up to the Desired Standard*

Fig. 10-1. *Spare the Rod, Spoil the Child*. Huvanco, Ilford, England. 1930s. 9½″ × 7¾″, 140 hand-cut plywood pieces. Cardboard box, 5½″ × 8½″. Artist is Cecil Aldin.

Fig. 10-2. *Song of the Lark*. Globe Puzzle Co., Boston, Mass. Circa 1909. 13½″ × 10″, 305 hand-cut wood pieces. Cardboard box, 5¼″ × 7¾″. Artist is Jules Breton.

Fig. 10-4. *Land of Counterpane*. Little Cut-Up series. H. E. Hamlen, Chicopee, Mass. 1930s. 9½″ × 8″, 51 hand-cut plywood pieces. Cardboard box, 5¼″ × 6¼″. Picture is one of Clara M. Burd's illustrations for *A Child's Garden of Verses* by Robert Louis Stevenson.

Fig. 10-3. *Puss 'n Boots*. Unknown maker. 1910s. 9½″ × 7¼″, 91 hand-cut wood pieces. Cardboard box, 5¼″ × 8¼″. Artist is H. M. Brock.

Fig. 10-5. *Picture Puzzles of Animals*. Saalfield Publishing Co., Akron, Ohio. 1930s. Set of three die-cut cardboard puzzles, each 9¾″ × 7¾″, approx. 30 pieces. Puzzles include 1) Girl feeding lambs, 2) Boy and girl with geese, 3) Children feeding poultry, but not the cover illustration. All are from Gladys E. Toon's *Animal Story Book* illustrated by Clara M. Burd. Serial no. 560.

Fig. 10-6. *Watering the Calf*. Swastika series. Helen Haskell Noyes, New York, N.Y. 1920s. 10½″ × 8″, 144 hand-cut plywood pieces, including one signature piece of swastika. Cardboard box, 4¼″ × 4¼″. Illustration by Clara M. Burd is from Gladys E. Toon's *Animal Story Book*.

Fig. 10-7. *Grandfather Frog Gets a Ride*. [Madmar Quality Co., Utica, N.Y.] 1930s. Set of four die-cut cardboard puzzles, each 9″ × 12″, 12 pieces. Cardboard box, 9½″ × 12½″, with one guide picture. Others in set include 1–2) two Raggedy Ann and Andy pictures by Johnny Gruelle (illustrated in Figs. 10-19 and C-31), 3) Digger the Badger. The artist for Digger the Badger and Grandfather Frog is Harrison Cady. (Courtesy of the Siegels)

Fig. 10-8. *Central Park — Winter*. Pine Tree Puzzle series. Waman S. Hassett. 1930s. 8½″ × 13½″, 212 hand-cut plywood pieces. Cardboard box, 5¼″ × 6¼″. A reproduction of a Currier & Ives print.

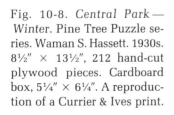

176

Fig. 10-9. *Snowbound*. Currier and Ives American Railroad Scenes series. Joseph K. Straus, Brooklyn, N.Y. Circa 1950. 8½" × 13", 200 hand-cut plywood pieces. Cardboard box, 6¼" × 9".

Fig. 10-10. *Double Image: Apparition of the Invisible Bust of Voltaire*. Springbok Editions, Inc., New York, N.Y. Copyright 1965. 20¼" diameter, 500 die-cut cardboard pieces. Cardboard box, 14¼" diameter, with guide picture. Salvador Dali incorporated puzzle pieces into this picture, commissioned by Springbok.

Fig. 10-11. [*Fishing*]. Unknown maker. 1920s. 12½" × 10", 71 hand-cut wood pieces. Box not extant. Artist is Grace Drayton (Wiedersheim) who also drew the Campbell Kids.

Fig. 10-12. *4 Picture Puzzles for Children*. Milton Bradley Co., Springfield, Mass. 1940s. Set of four die-cut cardboard puzzles, each 10¼″ × 13¼″, 40 pieces, including figure pieces. Cardboard box, 10½″ × 13½″, with guide picture for one puzzle. Puzzles illustrated by H. Boylston Dummer also include: 1) Swimming hole, 2) Ice skating. Serial no. 4220.

Fig. 10-13. *Land of Dreams*. Dee-Gee It's A Corker series. Detroit Gasket & Mfg. Co., Detroit, Mich. 1930s. 10″ × 8″, 190 hand-cut cork pieces. Cardboard box, 6¼″ × 6¼″. Artist is R. Atkinson Fox.

Fig. 10-14. *Romance Canyon*. Big 10 Picture Puzzle. 1930s. 15¼″ × 10½″, 280 die-cut cardboard pieces. Cardboard box, 7¼″ × 5¼″ with small guide picture. Artist is R. Atkinson Fox.

Fig. 10-15. *A Gibson Picture*. [Puzzles for Grown Ups and Shut Ins]. Circa 1909. 9¼″ × 15″, 162 hand-cut wood pieces. Cardboard box, 4¼″ × 8¼″. Artist is Charles Dana Gibson.

Fig. 10-16. *Upsetting Their Calculations.* Pastime series. Parker Brothers, Inc., Salem, Mass. 1932. 16¼″ × 25¼″, 519 hand-cut plywood pieces, including figure pieces. Cardboard box, 10″ × 10″. Artist is Philip R. Goodwin.

Fig. 10-17. *Mid-Stream.* Sanford Puzzles. 1930s. 8¾″ × 13″, 203 hand-cut plywood pieces. Cardboard box, 5¼″ × 9½″. Artist is Philip R. Goodwin.

Fig. 10-18. *Log Riders.* Pastime series. Parker Brothers, Inc., Salem, Mass. 1920s. 9¼″ × 13¾″, 188 hand-cut plywood pieces, including figure pieces. Cardboard box, 5¼″ × 8¼″. Artist is Philip R. Goodwin.

Fig. 10-19. *Grandfather Frog Gets a Ride.* [Madmar Quality Co., Utica, N.Y.] 1930s. Set of four die-cut cardboard puzzles, each 9″ × 12″, 12 pieces. Cardboard box, 9½″ × 12½″, with guide picture for Grandfather Frog (illustrated in Fig. 10-7). Others in set include: 1) Digger the Badger, and 2) Raggedy Ann and Andy's dance (illustrated in color section). The artist for the Raggedy Ann and Andy pictures is Johnny Gruelle. (Courtesy of the Siegels)

Fig. 10-20. *Mystery Picture Puzzle.* Madmar Quality Co., Utica, N.Y. 1930s. 8″ × 12¼″, 32 hand-cut pressboard pieces. Double-sided puzzle, shows witch on broomstick on reverse. Cardboard box, 8″ × 12″, with guide picture for witch side. Artist is Johnny Gruelle.

Fig. 10-21. *His Sailor Boy.* Jig-O-RamA Locktite series. Gold Seal Toy Co., Dundee, Ill. 1930s. 10″ × 8″, approx. 280 hand-cut plywood pieces in three layers. Cardboard box, 9¼″ × 12¼″. Contains 9″ × 12″ wood frame that holds assembled puzzle. The layering of the picture creates a three-dimensional effect. Artist is H. Hintermeister.

Fig. 10-22. *Shattered Hopes.* Eveready Specialties Mfg. Co., New York, N.Y. 1930s. 7″ × 10″, 102 hand-cut plywood pieces, including figure pieces. Cardboard box, 8¼″ × 10¼″. Artist is H. Hintermeister.

Fig. 10-23. *Look Out Gramp!* Deluxe series. Tuco Work Shops, Lockport, N.Y. 1940s. 20″ × 16″, 300–500 die-cut cardboard pieces. Cardboard box, 9¼″ × 7¼″, with guide picture. Artist is H. Hintermeister.

Fig. 10-24. *Happy Times Picture Puzzles.* Parker Brothers Inc., Salem, Mass. Circa 1905. Set of three hand-cut cardboard puzzles, each 9″ × 12½″, 15 pieces. Cardboard box, 9″ × 12¾″, with guide picture for one puzzle. Others in set include: 1) Donkey ride, 2) Children in the woods. Artist is Maud Humphrey.

Fig. 10-25. *Little Miss Muffet*. Art Picture Puzzle series. K. R. Lunn, Brookline, Mass. Circa 1909. 8″ × 6″, 71 hand-cut wood pieces. Cardboard box, 2¾″ × 4¼″. Artist is M. L. Kirk.

Fig. 10-27. *The Woman in the Doorway*. Ye Squirlijig series. Marjorie Bouvé, Brookline, Mass. Circa 1909. 11″ × 8¾″, 127 hand-cut wood (mahogany) pieces, with irregular edge. Cardboard box, 4¾″ × 5¾″. Artist is Frank X. Leyendecker.

Fig. 10-26. *The Black Kitten*. Dorothy Dainty series. Parker Brothers, Inc., Salem, Mass. 1910s. 7½″ × 5¾″, 29 hand-cut plywood pieces. Cardboard box, 8¼″ × 6¼″, with guide picture. Artist is M. L. Kirk.

183

Fig. 10-28. *Carnival of Harlequin*. Springbok Editions, Inc., New York, N.Y. Copyright 1965. 13½″ × 19″, 404 die-cut cardboard pieces. Cardboard box, 6″ × 14″. Contains guide picture. Artist is Joan Miro.

Fig. 10-29. *Cleopatra's Barge*. Pastime series. Parker Brothers, Inc., Salem, Mass. 1932. 12¾″ × 16″, 334 hand-cut plywood pieces, including figure pieces. Cardboard box, 5½″ × 9¼″. Artist is Maxfield Parrish.

Fig. 10-30. *Garden of Allah*. Pastime series. Parker Brothers, Inc., Salem, Mass. 1940s. 9″ × 18¼″, 252 hand-cut plywood pieces, including figure pieces. Cardboard box, 5½″ × 9¼″. Artist is Maxfield Parrish.

Fig. 10-31. *Peter Rabbit Puzzles*. Harter Publishing Co., Cleveland, Ohio. 1930s. Set of four die-cut cardboard puzzles, each 9½" × 7¼", approx. 15 pieces. Cardboard box, 10" × 8". Other puzzles in set include 1) Rabbit family, 2) Grandma rabbit shopping, 3) Peter Rabbit in bed with chills. Artist is Fern Bisel Peat.

Fig. 10-32. *A Dream*. Unknown maker with initials E.M.B. Circa 1909. 8¼" × 7¾", 184 hand-cut wood pieces. Cardboard box, 2¾" × 6¾". Artist is Jessie Willcox Smith.

Fig. 10-33. *Turning the Leaves*. Zeitvertreib Company, Waterbury, Conn. 1908. 9½" × 9¼", 128 hand-cut wood pieces. Cardboard box, 5" × 6¼". Artist is Jessie Willcox Smith.

Fig. 10-34. [*Picture Book*]. Unknown maker. 1920s. 7¼" × 8½", 50 hand-cut plywood pieces. Box not extant. Artist is Jessie Willcox Smith.

11 AMERICA ON THE MOVE

SHIPS, TRAINS, cars, airplanes—all these conjure up the magic of travel to new places. And over the years transportation, embodying the newest technological developments, has been a source of national pride in the United States. Children and adults alike have been fascinated by the speed and style of the various modes of travel. It is no accident that sets of transportation puzzles have been perennial favorites of both manufacturers and customers.

This chapter has five sections, covering ships, trains, road vehicles (carriages, bicycles, cars, trucks), aviation, and mixed subjects.

The color section includes the following items in addition to those described in this chapter:

- *Fire Engine Picture Puzzle*
- *Cut Up Locomotive*
- *American Boy and Girl Picture Puzzles*

▪ Ships

Fig. 11-1. *The Yacht Puzzle.* Milton Bradley & Co., Springfield, Mass. 1870s. 9¾″ × 11½″, 31 sliced cardboard pieces. Wood box, 5½″ × 6¾″.

Fig. 11-2. *Picture Puzzle: Pilgrim of Fall River.* McLoughlin Brothers, New York, N.Y. Circa 1886. 17¼″ × 23¼″, 48 hand-cut pressboard pieces. Wood frame and cardboard box, 9″ × 12″.

Fig. 11-3. *Steamship Picture Puzzle: St. Paul.* McLoughlin Brothers, New York, N.Y. Copyright 1896. 12¼″ × 33¼″, 64 hand-cut pressboard pieces. Wood frame and cardboard box, 7¾″ × 19¼″.

Fig. 11-4. *Steamship Puzzle.* Milton Bradley Co. Springfield, Mass. Circa 1905. 14¼″ × 20¼″, 24 hand-cut cardboard pieces. Cardboard box, 12¼″ × 12¼″. Serial no. 4024.

Fig. 11-5. *Boat Picture Puzzle.* Madmar Quality Co., Utica, N.Y. 1930s. Set of two die-cut cardboard puzzles, each 9″ × 7″, 12 pieces. Cardboard box, 9¼″ × 7¼″, with guide picture for one puzzle. Serial no. 311.

Fig. 11-6. *Queen Elizabeth.* Victory series. G. J. Hayter & Co., Ltd., Bournemouth, England. 1950s. 9½″ × 12½″, 175 hand-cut plywood pieces. Cardboard box, 7½″ × 9½″ with guide picture.

▪ Trains

Fig. 11-7. *Little Folks' New Dissected Pictures.* Davis, Porter & Co., Philadelphia, Pa. 1865. 7″ × 11″, 17 hand-colored and hand-cut pieces. Wood box, 8″ × 6¼″. Double-sided puzzle, shows city scenes on reverse. The same print of the Pennsylvania Railroad appears on some puzzles produced by Thomas S. Wagner at the same time. (Courtesy of the Siegels)

Fig. 11-8. *The Smashed Up Locomotive.* Milton Bradley & Co., Springfield, Mass. In production 1870 to circa 1900. 8″ × 23¾″, 64 sliced and die-cut cardboard pieces. Wood box, 6¾″ × 8½″. This puzzle was also sold in a cheaper edition with a cardboard box. (Courtesy of the Siegels)

Fig. 11-9. *Our Trains*. J. W. Spear & Son, England. Circa 1920. Set of three hand-cut cardboard puzzles, each 5″ × 6¾″, 12 pieces. Cardboard box, 5¼″ × 7¼″ shows picture of one of the three trains in the set.

Fig. 11-10. *Locomotive Puzzle*. Parker Brothers, Inc., Salem, Mass. Circa 1920. 12½″ × 30″, 48 hand-cut cardboard pieces. Cardboard box, 15¾″ × 12″.

Fig. 11-11. *Pennsylvania Railroad*. Unknown maker, Spring City, Pa. 1933. 16″ × 24″, 700 hand-cut plywood pieces. Wood box, 5½″ × 17¾″. Maker used print from Pennsylvania Railroad calendar drawn by Grif Teller.

Fig. 11-12. *King George V Engine*. Great Western Railway series. Chad Valley Co., Ltd., Harborne, England. 1930s. 8½″ × 22″, 207 hand-cut plywood pieces, with irregular edge. Cardboard book-like box, 9½″ × 6¼″.

Fig. 11-13. *Prairie Fires of the Great West.* Lydia H. Williamson, West Chester, Pa. 1958. 8½″ × 13½″, 206 hand-cut plywood pieces. Cardboard box, 5¾″ × 8½″. Reproduction of a Currier & Ives print.

▪ Road Vehicles

Fig. 11-14. *Tally Ho Puzzle.* Seymour Lyman, New York, N.Y. Copyright 1878. 13¼″ × 28½″, 30 sliced cardboard pieces. Cardboard box, 6¾″ × 9¾″.

Fig. 11-15. *In the Bois de Boulogne.* Unknown maker. Circa 1909. 12″ × 20″, 408 hand-cut wood pieces. Cardboard box, 5¼″ × 10¼″. Artist is Ludovici.

Fig. 11-16. *Up to Mischeif (sic)*. Brain Storm series. International Wood-Working Co., Jersey City, N.J. Circa 1909. 9¾" × 14½", 150 hand-cut plywood pieces. Cardboard box, 6¾" × 6¾". (Courtesy of the Siegels)

Fig. 11-17. *The Veteran Motor Car*. Springbok Editions, New York, N.Y. 1966. 14" diameter, 194 hand-cut plywood pieces. Cardboard box, 14¼" × 14¼", with guide picture.

Fig. 11-18. *The Great White Way Across Iran.* Deluxe series. Tuco Work Shops, Lockport, N.Y. 1940s. 15″ × 19½″, 357 die-cut cardboard pieces. Cardboard box, 9¼″ × 7¼″, with small guide picture.

Fig. 11-19. *Fire Engine Puzzle.* Peter G. Thomson, Cincinnati, Ohio. 1880s. 12″ × 16″, 31 sliced cardboard pieces. Cardboard box, 5½″ × 6½″ with guide picture. (Courtesy of the Siegels).

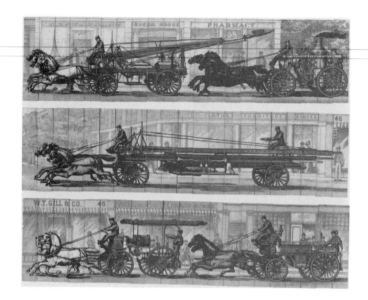

Fig. 11-20. *Fire Department Puzzle*. Milton Bradley Co., Springfield, Mass. 1910s. 5″ × 59″, 63 sliced cardboard pieces. Cardboard box. (Courtesy of John Seymour)

Fig. 11-21. *Five Little Firemen*. Little Golden Picture Puzzle series no. 1. Whitman Publishing Co., Racine, Copyright 1949, 7½″ × 6″, 10 die-cut cardboard pieces including one figure piece. Cardboard box, 8″ × 6½″, with guide picture. Series contained six puzzles, each showing cover art for a Little Golden Book. There were four different series and a total of 24 puzzles.

▪ Aviation

Fig. 11-22. *Puzzle Box of Airships*. Ernest Nister, London, England, and E. P. Dutton & Co., New York, N.Y. Circa 1905. Set of four hand-cut cardboard puzzles, each 8″ × 9¾″, 20 pieces. Cardboard box, 8½″ × 10¼″, with one guide picture of dirigible over London (illustrated in color section). Others in set include: 1) Dirigible over a river, 2) Dirigible at sea, 3) Plane.

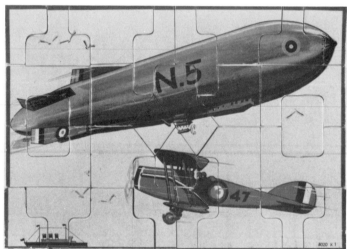

Fig. 11-23. *Aeroplane* Puzzle. Milton Bradley Co., Springfield, Mass. 1930s. 6½″ × 9½″, 30 die-cut cardboard pieces. Double-sided puzzle. Cardboard box, 7″ × 9¾″, with one guide picture. Serial no. 4020.

Fig. 11-24. *Jolly Time Puzzles.* All-Fair. 1930s. Set of two die-cut cardboard puzzles, each 8¼″ × 10″, 25 pieces including figure pieces. Cardboard box, 8½″ × 10¼″, with guide picture for one puzzle.

▪ Mixed Subjects

Fig. 11-25. *Fire-Engine Scroll Puzzle.* McLoughlin Brothers, New York, N.Y. Set of three die-cut cardboard puzzles, each 10″ × 16½″, 24 pieces. Cardboard box, 10½″ × 17″. Contains three guide pictures. Serial no. 7050.

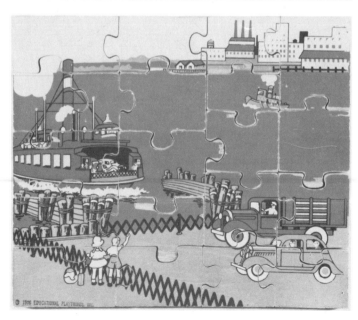

Fig. 11-26. [*Ferry Pier*]. Educational Playthings, Inc. Copyright 1936. 10″ × 12″, 20 hand-cut plywood pieces. Box not extant.

Fig. 11-27. *Transportation Scene.* Daintee Toys, Inc. Brooklyn, N.Y. Circa 1940. Frame tray puzzle 9½″ × 11½″, 12 hand-cut plywood pieces. Cardboard box, 9¾″ × 12″.

Fig. 11-28. *The Big Treasure Box of Jigsaw Puzzles.* Grosset & Dunlap, New York, N.Y. Copyright 1952. Set of three die-cut cardboard frame puzzles, each 9¾″ × 16½″, approx. 32 pieces. Cardboard box, 10¼″ × 17¼″, with guide picture for one puzzle. Other puzzle in set is fire engine.

12 SPECIAL DAYS

HOLIDAYS and celebrations have always been occasions for presenting puzzles as gifts. So it is no surprise that many puzzles take such special days as their subjects. The puzzles in this chapter reflect the changing celebrations of holidays over the years. For example, the tall lean Father Christmas of the mid-nineteenth century has become the rotund jolly Santa Claus of today.

Puzzles in this chapter are grouped by the holiday they represent, including: Valentine's Day, Christmas, Birthdays and Anniversaries, and New Year's, Easter, Thanksgiving, etc.

The color section includes the following items in addition to those described in this chapter:

- [*Happy New Year 1932*]
- *Sheer Bliss*
- [*Santa Claus ABC Blocks*]
- [*Santa Claus Frame Tray Puzzle*]

▪ Valentine's Day

Fig. 12-1. [*Valentine Puzzle*]. Parker Brothers, Salem, Mass. Copyright 1909. 4½″ × 4¼″, 15 hand-cut plywood pieces. Cardboard box, 2″ × 3″. Puzzle continues poem on box by Marion Cable.

Fig. 12-2. *To My Valentine.* Unknown maker. Circa 1909. 3½″ × 5½″, 30 hand-cut plywood pieces, including figure pieces. Cardboard box, 5¾″ × 3¾″, shows different Valentine card.

Fig. 12-4. *A Narrow Escape.* Unknown maker. Circa 1909. 10¼″ × 9½″, 132 hand-cut wood pieces, with irregular edge. Cardboard box, 4½″ × 7″. Cut from magazine cover drawn by J. C. Leyendecker.

Fig. 12-3. *To My Valentine.* Unknown maker. Circa 1909. 5½″ × 3½″, 30 hand-cut plywood pieces, including figure pieces. Cardboard box, 5¾″ × 3¾″, shows different Valentine card.

Fig. 12-5. *A Valentine for You*. Hallmark Cards, Kansas City, Mo. 1940s. 6½″ × 5¼″, 29 die-cut cardboard pieces, including figure pieces. Cloth mailing sack 4″ × 3″.

▪ Christmas

Fig. 12-6. *Peaceful Valley*. Big Star Series. 1930s. 10¼″ × 13¾″, 252 die-cut cardboard pieces. Cardboard box, 6½″ × 4¾″, with small guide picture.

Fig. 12-7. *Nellie's Christmas Eve.* Aunt Louisa's Cube Puzzles series. McLoughlin Brothers, New York, N.Y. Circa 1880. 10½″ × 8¾″, 30 wood cubes that make six different pictures. Wood box, 11½″ × 10″. Enclosed story booklet contains illustrations of all six sides of puzzle.

Fig. 12-8. *Christmas Eve.* Superior Picture Puzzles. Arthur G. Grinnell, New Bedford, Mass. Circa 1909. 6¼″ × 13¾″, 152 hand-cut plywood pieces. Cardboard box, 4″ × 7″.

Fig. 12-9. [*Christmas Toys*]. Unknown German maker. Circa 1860. 3″ × 4″, 12 hand-colored wood cubes that make six different pictures. Wood box, 3¾″ × 5″, contains five hand-colored guide pictures, with sixth picture on box lid. Other pictures show farming and coaching scenes. Upper left cube shows part of another scene.

Fig. 12-10. [*Holiday Puzzle*]. Unknown German maker. Circa 1900. 4½" × 3", 6 hand-cut wood cubes that make six different pictures. Cardboard box, 4¾" × 3½", contains five guide pictures, with sixth picture on box lid. Set also includes: 1) Girl at Christmas tree, 2) Easter Bunny (illustrated in Easter section in this chapter), 3) Girl with bunnies, 4) Sailor Boy, 5) Boy with pet bird.

Fig. 12-11. *Carnival in Russia*. Picture Puzzle Exchange, Boston, Mass. Circa 1909. 12" × 20", 270 hand-cut wood pieces. Cardboard box, 4¾" × 7".

Fig. 12-12. *Tally-Ho Scroll Puzzle*. McLoughlin Brothers, New York, N.Y. Copyright 1894. 12" × 24¼", 60 hand-cut cardboard pieces. Cardboard box, 10" × 15", with guide picture. (Courtesy of the Siegels)

Fig. C-33

Fig. C-34

Fig. C-35

Fig. C-36

Chapter 11

Fig. C-33. *Cut Up Locomotive.* Parker Brothers, Salem, Mass. Circa 1900. 11¼″ × 27¾″, 36 hand-cut cardboard pieces. Cardboard box, 11¾″ × 14¾″. **Fig. C-34.** *Fire Engine Picture Puzzle.* McLoughlin Brothers, New York, N.Y. Copyright 1887. 18″ × 25″, 68 hand-cut pressboard pieces. Wood frame and cardboard box, 9″ × 12¼″. **Fig. C-35.** *American Boy and Girl Picture Puzzles.* Saalfield Publishing Co., Akron, Ohio. 1940s. Set of four die-cut cardboard puzzles, each 9½″ × 7½″, 22 pieces. Cardboard box, 10″ × 7¾″, with guide picture for puzzle of boy watching planes. Other puzzles show: 1) traffic jam, 2) children at campfire, 3) Old sailor showing model ship to boy. Serial no. 1702. **Fig. C-36.** *Puzzle Box of Airships.* Ernest Nister, London, and E. P. Dutton & Co., New York, N.Y. Circa 1905. Set of four hand-cut cardboard puzzles, each 8″ × 9¾″, 20 pieces. Box and another puzzle are illustrated in Chapter 11.

Fig. C-37

Fig. C-38

Fig. C-39

Fig. C-40

Chapter 12

Fig. C-37. *Sheer Bliss.* Par Company, Ltd., New York, N.Y. Circa 1947. 16″ × 27″, 825 hand-cut mahogany plywood pieces, including figure pieces and irregular edge. Cardboad box. Par time is "Forever and Ever." (Courtesy of the Trowbridges; photo by Allan Detrich) **Fig. C-38.** *[Santa Claus ABC Blocks].* McLoughlin Brothers, New York, N.Y. Circa 1890. Double-sided 1″-thick blocks with letters of alphabet on reverse. 20″ × 14¾″, 25 hand-cut wood pieces. Box not extant. (Courtesy of the Siegels) **Fig. C-39.** *[Happy New Year 1932].* Unknown maker. 1930s. 10½″ × 8½″, about 150 hand-cut plywood pieces. Cardboard box, 6½″ × 9″. **Fig. C-40.** *[Santa Claus Frame Tray Puzzle].* Whitman Publishing Co., Racine, Wisc. 1950s. 14½″ × 11½″, about 50 die-cut cardboard pieces. Serial no. 4424.

Fig. C-41

Fig. C-42

Fig. C-44

Fig. C-43

Chapter 13

Fig. C-41. *Keeper of the Flame.* Squarecut Puzzle Co., New York, N.Y. 1940s. 16¾" × 22", 520 square die-cut cardboard pieces in frame. Cardboard box, 17½" × 11½", with small guide picture. Katherine Hepburn and Spencer Tracy played the starring roles.   **Fig. C-42.** *Hollywood on Parade.* Consolidated Lithographing Corp., Brooklyn, N.Y. Circa 1933. 7" × 9", 68 die-cut cardboard pieces, including figure pieces. Paper envelope, 9½" × 7¼", with small guide diagram.   **Fig. C-43.** *Ed Wynn Picture Puzzle: No. 1, Fire Chief.* Viking Mfg. Co., Boston, Mass. Circa 1933. 14" × 11", 203 die-cut cardboard pieces. Cardboard box, 8" × 10". Another edition of this puzzle has figure pieces spelling "The Fire Chief" cut into the puzzle.   **Fig. C-44.** *Hopalong Cassidy Puzzles.* Milton Bradley Co., Springfield, Mass. Copyright 1950. Set of three die-cut cardboard puzzles, each 9" × 12", 40 pieces, including figure pieces. Cardboard box, 12½" × 9½", with guide picture for one puzzle. Others in set include: 1) Closeup of Hoppy and Topper, 2) Hoppy with Topper. Serial no. 4025. Royalty records show that 635,838 copies of this set were produced in 1950–52.

Fig. C-45

Fig. C-46

Fig. C-47

Fig. C-48

Chapter 13

Fig. C-45. *Flash Gordon.* Milton Bradley Co., Springfield, Mass. Copyright 1951. Set of three die-cut cardboard puzzles, each 12″ × 9″, approximately 30 pieces, including figure pieces. Box and another puzzle are illustrated in Chapter 13. **Fig. C-46.** *Mickey Mouse Jig-Saw Puzzle.* Chad Valley Co., Ltd., Harborne, England. 1930s. 10″ × 14″, 200 hand-cut plywood pieces. Cardboard box, 10½″ × 14½″, with guide picture. **Fig. C-47.** *Bringing Up Father: 4 Picture Puzzles.* Saalfield Publishing Co., Akron, Ohio. Copyright 1932. Set of four die-cut cardboard puzzles, each 7¾″ × 9½″, approximately 35 pieces. Box and another puzzle are illustrated in Chapter 13. **Fig. C-48.** *Little Orphan Annie.* Famous Comics Jig Saw no. 1. Stephens Kindred & Co., New York, N.Y; distributed by Novelty Distributing Co., Newark, N.J. 12¼″ × 13″, 255 die-cut cardboard pieces. Box is illustrated in Chapter 13.

Fig. C-49

Fig. C-50

Fig. C-51

Fig. C-52

Chapter 14

Fig. C-49. *Try for a Speed Record.* Victor Talking Machine Co., Camden, N.J. Patented 1908. 8½″ diameter, 35 die-cut cardboard pieces. Paper envelope, 7¼″ × 4″. (Courtesy of the Siegels) **Fig. C-50.** *Hood's Rainy Day and Balloon Puzzles.* C. I. Hood & Co., Lowell, Mass. Copyright 1891. 10″ × 15″, 34 die-cut cardboard pieces. Double-sided, shows hot air balloon on reverse. Cardboard box, 7½″ × 5″, with key diagrams. Contains two advertising brochures. Other editions of this puzzle have slight variations in the picture and box designs. **Fig. C-51.** *Clemens' Silent Teacher: The World/White Sewing Machines.* C. E. Hartman, Utica, N.Y. Circa 1900. 15¾″ × 11″, 22 hand-cut wood pieces. Double-sided, with map of world on reverse. Cardboard box, 7″ × 9″, is similar to the one illustrated in Chapter 2. **Fig. C-52.** *40th Anniversary.* Spear's Department Store, Pittsburgh, Penna. 1933. 11″ × 8½″, approximately 150 die-cut cardboard pieces. Paper envelope, 11″ × 9″.

Fig. C-53

Fig. C-54

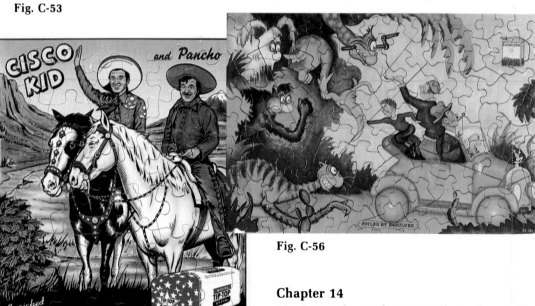

Fig. C-56

Fig. C-55

Chapter 14

Fig. C-53. *Where's the Fire?* Hills Brothers Coffee, Inc., San Francisco, Calif. Copyright 1933. 14¾" × 10¾", approximately 200 die-cut cardboard pieces, irregular outline. Cardboard box, 4½" × 5¾". **Fig. C-54.** *Is That You Santa Claus?* Eveready Flashlight & Batteries. 1930s. 12" × 8¾", 60 die-cut cardboard pieces. Paper envelope, 12½" × 9¼", with guide diagram. Artist is Frances Tipton Hunter. **Fig. C-55.** *Cisco Kid.* Tip-Top Bread (Ward Baking Co.), manufactured by Specialty Adv. Service, New York, N.Y. Copyright 1953. Frame puzzle, 8¼" × 7¼", 36 die-cut cardboard pieces. Glassine envelope, 7¾" × 8½", with guide diagram. **Fig. C-56.** *Foiled by Essolube.* Esso. 1930s. 11¼" × 17¼", 150 die-cut cardboard pieces, including figure pieces. Paper envelope, 17½" × 11½". Dr. Seuss drew the picture on this puzzle.

Fig. C-57

Fig. C-58

Fig. C-59

Fig. C-60

Chapter 15

Fig. C-57. *[Feeding the Ducks].* Parker Brothers, Inc., Salem, Mass. 1930s. 9¼″ × 13″, 214 hand-cut plywood pieces. Cardboard box, 5¼″ × 7¼″. **Fig. C-58.** *3 Kiddies' Jigsaw Puzzles.* Jaymar Specialty Co., New York, N.Y. Circa 1950. Set of three die-cut cardboard puzzles, each 8½″ × 11″, 24 pieces. Cardboard box, 11¼″ × 9″. See Chapter 13 for puzzle illustration. **Fig. C-59.** *3 Perfect Children's Puzzles.* Consolidated Paper Box Co., Somerville, Mass. 1940s. Set of three die-cut cardboard puzzles, each 9½″ × 7¼″, 50 pieces. Cardboard box, 7¾″ × 10″. Set includes: 1) St. Bernard watching sleeping child, 2) Farm boy with dog, 3) Puppy. Serial no. 310. **Fig. C-60.** *[Asian Harbor].* Chad Valley Works, Harborne, England. 1920s. 11¼″ × 16″, 196 hand-cut plywood pieces. Cardboard box, 7″ × 9¾″.

Fig. C-61

Fig. C-62

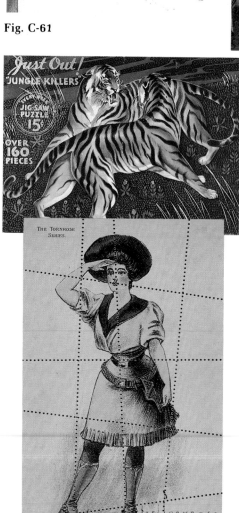

Fig. C-64

Fig. C-63

Chapter 16

Fig. C-61. *Popinjay's Jig-Puz Book.* John Leng & Co., Ltd., London, England. 1930s. 10″ × 7½″ book, with ten pages. Five pages hold die-cut cardboard frame tray puzzles, each 8″ × 6¼″, 48 pieces. See Chapter 16 for another illustration. **Fig. C-62.** *Murder By the Stars.* Mystery-Jig series. Einson-Freeman Co., Inc., Long Island City, N.Y. 1933. 14″ × 20″, 300 die-cut cardboard pieces, including figure pieces. Box is illustrated in Chapter 16. **Fig. C-63.** *Jungle Killers* Poster. Einson-Freeman Co., Inc., Long Island City, N.Y. 1933. 10¼″ × 14¼″ cardboard poster, advertising Every Week Puzzle no. 20. **Fig. C-64.** *Looking for You.* Tornrose series. Unknown postcard maker, Germany. Copyright 1907. 5½″ × 3½″, 20 perforated paper pieces.

Fig. 12-13. *Santa Claus Puzzle Box*. Milton Bradley Co., Springfield, Mass. 1910s. Set of three hand-cut cardboard puzzles, each 9″ × 12½″, 15 pieces. Cardboard box, 9¼″ × 13″, with guide picture. Puzzles include: 1) Santa in auto, 2) Descent down chimney, 3) Santa at Christmas tree. Serial no. 4217.

Fig. 12-14. *Dissected A.B.C.* J. Ottmann Lith. Co., New York, N.Y. Circa 1910. 24 sliced cardboard pieces. Cardboard box, 10″ × 11½″. Puzzle shows only alphabet, not Santa Claus.

Fig. 12-15. *Watching for Santa Claus.* Interlocked Picture Puzzle Co., Newton Lower Falls, Mass. 1930s. 8½″ × 10½″, 115 hand-cut plywood pieces. Cardboard box, 4¾″ × 7¼″.

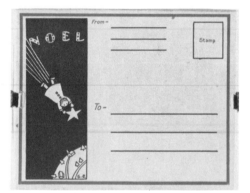

Fig. 12-16. *And Laying a Finger Aside of His Nose.* [Fifield family cutter, Swampscott, Mass.] 1916. 11″ × 6½″, 139 hand-cut plywood pieces. Cardboard box, 4″ × 7″.

Fig. 12-17. *Noel.* C. S. Hammond & Co., Brooklyn, N.Y. 1930s. 4½″ × 3½″, 24 hand-cut plywood pieces. Cardboard mailing box, 4″ × 6″. (Courtesy of the Siegels)

Fig. 12-18. *The Season's Greetings*. Harry N. Walker, (Massachusetts?). 1930s. 4″ × 5″, 30 hand-cut plywood pieces. Cardboard mailing box, 2½″ × 4″.

Fig. 12-19. *Xmas Greeting Puzzle*. J.D. Series. James I. DeHaven, Lancaster, Pa. 1930s. 4¼″ × 5½″, 34 hand-cut plywood pieces. Cardboard box, 3″ × 4½″.

▪ Birthdays and Anniversaries

Fig. 12-20. *The Christening.* Pastime series. Parker Brothers, Inc., Salem, Mass. 1920s. 10″ × 14″, 226 hand-cut plywood pieces, including figure pieces. Cardboard box, 4½″ × 9″.

Fig. 12-21. *Birthday Wishes.* Unknown German maker. Circa 1909. 3½″ × 5½″, 20 perforated cardboard pieces. Postcard back for mailing.

Fig. 12-22. *Many Happy Returns of the Day.* Unknown German maker. Circa 1909. 3½″ × 5½″, 20 perforated cardboard pieces. Postcard back for mailing.

Fig. 12-23. *Wedding Bells.* Unknown maker. Circa 1909. 13″ × 19¾″, 288 hand-cut wood (mahogany) pieces. Cardboard box, 8¼″ × 6″.

▪ New Year's, Easter, Thanksgiving, etc.

Fig. 12-24. *The New Boarder.* Zeitvertreib Company, Waterbury, Conn. 1908. 10¾″ × 8½″, 141 hand-cut wood pieces. Cardboard box, 5″ × 6″.

Fig. 12-25. *Erin Go Bragh.* Unknown maker. 1930s. 3½″ × 5½″, 29 hand-cut plywood pieces. Box missing.

Fig. 12-26. *Mardi Gras Dancer.* Andrew L. Galles, Buffalo, N.Y. One of a set of four hand-cut plywood Party Puzzles, each 5″ × 8″, about 50 pieces. Cardboard box, 5½″ × 10½″. Other puzzles in set include: 1) *Modern Pirate,* 2) *Tense Moments,* 3) *Don't Lose Him Dad.*

Fig. 12-27. [*Holiday Puzzle*]. Unknown German maker. Circa 1900. 4½″ × 3″, 6 hand-cut wood cubes that make six different pictures. Cardboard box, 4¾″ × 3½″, contains five guide pictures, with sixth picture on box lid. Set also includes: 1) Girl at Christmas tree, 2) Father Christmas (illustrated in Christmas section of this chapter), 3) Girl with bunnies, 4) Sailor Boy, 5) Boy with pet bird.

Fig. 12-29. *Thanksgiving*. Fifield family cutter, Swampscott, Mass. Circa 1909. 12″ × 9½″, 134 hand-cut wood pieces, with irregular edge. Cardboard box, 4½″ × 7″.

Fig. 12-28. *Easter Eggs*. Patience Puzzle. R & J Specialty Co., New York, N.Y. Circa 1909. 16½″ × 10½″, 300 hand-cut wood pieces. Cardboard box, 5¼″ × 7¼″.

Fig. 12-30. *Thanksgiving*. Jig of the Week Puzzle No. 8. University Distributing Co., Cambridge, Mass. 1932. 10¼″ × 13½″, 300 die-cut cardboard pieces. Cardboard box, 7¼″ × 7¼″.

13 THERE'S NO BUSINESS LIKE SHOW BUSINESS

THE BLOSSOMING of jigsaw puzzles during the Great Depression coincided with both the early years of talking pictures and the development of some of the most memorable radio programming. Americans' fascination with these two media spilled over into puzzles. The 1932–33 period brought such new items as the Movie Cut-Ups weekly puzzle and numerous puzzles offered as radio premiums. Entertainers of all types, from Eddie Cantor to Greta Garbo, appeared on puzzles. Comic and cartoon characters too were cut into pieces to be reconstructed by eager fans. Mickey Mouse, created by Walt Disney in 1928, showed up on Saalfield Publishing Company puzzles by 1933, as did Maggie and Jiggs, Tillie the Toiler, and many others.

Licensing of entertainment and comic characters for jigsaw puzzles has continued at a brisk rate ever since the Depression. Virtually every Disney character, from comic books to movies, has decorated a puzzle. During the 1950s television stars, especially cowboy heroes, took the place on puzzles that movie and radio stars had occupied before World War II.

This chapter contains five sections, dealing with: Hollywood (including animated features), radio personalities, television, comic characters, and wild west and super heroes.

Some individuals appear in more than one category such as Bill Boyd who had a successful early acting career in Hollywood before he moved into his most famous cowboy hero role as Hopalong Cassidy. The indexes can help locate specific characters. The color section includes the following items in addition to those described in this chapter:

- *Hollywood on Parade*
- *Keeper of the Flame*
- *Ed Wynn Picture Puzzle: No. 1, Fire Chief*
- *Mickey Mouse Jig-Saw Puzzle*
- *Hopalong Cassidy Puzzles*

▪ Hollywood

Fig. 13-1. *Movie-Land Cut Ups*. Wilder Mfg. Co., St. Louis, Mo. 1930s. Set of four die-cut cardboard puzzles, each 8″ × 10″, 12 to 20 pieces. Cardboard box, 8½″ × 10½″. Set includes: 1) Our Gang, 2) Harry Langdon, 3) Mickey (Himself) McGuire, 4) Only the Brave.

Fig. 13-2. *Movie-Land Puzzle*. Milton Bradley Co., Springfield, Mass. Copyright 1926. Set of two die-cut cardboard puzzles, each 8″ × 10″, 55 pieces. Cardboard box, 8½″ × 10½″. Set includes: 1) Our Gang, 2) William Boyd and Elinor Fair in *The Yankee Clipper*. Serial no. 4975.

Fig. 13-3. *Babes in Toyland.* Whitman Publishing Co., Racine, Wisc. Copyright 1961. Frame tray puzzle 14½″ × 11½″, approx. 25 die-cut cardboard pieces, including figure pieces. Serial no. 4454.

Fig. 13-4. *Chitty Chitty Bang Bang.* Whitman Publishing Co., Racine, Wisc. Copyright 1968. Set of four die-cut cardboard frame tray puzzles, each 10″ × 8″, approx. 15 pieces. Cardboard box, 10½″ × 8½″, with four guide pictures. Puzzles show scenes from the movie starring Dick Van Dyke.

Fig. 13-5. *Mary Poppins.* Jaymar Specialty Co., New York, N.Y. Copyright 1964. Frame tray puzzle 9¾″ × 12¾″, 30 die-cut cardboard pieces. Serial no. 2315.

217

Fig. 13-6. *101 Dalmatians.*
Jaymar Specialty Co., New
York, N.Y. Copyright 1960.
Frame tray puzzle 9¾" ×
12¾", 30 die-cut cardboard
pieces.

Fig. 13-7. *Peter Pan.* Whitman Publishing Co.,
Racine, Wisc. Copyright 1952. Set of six die-
cut cardboard frame puzzles, each 11½" × 9¾",
approx. 20 pieces, including figure pieces.
Cardboard box, 12" × 10¼". Puzzles include:
1) Peter and children flying, 2) Peter and Wendy
at lagoon, 3) Captain Hook and crew, 4) Captain
Hook and first mate, 5) Lost boys captured by
Indians, 6) Peter Pan and Captain Hook fight-
ing. Serial no. 5617.

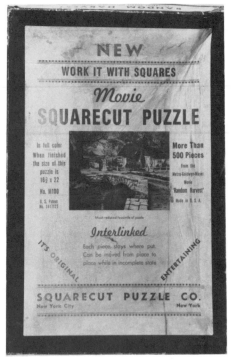

Fig. 13-8. *Random Harvest.* Squarecut Puzzle
Co., New York, N.Y. Circa 1942. 16¾" × 22"
522 square die-cut cardboard pieces in frame.
Cardboard box, 17" × 11½", with small guide
picture. Ronald Colman and Greer Garson played
the starring roles.

218

Fig. 13-9. *Sleeping Beauty*. Whitman Publishing Co., Racine, Wisc. Copyright 1958. Frame tray puzzle 14½″ × 11½″, approx. 40 die-cut cardboard pieces.

Fig. 13-10. *Snow White and the Seven Dwarfs*. Jaymar Specialty Co., New York, N.Y. Copyright 1952. Frame tray puzzle 11″ × 14″, 35 die-cut cardboard pieces. Serial no. 2596.

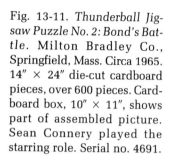

Fig. 13-11. *Thunderball Jigsaw Puzzle No. 2: Bond's Battle*. Milton Bradley Co., Springfield, Mass. Circa 1965. 14″ × 24″ die-cut cardboard pieces, over 600 pieces. Cardboard box, 10″ × 11″, shows part of assembled picture. Sean Connery played the starring role. Serial no. 4691.

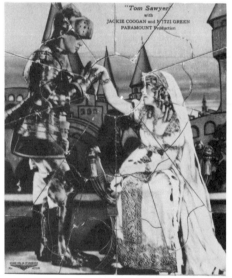

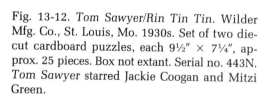

Fig. 13-12. *Tom Sawyer/Rin Tin Tin*. Wilder Mfg. Co., St. Louis, Mo. 1930s. Set of two die-cut cardboard puzzles, each 9½″ × 7¼″, approx. 25 pieces. Box not extant. Serial no. 443N. *Tom Sawyer* starred Jackie Coogan and Mitzi Green.

Fig. 13-13. *White Eagle*. Movie Cut-Ups No. 13. Movie Cut-Ups Co. Inc., Peabody, Mass. Circa 1933. 10¼″ × 13¼″, 300 die-cut cardboard pieces. Cardboard box, 7¼″ × 7¼″. Buck Jones starred.

Fig. 13-14. *Bogart*. Star Puzzle series. Adult Leisure Products Corp., Locust Valley, N.Y. Copyright 1967. 18″ diameter, 300 die-cut cardboard pieces, including figure pieces. Metal film-type cannister, 9½″ diameter, with small guide picture.

Fig. 13-15. *Fields*. Star Puzzle series. Adult Leisure Products Corp., Locust Valley, N.Y. Copyright 1969. 18¼″ diameter, 300 die-cut cardboard pieces, including figure pieces. Metal film-type cannister, 9½″ diameter, with small guide picture.

Fig. 13-16. [*Greta Garbo*]. Allied Radio Corp., Chicago, Ill. 1935. 12″ × 8½″, 50 die-cut cardboard pieces. Paper envelope, 7″ × 10″.

Fig. 13-18. *Laurel & Hardy*. Unknown maker. 1940s. 8½″ × 6¾″, 50 die-cut cardboard pieces. Envelope not extant.

Fig. 13-17. *Esky Gift Kit: Susan Hayward*. Esquire, Inc. Copyright 1943. 13½″ × 9½″, 81 die-cut cardboard pieces. Paper envelope, 14¼″ × 10¼″, with guide picture. Contains 1944 Varga girl calendar.

Fig. 13-19. *Norma Shearer*. Movie Mix-Up! series. Dell Publishing Co., Inc., New York, N.Y. 12″ × 8½″, 150 die-cut cardboard pieces. Paper envelope, 12½″ × 8½″.

▪ Radio Personalities

Fig. 13-21. *Clara, Lu' n' Em at the Capitol.* Palmolive, Chicago, Ill. 1930s. 12″ × 9″, 179 die-cut cardboard pieces. Paper envelope, 6½″ × 9½″. Contains letter from Clara, Lu, and Em whose radio show in the early 1930s was sponsored by Palmolive.

Fig. 13-20. *Eddie Cantor Jig-Saw Puzzle.* Radio Stars series no. 1. Einson-Freeman Co., Long Island City, N.Y. Copyright 1933. 14¾″ × 10″, over 200 die-cut cardboard pieces. Cardboard box, 10″ × 7″, is illustrated in Chapter 2.

Fig. 13-22. *Gambling's Gang.* Thom McAn. 1932. 10¼″ × 13″, 100 die-cut cardboard pieces. Double-sided puzzle with Thom McAn shoes advertisement on reverse. Envelope not extant.

Fig. 13-23. *The Goldbergs Puzzle*. Pepsodent Co., Chicago, Ill. Copyright 1932. 8″ × 10″, 59 die-cut cardboard pieces. Paper envelope, 8¼″ × 10¼″.

Fig. 13-24. *Just Breezing Along*. Jake and Lena Radio Jig Saw Puzzle. Olman Music Corporation, New York, N.Y. Copyright 1933. 11¼″ × 14¼″, 300 die-cut cardboard pieces. Cardboard box, 8½″ × 6″. This puzzle was also distributed by Sohio, which held the copyright.

Fig. 13-25. *Charlie McCarthy Picture Puzzles.* Whitman Publishing Co., Racine, Wisc. Copyright 1938. Set of two die-cut cardboard puzzles, each 7½ × 10″, 42 pieces. Cardboard box, 10½″ × 7½″. Puzzles show: 1) Edgar Bergen and Charlie at breakfast, 2) Edgar brushing Charlie's teeth.

Fig. 13-26. *Ed Wynn Picture Puzzle: No. 2, The Fire Alarm.* Viking Mfg. Co., Boston, Mass. Circa 1933. 11″ × 14¼″, approx. 200 die-cut cardboard pieces, including figure pieces that spell out "The Fire Alarm." Cardboard box, 8¼″ × 10¼″.

▪ Television

Fig. 13-27. *Ding Dong School*. National Mask & Records. 1950s. Frame tray puzzle 11½″ × 8½″, 10 hand-cut plywood pieces, including figure pieces.

Fig. 13-28. *Howdy Doody: 3 Puzzles*. Milton Bradley Co., Springfield, Mass. 1950s. Set of three die-cut cardboard puzzles, each 12″ × 9″, 32 pieces, including figure pieces. Cardboard box, 12¼″ × 9½″, with guide picture for Howdy Doody puzzle. Others in set show: 1) Princess SummerFallWinterSpring, 2) Entire gang. Serial no. 4121.

Fig. 13-29. *The Mod Squad*. Milton Bradley Co., Springfield, Mass. Copyright 1969. 20″ × 14¼″, 513 die-cut cardboard pieces. Cardboard box, 14½″ × 9½ with guide picture. Serial no. 4089.

▪ Comic and Cartoon Characters

Fig. 13-30. *Blondie Jig-Saw Puzzle.* Supplement to the Sunday Inquirer, Philadelphia, Pa. Copyright 1933. Frame puzzle 8″ × 10″, 49 die-cut cardboard pieces. No envelope or box.

Fig. 13-31. *Blondie and Dagwood Interchangeable Blocks.* Gaston Mfg. Co., Cincinnati, Ohio. Copyright 1951. 6½″ × 10¾″, 20 hand-cut wood blocks, with pictures on four sides. Cardboard box, 6¾″ × 11″. Pieces can be rearranged to form over one trillion different expressions.

Fig. 13-32. *Bringing Up Father: 4 Picture Puzzles.* Saalfield Publishing Co., Akron, Ohio. Copyright 1932. Set of four die-cut cardboard puzzles, each 7¾″ × 9½″, approx. 35 pieces. Cardboard box, 8¼″ × 10″, with guide picture for one puzzle. Other puzzles in set are: 1) Maggie evicting Jiggs (illustrated in color section), 2) Maggie and Jiggs in formal attire, 3) Jiggs playing cards at the Dinty Moore cafe. Serial no. 909.

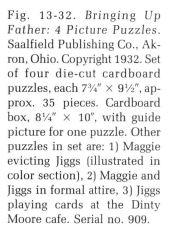

Fig. 13-33. *The Brownie Blocks.* McLoughlin Brothers, New York, N.Y. Copyright 1891. 10″ × 12½″, 20 hollow wood cubes that make six different pictures. Wood frame and cardboard box, 11″ × 15″. Contains booklet of guide diagrams.

Fig. 13-34. *Bugs Bunny*. Jaymar Specialty Co., New York, N.Y. 1950s. Frame tray puzzle 9¾″ × 12¾″, approx. 30 die-cut cardboard pieces. Serial no. 2389–3.

Fig. 13-35. *Don Winslow of the Navy*. Your Favorite Funnies Series. Jaymar Specialty Co., New York, N.Y. 1940s. 9½″ × 14¼″, 136 die-cut cardboard pieces, including figure pieces. Cardboard box, 5½″ × 7½″.

Fig. 13-36. *Donald Duck.* Jaymar Specialty Co., New York, N.Y. Circa 1950. 14″ × 21½″, 327 die-cut cardboard pieces, including figure pieces. Cardboard box, 7″ × 10″, with small guide picture.

Fig. 13-37. *The Gumps.* Famous Comics Jig Saw no. 2. Stephens Kindred & Co., New York, N.Y. Distributed by Novelty Distributing Co., Newark, N.J. 1930s. 11¾″ × 13″, 255 die-cut cardboard pieces. Cardboard box, 7¼″ × 7¼″.

Fig. 13-38. *Joe Palooka Jig-Saw Puzzle.* Supplement to the Sunday Inquirer, Philadelphia, Pa. Copyright 1933. Frame puzzle 8″ × 10″, 42 die-cut cardboard pieces. No envelope or box.

Fig. 13-39. *Just Kids: 4 Picture Puzzles.* Saalfield Publishing Co., Akron, Ohio. Copyright 1932. Set of four die-cut cardboard puzzles, each 7½″ × 9½″, approx. 33 pieces. Cardboard box, 8¼″ × 10″, with guide picture for one puzzle. Others in set include: 1) See Saw, 2) Fishing, 3) Saturday night stroll. Serial no. 910.

Fig. 13-40. *Li'l Abner*. Jaymar Specialty Co., New York, N.Y. Copyright 1952. Frame tray puzzle 14″ × 11″, 35 die-cut cardboard pieces. Serial no. 2594.

Fig. 13-41. *Little Orphan Annie*. Famous Comics Jig Saw no. 1. Stephens Kindred & Co., New York, N.Y. Distributed by Novelty Distributing Co., Newark, N.J. 12¼″ × 13″, 255 die-cut cardboard pieces. Puzzle is illustrated in color section. Cardboard box, 7¼″ × 7¼″.

Fig. 13-42. *Mickey Mouse*. Jaymar Specialty Co., New York, N.Y. 1950s. 13¾″ × 21½″, 300 die-cut cardboard pieces, including figure pieces. Cardboard box, 7″ × 10″, with guide picture.

Fig. 13-43. *Mickey Mouse Comic Picture Puzzle.* Parker Brothers, Inc., Salem, Mass. Circa 1952. Set of four sequenced die-cut cardboard puzzles, each 6″ × 17½″, 16 pieces. Cardboard box, 7″ × 18″.

Fig. 13-44. *Moon Mullins/ Cottage of Dreams*. Double Set series. Louis Marx & Co., New York, N.Y. 1930s. 7″ × 9½″, 150 hand-cut plywood pieces. Double-sided, with pastoral scene on reverse. Cardboard box, 10″ × 7½″.

Fig. 13-45. *3 Kiddies' Jigsaw Puzzles*. Jaymar Specialty Co., New York, N.Y. Circa 1950. Set of three die-cut cardboard puzzles, each 8½″ × 11″, 24 pieces. Cardboard box, 11¼″ × 9″, is illustrated in color section. Set includes: 1) Mickey Mouse, 2) Donald Duck, 3) Pluto.

Fig. 13-46. *Popeye Jigsaw Puzzle.* Jaymar Specialty Co., New York, N.Y. 1950s. 13¾″ × 18¾″, 108 die-cut cardboard pieces. Cardboard box, 10¼″ × 7¾″, with guide picture. Serial no. 7964–29.

Fig. 13-47. *Prince Valiant Junior Picture Puzzle.* Built-Rite Junior series. Warren Paper Products, Lafayette, Ind. 1954–55. 17″ × 11″, 96 die-cut cardboard pieces. Cardboard box, 6¾″ × 8″, with partial guide picture. Serial no. 100. There were six different Prince Valiant subjects in this series.

Fig. 13-48. *Bump Hopes It's A Whale*. Reg'lar Fellers Series. Selchow & Righter Co., New York, N.Y. Circa 1933. 6″ × 8″, 70 hand-cut plywood pieces, including figure pieces. Cardboard box, 4½″ × 7¼″.

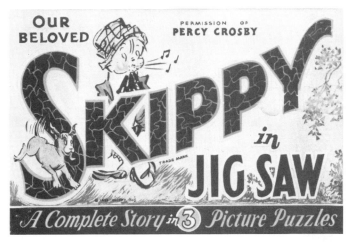

Fig. 13-49. *Skippy*. Consolidated Paper Box Co., Somerville, Mass. Copyright 1933. Set of three die-cut cardboard puzzles, each 6¾″ × 10½″, approx. 30 pieces. Cardboard box, 7″ × 10¾″. Puzzles show three scenes from a mini-story "Spring is come." Serial no. 730.

Fig. 13-50. *Walt Disney Jigsaw Puzzle: Tortoise and the Hare*. Jaymar Specialty Co., New York, N.Y. 1940s. 13¾″ × 21¾″, 300 die-cut cardboard pieces, including figure pieces. Cardboard box, 7″ × 10″, with small guide picture.

Fig. 13-51. *Yellow Kid Puzzle.* McLoughlin Brothers, New York, N.Y. Copyright 1896. 25½" × 18¾", 68 hand-cut pressboard pieces. Cardboard box, 13" × 12½". (Courtesy of the Siegels)

Fig. 13-52. *Yogi Bear.* Whitman Publishing Co., Racine, Wisc. Copyright 1961. Frame tray puzzle 14½" × 11½", approx. 30 die-cut cardboard pieces. Serial no. 4420.

▪ Wild West and Super Heroes

Fig. 13-53. *Broken Arrow.* Built-Rite series. Warren Paper Products Co., Lafayette, Ind. 1957–60. Set of four die-cut cardboard frame tray puzzles. Two are 13½" × 11", approx. 25 pieces each; two are 6¾" × 10¾", approx. 10 pieces each. Cardboard box, 14" × 11", with guide picture for one puzzle. Others in set include: 1) Broken Arrow and others in cart, 2) Broken Arrow and others talking to a white man, 3) Broken Arrow and others on horseback.

Fig. 13-54. *Hopalong Cassidy: 3 Film Puzzles.* Milton Bradley Co., Springfield, Mass. Copyright 1950. Set of three die-cut cardboard puzzles, each 9¼″ × 12″, 40 pieces, including figure pieces. Cardboard box, 9½″ × 12½″, with guide picture for one puzzle. Others in set include: 1) Hoppy riding Topper, 2) Hoppy taking aim. Serial no. 4105.

Fig. 13-56. *Cisco Kid.* Saalfield Publishing Co., Akron, Ohio. Copyright 1950. Frame tray puzzle 11½″ × 10¼″, approx. 25 pieces, including figure pieces. Serial no. 7348.

Fig. 13-55. *Clint Walker, Star of Cheyenne.* Milton Bradley Co., Springfield, Mass. Copyright 1959. Frame tray puzzle 14¼″ × 10″, approx. 35 die-cut cardboard pieces, including figure pieces. Serial no. 4508–X10.

Fig. 13-57. *Tom Corbett Space Cadet*. Saalfield Publishing Co., Akron, Ohio. Copyright 1950. Frame tray puzzle 11½″ × 10½″, approx. 35 die-cut cardboard pieces. Serial no. 7320.

Fig. 13-59. *Hugh O'Brien as Wyatt Earp*. Whitman Publishing Co., Racine, Wisc. Circa 1960. Frame tray puzzle 14½″ × 11½″, 40 die-cut cardboard pieces. Serial no. 4427:29.

Fig. 13-58. *Davy Crockett*. Whitman Publishing Co., Racine, Wisc. Copyright 1955. Frame tray puzzle 14¾″ × 11¼″, approx. 30 pieces including figure pieces.

Fig. 13-60. *Flash Gordon*. Milton Bradley Co., Springfield, Mass. Copyright 1951. Set of three die-cut cardboard puzzles, each 12″ × 9″, approx. 30 pieces, including figure pieces. Cardboard box, 12¼″ × 9½″, with guide picture for one puzzle. Others in set include: 1) Attack scene (illustrated in color section), 2) Riding a rocket. Serial no. 4221.

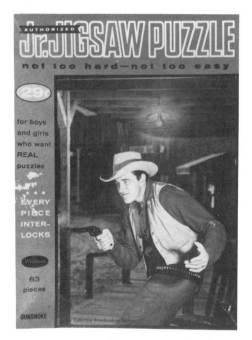

Fig. 13-62. *Monte Hale in "The Missourians"*. Unknown maker. Circa 1950. 6″ × 6½″, 27 hand-cut masonite pieces. The uncut puzzle picture was printed on the back of Quaker Puffed Wheat cereal boxes, with instructions on how to make and use the puzzle.

Fig. 13-61. *Gunsmoke*. Jr. Jigsaw Puzzle series no. 302. Whitman Publishing Co., Racine, Wisc. Circa 1960. 18″ × 14″, 63 die-cut cardboard pieces. Cardboard box, 9¼″ × 7″, with guide picture. Serial no. 4404:29.

Fig. 13-64. *Lone Ranger Picture Puzzle.* Whitman Publishing Co., Racine, Wisc. Copyright 1953. Frame tray puzzle 14½″ × 11½″, approx. 25 die-cut cardboard pieces, including figure pieces. Serial no. 2610:29.

Fig. 13-63. *Gabby Hayes.* Milton Bradley Co., Springfield, Mass. Copyright 1950. Frame tray puzzle 14½″ × 10¼″, 45 die-cut cardboard pieces, including figure pieces. Serial no. 4308–X4.

Fig. 13-65. *Captain Marvel Picture Puzzle: No. 1, One Against Many.* Fawcett Publications, Inc., Minneapolis, Minn. Circa 1940. 6¾″ × 9″, 32 die-cut cardboard pieces, including figure pieces that spell out "Shazam." Paper envelope, 10″ × 7″, with guide picture.

Fig. 13-66. *Tom Mix and His New Horse Tony Jr.* Rexall Drug Stores. 1930s. 9¾″ × 13″, 125 die-cut cardboard pieces. Paper envelope, 10″ × 13¼″.

Fig. 13-67. *Sergeant Preston and His Dog "Yukon King."* Milton Bradley Co., Springfield, Mass. 1950s. Frame tray puzzle 14½″ × 10¼″, 45 die-cut cardboard pieces. Serial no. 4308−X2.

Fig. 13-68. *Roy Rogers.* Whitman Publishing Co., Racine, Wisc. Copyright 1950. Frame tray puzzle 11½″ × 9¼″, 15 die-cut cardboard pieces. Serial no. 2982.

Fig. 13-69. *Walt Disney's Zorro: The Duel.* Jaymar Specialty Co., New York, N.Y. 1950s. 10″ × 14″, 104 die-cut cardboard pieces. Cardboard box, 6¾″ × 10″, with guide picture. Serial no. 8610.

14 PIECES FROM MADISON AVENUE

ADVERTISING PUZZLES date from the 1870s, when manufacturers first realized that people might enjoy reassembling pieces that depicted a company's products. As Chapter 1 details, although advertising puzzles have appeared on a fairly regular basis since 1880, the heyday of the advertising puzzle came in the depths of the Great Depression. In 1932–33 hundreds, and perhaps thousands of companies gave away puzzles as premiums to their customers.

Most of the firms that issued advertising puzzles did not actually manufacture the puzzles themselves. Although virtually no records remain of the business arrangements, it is clear that the puzzle production itself (gluing, die-cutting, and packaging) was subcontracted to large-scale puzzle manufacturers such as Einson-Freeman. The issuing company was generally responsible for providing the original art for the puzzles. But in the 1930s some puzzle manufacturers even sold generic puzzles (usually traditional scenic subjects) for use as advertising premiums; they would then package these puzzles in specially printed envelopes with the issuing companies' advertising messages. Since the advertising images on these examples appear only on the envelope and not on the puzzle, they are of less interest to collectors interested in the history of advertising.

Advertising puzzles suffer more loss in value than other puzzles when the original packaging is lost, because then part or even all of the advertising message is gone. Booklets and other inserts with product information are also important with these puzzles.

Most individual advertising puzzles were in production for less than a year, so copyright dates are quite reliable guides to issuing dates. These puzzles range in size from small children's puzzles to 150–250 piece adult puzzles. Many of the envelopes during the 1930s listed the times expected for children of different ages or adults to complete the puzzle.

Unlike the puzzles depicted in other chapters, virtually all of the advertising puzzles are die-cut from cardboard. Since the puzzles were being given away rather than sold, the issuing companies used the least costly technology available. Advertising puzzles were usually packaged in paper envelopes rather than boxes for the same reason.

Some puzzles with advertising messages are not true advertising puzzles, particularly if they are hand-cut wood puzzles. Amateur, and even professional cutters have always been eclectic in their choices of prints for their puzzles. The Cream of Wheat puzzle illustrated below is a good example of one that was surely made by an amateur from a magazine print.

This chapter presents the advertising puzzles in *alphabetical order, usually by the name of the issuing company.* However, in some cases the brand name of the product appears on the puzzle instead of the company name; these puzzles are thus alphabetized by brand name. The color section includes puzzles advertising the following products in addition to those described in this chapter:

- Eveready batteries
- Essolube
- Hills Brothers coffee
- Hood's Sarsaparilla
- Spear's Department Store
- Tip-Top Bread
- Victor Talking Machine
- White sewing machines and bicycles

Fig. 14-1. *A & P Coffee Experts at the Plantation.* Great Atlantic and Pacific Tea Co., New York, N.Y. Circa 1933. 8½″ × 10″, approx. 100 die-cut cardboard pieces. Paper envelope, 9″ × 10½″.

Fig. 14-2. *Armstrong Quaker Rugs.* Armstrong Cork Co., Lancaster, Pa. Circa 1933. 5½″ × 8½″, 15 die-cut cardboard pieces. Cardboard folder, 9″ × 6″.

Fig. 14-3. *Black Cat Hosiery.* Black Cat Hosiery Co., Kenosha, Wisc. Circa 1909. 7" × 5", 60 die-cut cardboard pieces. Paper envelope, 4" × 3".

Fig. 14-4. *Sparkalong Burgess.* Burgess Battery Co. Copyright 1952. 4" × 6" frame puzzle, approx 15 die-cut cardboard pieces. Glassine envelope, 4¼" × 6¼".

Fig. 14-5. *Campbell Kids.* Campbell Soup Co., Camden, N.J. Manufactured by Jaymar Specialty Co., Brooklyn, N.Y. Circa 1965. Frame tray puzzle, 9¾" × 12¾", 30 die-cut cardboard pieces. Artist is Grace G. Drayton.

Fig. 14-6. *Spanish Galleon.* Campfire or Angelus Marshmallows. 1930s. 9¾" × 6¾", 48 die-cut cardboard pieces. Paper envelope, 10" × 7". No. 4 in the series.

Fig. 14-7. *Old Fashioned New England Country Store.* Chase & Sanborn. Circa 1909. 6″ × 8″, 63 die-cut cardboard pieces. Cardboard box, 2½″ × 3¼″.

Fig. 14-8. *Chevrolet School Bus.* Chevrolet Motor Co. Copyright 1932. 7½″ × 13½″, approx. 35 die-cut cardboard pieces. Double-sided, shows mechanical features on reverse. Cardboard box, 8″ × 14″, with guide picture of bus exterior.

Fig. 14-9. *Jack and Ann Visit Old Chief-Tan.* Chief-Tan Shoes. 1930s. 3¾″ × 6½″, 18 die-cut cardboard pieces. Envelope not extant.

Fig. 14-10. *Brownie Town Picture Puzzle*. Clean Up & Paint Up Campaign Committee, Boston, Mass. Circa 1910s. 7½″ × 5″, 32 hand-cut plywood pieces. Cardboard box, 5¼″ × 4¼″.

Fig. 14-11. *Buffalo Bill*. Cocomalt. R. B. Davis Co., Hoboken, N.J. Copyright 1933. 10″ × 6½″, 65 die-cut cardboard pieces. Paper envelope, 10½″ × 7″, with guide diagram.

Fig. 14-12. *The Flying Family.* Cocomalt. R. B. Davis Co., Hoboken, N.J. Copyright 1932. 9¼" × 12¼", 65 die-cut cardboard pieces, including figure pieces. Paper envelope, 9½" × 12½", with guide diagram. Contains 4-page brochure on how to become a flight commander. The Hutchinson family had a radio program about their flying adventures.

Fig. 14-13. *Use Coe's Fertilizer.* E. Frank Coe Co., New York, N.Y. Circa 1909. 8" × 8", 99 hand-cut wood pieces. Box not extant.

Fig. 14-14. *First Stars and Stripes on the Ocean.* Continental Fire Insurance, New York, N.Y. Circa 1909. 4¾″ × 7½″, 55 hand-cut cardboard pieces. Cardboard frame 6″ × 8½″.

Fig. 14-15. [*Cowboy's Mailbox.*] Cream of Wheat. Circa 1909. 14¼″ × 9½″, 112 hand-cut wood pieces. Artist is N. C. Wyeth. Box not extant. Probably made by amateur from magazine print. (Courtesy of the Siegels)

Fig. 14-16. *Cruikshank's Little Cooks.* Cruikshank Brothers Co., Pittsburgh, Pa. 1930s. 7″ × 9¾″, approx. 25 die-cut cardboard pieces. Double-sided puzzle, reverse shows: "No thanks," said Banks, "I want Cruikshanks." Paper envelope, 7¼″ × 10″.

Fig. 14-17. *Baby Ruth.* Curtiss Candy Co., Chicago, Ill. 1930s. 5½″ × 7½″, 45 die-cut cardboard pieces. Double-sided puzzle, reverse shows array of Curtiss products. Envelope not extant. Artist is J. F. Kernan.

Fig. 14-18. *The Big Sport from Dayton.* Dayton Tires. 1950s. 12″ × 9″ frame tray puzzle, 18 die-cut cardboard pieces.

Fig. 14-19. *For Every Job the Dearborn Truck.* Dearborn Truck Co., Chicago, Ill. 1930s. 7″ × 10½″, 30 die-cut paper pieces. Paper envelope, 4″ × 6½″.

Fig. 14-20. *Psyche.* Dif Corp., Garwood, N.J. (Puzzle manufacturer is Einson-Freeman Co., Long Island City, N.Y.) Circa 1933. 12″ × 9½″, 125 die-cut cardboard pieces. Paper envelope, 12½″ × 9¾″, with small guide diagram.

Fig. 14-21. *The 1959 Edsel.* Ford Motor Co., Detroit, Mich. Distributed by Lakeside Motors, Ebensburg, Pa. 1958. 4″ × 7″ paper card with six puzzle pieces to punch out and assemble.

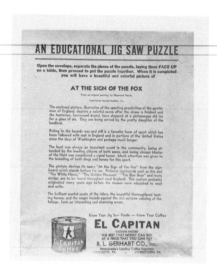

Fig. 14-22. *At the Sign of the Fox.* El Capitan Coffee, R. L. Gerhart Co., Inc., Lancaster and Johnstown, Pa. 1930s. 7″ × 9″, 40 die-cut cardboard pieces. Paper envelope, 9½″ × 7½″.

Fig. 14-23. *The Everett Piano.* Everett Piano Co., Boston, Mass. Distributed by John Church Co., Cincinnati, Ohio. Circa 1890. 8½″ × 6½″, 16 sliced cardboard pieces. Cardboard folder 3¾″ × 5½″.

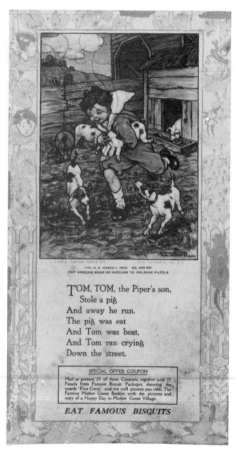

Fig. 14-24. *Tom, Tom the Piper's Son.* Famous Biscuits. Patented 1910. 10″ × 5½″ frame puzzle, 39 die-cut cardboard pieces. Envelope not extant. Artist is Clara Burd.

Fig. 14-25. *Vitamin "D" Bread*. Fischer. 1930s. 7" × 9¼", 49 die-cut cardboard pieces. Paper envelope, 9½" × 7¼", with guide diagram.

Fig. 14-26. *Folger's Coffee*. Folger's Coffee Co., San Mateo, Calif. Circa 1965. 10½" × 8", 56 die-cut cardboard pieces. Cardboard and metal container 3½" high, 2½" diameter resembles coffee can.

Fig. 14-27. *Carlene Fuller, the Fuller Girl*. Fuller's Magnesia Dental Cream. 1930s. 8¾" × 6½", 45 die-cut cardboard pieces. Paper envelope, 9" × 7".

Fig. 14-28. *Portable Appliances*. General Electric, Schenectady, N.Y. Circa 1960. 10½″ × 15″, 104 die-cut cardboard pieces. Plastic bag, 5″ × 7½″, contains small guide picture.

Fig. 14-29. *Puzzle Board: Thoroughbreds*. Goodrich Tire, Akron, Ohio. 1930s. 11″ × 14″ frame tray puzzle, approx. 95 die-cut cardboard pieces. Horses cut on outlines can be inserted in slots on back of frame for display. Puzzle is double-sided, shows tire on reverse. Paper envelope, 14¼″ × 11¼″. Serial no. 4094.

Fig. 14-30. *The Goodrich Silver Fleet at Niagara Falls.* Goodrich Tire, Akron, Ohio. 1930s. 7½" × 9¾", approx 50 die-cut cardboard pieces. Paper envelope, 8" × 10".

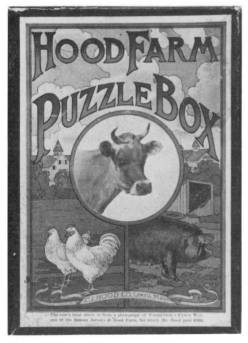

Fig. 14-31. *Hood Farm Puzzle Box.* C. I. Hood Co., Lowell, Mass. Copyright 1905. Set of three double-sided, die-cut cardboard puzzles, each 7¾" × 10½", 20 pieces. Cardboard box, 7" × 5¼". Contains list of Hood's medicines. Other puzzles in set show various farm scenes and a mother giving Hood's Sarsaparilla to her children.

Fig. 14-32. *Hood's Four-In-One Puzzle*. C. I. Hood Co., Lowell, Mass. Copyright 1896. 11¼″ × 18½″, 34 die-cut cardboard pieces. Cardboard box, 5″ × 7″. Contains 32 page booklet with testimonials for Hood's products and key diagrams. Pieces can be rearranged to form four separate puzzles including: 1) U.S. map, 2) View of Hood factory, 3–4) Hood's slogans.

Fig. 14-33. *Hood's Panama Canal Puzzle*. C. I. Hood Co., Lowell, Mass. Circa 1914. 5½″ × 14″, 22 die-cut cardboard pieces. Double-sided, with elevation showing canal locks on the reverse. Cardboard box, 5″ × 3¾″. Contains two advertising brochures and a brochure about the Panama Canal. (Courtesy of the Siegels)

Fig. 14-34. *Jap Rose Soap.* Kirk Co. 1910s. 7″ × 7″, 50 hand-cut plywood pieces. Box not extant.

Fig. 14-35. *South Pole Flight.* Kolynos Co., New Haven, Conn. 1933. 12″ × 8½″, approx. 150 die-cut cardboard pieces. Paper envelope, 9½″ × 12½″. Probably manufactured by Einson-Freeman Co., Long Island City, N.Y., which produced the same title under its own label.

Fig. 14-36. *Listerine.* Lambert Pharmacal Co., St. Louis, Mo. 1930s. 11″ × 13¾″, 50 die-cut cardboard pieces. Paper envelope, 11¼″ × 14¼″. Premium from the Phillips Lord Country Doctor radio program, sponsored by Listerine. Artist is Frances Tipton Hunter.

Fig. 14-37. *Puzzle Tobacco.* Lottier's. 1890s. 10¼″ × 10½″, 16 hand-cut wood pieces. Box is not extant.

Fig. 14-38. *The Wayside Inn.* Lux Soap. 1930s. 10″ × 12¼″, 150 die-cut cardboard pieces. Paper envelope, 10½″ × 12½″, with guide diagram. Artist is Charles Allen Winter.

Fig. 14-39. *My Island of Dreams.* Lux Soap. 1930s. 9″ × 12¼″, 150 die-cut cardboard pieces. Paper envelope, 9½″ × 12½″, with guide diagram.

262

Fig. 14-40. *McKesson's Products*. McKesson & Robbins, Inc., Bridgeport, Conn. Copyright 1933. 14″ × 10½″, 150 die-cut cardboard pieces. Paper envelope, 14¼″ × 11″. Contains crossword puzzle and first-aid book. Contest awarded $1000 in prizes for identification of company products on puzzle.

Fig. 14-42. *Home Office*. Metropolitan Life Insurance Co., New York, N.Y. Circa 1909. 6½″ × 5″, 44 die-cut cardboard pieces. Envelope not extant.

Fig. 14-41. *Our Gang Jig-Saw Puzzle*. McKesson & Robbins, Inc., Bridgeport, Conn. Copyright 1932. 11″ × 14″, 80 die-cut cardboard pieces. Paper envelope, 14″ × 11¼″.

Fig. 14-43. *Toy Carnival.* Miller Rubber Products Co., Inc., Akron, Ohio. 1933. 7½" × 9¾", approx. 50 die-cut cardboard pieces. Paper envelope, 8" × 10".

Fig. 14-44. *Hauling 20 Mule Team Borax Out of Death Valley.* Pacific Coast Borax Co., New York, N.Y. Copyright 1933. 8" × 10½", 100 die-cut cardboard pieces, including 20 figure pieces of mules' heads. Paper envelope, 8¼" × 11". Contains insert with company history, ad, and two comic strips about Borax. Some examples of this puzzle were cut with different dies and have no figure pieces.

Fig. 14-45. *Pan-Am Pete.* Pan-American Products, New York, N.Y. Copyright 1933. 10" × 13¼", 100 die-cut cardboard pieces. Paper envelope, 13½" × 10¼", with guide diagram.

Fig. 14-46. *Help Your Friends to Help Themselves.* Personal Finance Co., Bangor, Me. Copyright 1933. 6″ × 9″, 49 die-cut cardboard puzzles. Envelope is not extant.

Fig. 14-47. *Post Toasties' Captain Better.* General Foods Corp., Battle Creek, Mich. Copyright 1932. 8″ × 9¾″, 50 die-cut cardboard pieces. Paper envelope, 8½″ × 10½″. Serial no. 9008.

Fig. 14-48. *Old Grist Mill Jig Cut Puzzle.* Potter Wrightington, Inc., Boston, Mass. 1930s. 8½″ × 7¼″, 49 die-cut cardboard pieces. Paper envelope, 5¼″ × 8¼″.

Fig. 14-49. [*Uncle Sam*]. Pratt Food Co., Philadelphia, Pa. Circa 1905. 6¼″ × 9″, 10 die-cut cardboard pieces. Paper envelope, 4¾″ × 6¾″. Double-sided with advertising text on reverse.

Fig. 14-50. *Adventures of Professor Oscar Quackenbush: Chasing Pink Elephants*. Procter & Gamble. Puzzle manufacturer is Akron Paper Products, Akron, Ohio. Copyright 1933. 7½″ × 9¾″, 50 die-cut cardboard pieces. Glassine envelope, 8″ × 10¼″. There were four different puzzles in the Quackenbush series.

Fig. 14-51. *Uncle Sam Recommends the Prophylactic Brush*. Florence Mfg. Co., Florence, Mass. Copyright 1908. 8½″ × 8½″, 54 die-cut cardboard pieces. Envelope not extant.

Fig. 14-52. *Dick Daring Underground*. Quaker Oats Co., Chicago, Ill. 1933. 9″ × 12″, 100 die-cut cardboard pieces, including figure pieces. Paper envelope, 6″ × 9″. Quaker Oats sponsored the Dick Daring radio program on NBC.

Fig. 14-53. *His Master's Voice.* RCA Victor, Inc. Copyright 1933. 10″ × 13″, approx. 165 die-cut cardboard pieces, including figure pieces of "Victor," Nipper, and phonograph. Cardboard box, 5¼″ × 3¼″, with design of radio.

Fig. 14-54. *Goofy Golf Puzzle No. 1: A Swiss-ituation.* Richfield Gasoline. 1930s. 9″ × 7″, 49 die-cut cardboard pieces. Paper envelope, 9½″ × 7½″, with golf lesson by Alex Morrison. One of a series of six, shows golfer shooting from an eagle's nest.

Fig. 14-55. *Goofy Golf Puzzle No. 4: A Tight Play in Scotland*. Richfield Gasoline. 1930s. 9″ × 7″, 49 die-cut cardboard pieces. Paper envelope, 9½″ × 7½″, with golf lesson by Alex Morrison. One of a series of six.

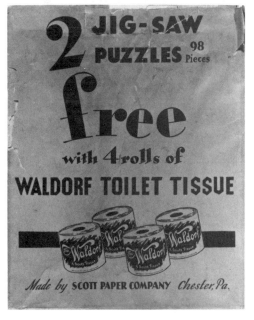

Fig. 14-56. *Innocence*. Waldorf Toilet Tissue, Scott Paper Co., Chester, Pa. 1930s. Set of two die-cut cardboard puzzles, each 9¼″ × 7¼″, 49 pieces. Paper envelope, 9½″ × 7½″. Artist is Lawson Wood. Other puzzle shows a sailboat.

Fig. 14-57. *Snellenburg's Toy Town.* Snellenburg's Department Store. Circa 1930. Jigsaw puzzle to cut out from paper sheet, 9″ × 18½″. Folds into packet, 9″ × 6″.

Fig. 14-58. *Sorosis Sets the Style in Shoes.* Sorosis Shoe Co., New Haven, Conn. Copyright 1909. 5¼″ × 5½″, 39 hand-cut wood pieces. Cardboard box, 4¼″ × 5¼″.

Fig. 14-59. *In Dutch.* Radio Jig Saw Puzzle No. 2, Standard Oil Co. of Ohio. Copyright 1933. 11″ × 14½″, 252 die-cut cardboard pieces. Cardboard box, 8¼″ × 6¼″. Contains guide picture with advertising on back. Sohio sponsored Gene, Glenn, Jake, and Lena's nightly radio program.

Fig. 14-60. *A Bully Time in Spain.* Radio Jig Saw Puzzle No. 3, Standard Oil Co. of Ohio. Copyright 1933. 11″ × 14½″, 252 die-cut cardboard pieces. Double-sided, shows Gene and Glenn on reverse. Cardboard box, 6¼″ × 8¼″. Contains guide picture with advertising.

Fig. 14-61. *Sunshine Lone Star Sugar Wafers.* L.-W.B. Co. Copyright 1932. 7″ × 9¼″, 40 die-cut cardboard pieces. Paper envelope, 9½″ × 7¼″, with guide diagram.

Fig. 14-62. *Jig-Play Puzzle.* Timken Silent Automatic Burner Co., Canton, Ohio. 1930s. 8½″ × 8″, 87 die-cut cardboard pieces. Paper envelope, 5″ × 7¼″.

Fig. 14-63. *Tip-Top Bread Kut Up Puzzle.* Ward Baking Co. Circa 1909. 3½" × 5", 28 die-cut cardboard pieces. Paper envelope, 3" × 5½".

Fig. 14-64. *Patriotic Jig-Saw Puzzle: U.S. Military Academy.* Ward Baking Co. Circa 1943. 8" × 10", approx. 100 die-cut cardboard pieces. Paper envelope, 8½" × 10½".

Fig. 14-65. *Tip-Top Circus.* Ward Baking Co. Copyright 1951. 7¼″ × 8¼″, 36 die-cut cardboard pieces. Paper envelope, 7¾″ × 8½″.

Fig. 14-66. *Circus Parade.* Toddy, Inc., New York, N.Y. Copyright 1932. 10″ × 13½″, 75 die-cut cardboard pieces, including figure pieces. Paper envelope. One of a series of six puzzles.

Fig. 14-67. *America's Cup Yacht Race.* Travel Series, Toddy, Inc., New York, N.Y. Copyright 1933. 13″ × 9¾″, 50 die-cut cardboard pieces, including figure pieces that spell "Toddy." Cardboard box, 13¼″ × 10″. Contains spinner for playing race game on assembled puzzle. Series included five different puzzle/games.

Fig. 14-68. *Treasure Hunt.* Travel Series, Toddy, Inc., New York, N.Y. Copyright 1933. 9¾″ × 13″, 50 die-cut cardboard pieces, including figure pieces that spell "Toddy." Cardboard box, 13¼″ × 10″. Contains spinner for playing race game on assembled puzzle.

Fig. 14-69. *Turkish Trophies.* American Tobacco Co., New York, N.Y. Circa 1909. Six different die-cut cardboard puzzles, each 2½″ × 3¼″, approx. 20 pieces. These were given out as tobacco inserts.

Fig. 14-70. *Bug Repair Kit.* Volkswagen. Circa 1968. 4¼″ × 10¾″, 9 die-cut paper pieces. Paper envelope, 4½″ × 3″.

Fig. 14-71. *Threshing Winter Wheat From Which Wheatena is Made.* Brother Cushman, Montclair, N.J. 1915. 3½″ × 5½″, 30 hand-cut wood pieces. Cardboard box, 3¼″ × 4″.

Fig. 14-72. *Jack O'Brien Jig Saw Puzzle No. 2: Jack O'Brien and the Penguins.* Wheaties. 1930s. 6″ × 7″, approx. 30 cardboard pieces cut from back of Wheaties box. Series included three other puzzles.

15 WHAT'S IN A BOX?

THE PRECEDING CHAPTERS, which are organized by subject matter, focus on puzzles with some special pictorial appeal. In addition, collectors in today's market can find a multitude of puzzles that are attractive and fun to work. It is impossible to show all of these in a book with limited space. This chapter, therefore, presents types of puzzles among the thousands of different adult puzzles produced in this century.

Pre-1935 puzzles for adults generally do not have a guide picture on the box. Nevertheless, many of the cardboard puzzles, and some of the wooden ones, were packaged in distinctive boxes that can easily be recognized. Later puzzles usually have a guide picture, which can be seen in the illustrations below. Although the puzzles themselves are not shown in this chapter, most have traditional scenic subjects.

The goal of this chapter is to deal with the *average* puzzle available in a given series. Thus the values given in the Price Guide must be interpreted carefully for this chapter. For a given item, the value applies only to it and to *similar* puzzles in the same series. However, a series of generally ordinary puzzles may include a few that are especially collectible; some of these items appear in the other chapters according to the subject matter or artist.

This chapter is organized *alphabetically by manufacturer*, or (in the case where the manufacturer's name does not appear on the box), by series. The color section includes boxes by the following companies in addition to those described in this chapter:

- Chad Valley Co.
- Jaymar Specialty Co.
- Parker Brothers, Inc.
- Consolidated Paper Box Co.

Fig. 15-1. *Hold It.* Big Star. 1930s. 13½″ × 10″, over 250 die-cut cardboard pieces. Cardboard box, 6½″ × 4¾″, with small guide picture. Serial no. 1010.

Fig. 15-2. *Grand Canyon Hues.* Big 10. 1940s. 15¼″ × 10¼″, over 275 die-cut cardboard pieces. Cardboard box, 7″ × 5¼″, with small guide picture.

Fig. 15-3. *Sunshine and Shadow.* Big Ben series. Milton Bradley Co., Springfield, Mass. 1940s. 22″ × 28″, 945 die-cut cardboard pieces. Cardboard box, 8″ × 13″, with small guide picture. Serial no. 4962.

Fig. 15-4. *Treasure Princess.* Buckingham Jig series. Milton Bradley Co., Springfield, Mass. 1930s. 15″ × 12″, 270 die-cut cardboard pieces. Cardboard box, 5″ × 8″. Serial no. 15.

Fig. 15-5. *Autumn on the River.* Croxley series. Milton Bradley Co., Springfield, Mass. Copyright 1965. 14″ × 20″, 500 die-cut cardboard pieces. Cardboard box, 8½″ × 10¼″, with guide picture. Serial no. 4611.

Fig. 15-6. *Banks of the Scheldt.* Wood Picture Puzzle series. Milton Bradley Co., Springfield, Mass. Circa 1940. 12″ × 16″, 252 die-cut composition board pieces. Cardboard box, 7″ × 9″, with small guide picture.

Fig. 15-7. *When Seconds Count.* Master Piece series, no. 2. Consolidated Lithographing Corp., Brooklyn, N.Y. Distributed by American News Co., Inc. and its branches. Circa 1933. 10″ × 12¼″, 304 die-cut cardboard pieces. Cardboard box, 7¼″ × 7¼″. Artist is H. Hintermeister.

Fig. 15-8. *Look Before You Leap.* Dubl-Thik Picture Puzzle. 1940s. 11½″ × 8¼″, 140 die-cut cardboard pieces. Cardboard box, 8″ × 4½″, with small guide picture.

Fig. 15-9. *Old Mill Run.* Circle-Cut series. E. E. Fairchild Corp, Rochester, N.Y. Copyright 1964. 17½″ × 22″, over 650 die-cut cardboard pieces. Cardboard box, 10¼″ × 12½″, with small guide picture.

Fig. 15-11. *Bull's Head Inn.* Fine Arts series. Saalfield Publishing Co., Akron, Ohio. 1950s. 16″ × 20″, 300 die-cut cardboard pieces. Cardboard box, 8½″ × 9″. Serial no. 7398.

Fig. 15-10. *Uninvited Guests.* Top-Hit series. E. E. Fairchild Corp., Rochester, N.Y. 1950s. 10½″ × 15″, 108 die-cut cardboard pieces. Cardboard box, 8¼″ × 7¼″, with guide picture.

Fig. 15-12. *Conquerors of Time and Space.* Marvel series. Samuel Gabriel Sons & Co., New York, N.Y. 1930s. 16″ × 22″, 432 die-cut cardboard pieces. Cardboard box, 8¼″ × 11″, with small guide picture.

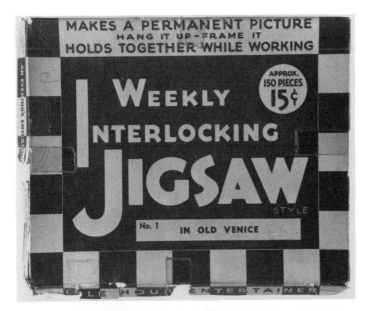

Fig. 15-13. *In Old Venice.* Weekly Interlocking series. Gelco Interlocking Puzzle Co., Chicago, Ill. Copyright 1933. 12″ × 8¾″, approx. 150 die-cut cardboard pieces. Cardboard box, 7¾″ × 9½″.

Fig. 15-14. *Sunshine and Shadows.* Jigette series. Hamblet Studios, Inc., Akron, Ohio. 1930s. 12″ × 16″, 250 die-cut cardboard pieces, including figure pieces. Cardboard box, 6¾″ × 8¾″.

Fig. 15-15. *Indian Village.* Happy Hour Puzzle, distributed by American News Co. and branches. Circa 1933. 10¼″ × 13¼″, 300 die-cut cardboard pieces. Cardboard box, 7¼″ × 7¼″. Picture is same as the Movie Cut-Ups puzzle, *White Eagle* (illustrated in Chapter 13).

Fig. 15-16. *Subtracting a Zero.* Modern Fighters for Victory series. Jaymar Specialty Co., New York, N.Y. Copyright 1942. 14″ × 21¾″, 306 die-cut cardboard pieces, including figure pieces. (Puzzle is illustrated in Chapter 2.) Cardboard box, 8″ × 10¼″, with small guide picture.

Fig. 15-17. *Winter's Embrace.* Jumble Jig, Philadelphia, Pa. 1930s. 11½″ × 9¾″, 304 die-cut cardboard pieces. Cardboard box, 7¼″ × 7¼″.

Fig. 15-18. *On the Loire.* Mayfair Jig. 1930s. 11¾″ × 15″, 204 die-cut cardboard pieces. Cardboard box, 7″ × 9″.

Fig. 15-19. *Hands Across the Sea.* Jiggity Jag series. Thomas D. Murphy Co., Red Oak, Iowa. 1930s. 7″ × 10″, 124 die-cut cardboard pieces. Paper envelope, 10¼″ × 7″.

Fig. 15-20. *Oriental Traders in Venice.* Pastime series. Parker Brothers, Inc., Salem, Mass. 1940s. 10½″ × 15½″, 255 hand-cut plywood pieces. Cardboard box, 5½″ × 9¼″.

Fig. 15-21. *Winter's Ermine Robe/Snowed In.* Perfect Double series. Consolidated Paper Box Co., Somerville, Mass. 1930s. 15½" × 10¼", 280 die-cut cardboard pieces. Cardboard box, 7¼" × 5¼", with one small guide picture.

Fig. 15-22. *Bloom of Spring.* Perfect Value-Plus series. Consolidated Paper Box Co., Somerville, Mass. 1930s. 10" × 14", over 250 die-cut cardboard pieces. Cardboard box, 6¾" × 4¾", with small guide picture. Serial no. 1410.

Fig. 15-23. *Lake Louise.* Perfect Picture Puzzle. Consolidated Paper Box Co., Somerville, Mass. 1940s. 15½" × 19½", over 375 die-cut cardboard pieces. Cardboard box, 9¾" × 7¼", with small guide picture.

Fig. 15-24. *Pride of the Farm.*
Picadilly Jig. 1930s. 12″ × 15″,
204 die-cut cardboard pieces.
Cardboard box, 6½″ × 10½″.

Fig. 15-25. *Dutch Gossip.* Zig-Zaw series. Pleasent (sic) Pastime Co., Philadelphia, Pa. Circa
1933. 11″ × 14″, 300 die-cut cardboard pieces.
Cardboard box, 7½″ × 7½″.

Fig. 15-26. *Louisa.* Popular
Picture Puzzle. Circa 1909. 7″
× 5″, 30 hand-cut plywood
pieces. Cardboard box, 5½″
× 7½″.

Fig. 15-27. *Flower of Japan.* R & J Specialty Co., New York, N.Y. Circa 1909. 7¾" × 6", 66 hand-cut wood pieces. Cardboard box, 4¼" × 5¾".

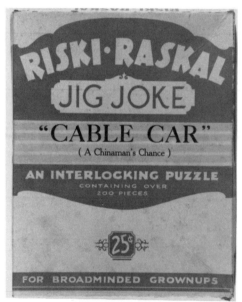

Fig. 15-29. *Trout Creek.* Essell series. George P. Schlicher & Son, Allentown, Pa. Circa 1933. 9" × 14½", over 200 die-cut cardboard pieces. Cardboard box, 7¼" × 7¼".

Fig. 15-28. *Cable Car.* Jig Joke series. Riski-Raskal Co., San Francisco, Calif. 1930s. 14½" × 10", 228 die-cut cardboard pieces. Cardboard box, 10" × 8".

Fig. 15-30. *Crossing the Mississippi.* Joseph K. Straus Products Corp., Brooklyn, N.Y. 1960s. 12″ × 15¾″, 280 hand-cut plywood pieces. Cardboard box, 6¾″ × 10″, with guide picture on bottom.

Fig. 15-31. *The Love That Keeps.* Gold Medal series. Transogram Co., Inc., New York, N.Y. 1930s. 12″ × 16″, over 200 die-cut cardboard pieces. Cardboard box, 6″ × 8″.

Fig. 15-32. *A Jewel of a Setting.* Tri-An-Mak-It Puzzle Co., Philadelphia, Pa. 1930s. 8″ × 10″, 93 hand-cut plywood pieces. Cardboard box, 6¼″ × 8¼″.

Fig. 15-33. *Mr. Pickwick and His Friends Arrive at the Blue Lion, Muggleton.* Zag-Zaw series. Raphael Tuck & Sons, Ltd., London, England. 1930s. 7″ × 11¾″, 171 hand-cut plywood pieces, including figure pieces. Cardboard box, 5¼″ × 8″, with small guide picture on bottom of box.

Fig. 15-34. *Bridal Veil Falls.* Tuco Work Shops, Lockport, N.Y. Circa 1933. 12″ × 16″, over 200 die-cut pressboard pieces. Cardboard box, 8½″ × 6½″.

Fig. 15-35. *Formal Opening of the White House.* Tuco Work Shops, Lockport, N.Y. 1930s. 15″ × 18¼″, 357 die-cut pressboard pieces. Cardboard box, 8½″ × 6¼″.

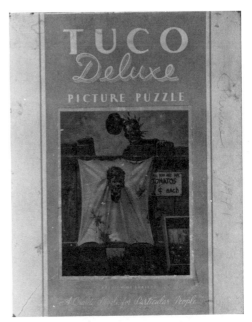

Fig. 15-36. *Highway in Holland.* Tuco Work Shops, Lockport, N.Y. 1930s. 16″ × 20″, 300 to 500 die-cut pressboard pieces. Cardboard box, 9¼″ × 7¼″, with guide picture.

Fig. 15-37. *A Bull's Eye.* Deluxe Series. Tuco Work Shops, Lockport, N.Y. 1930s. 19″ × 14¾″, 357 die-cut pressboard pieces. Cardboard box, 9¼″ × 7½″, with guide picture.

Fig. 15-38. *Morning Hunter.* Scenic series. Tuco Work-shops, Inc., Lockport, N.Y. Copyright 1957. 14¼″ × 21¼″, 408 die-cut cardboard pieces. Cardboard box, 9¼″ × 12″, with guide picture.

Fig. 15-40. [*Windjammer*]. Jig of the Week series, no. 1. University Distributing Co., Boston and Cambridge, Mass. 1932. 10″ × 13½″, 300 die-cut cardboard pieces. Cardboard box, 7¼″ × 7¼″.

Fig. 15-39. [*Boat Ride*]. Society series. Ullman Manufacturing Co., New York, N.Y. 5½″ × 7½″, 76 hand-cut plywood pieces. Cardboard box, 7¼″ × 5¼″.

Fig. 15-41. *Washington and Lafayette*. Jig Wood series. University Distributing Co., Cambridge, Mass. Circa 1933. 10″ × 13½″, 158 hand-cut plywood pieces. Cardboard box, 5″ × 7¼″.

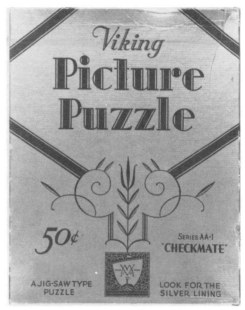

Fig. 15-42. *Battle of Bunker Hill.* Picture Puzzle Weekly series, no. B-1. Viking Mfg. Co., Inc., Boston, Mass. Circa 1933. 10¼″ × 14″, 175 die-cut cardboard pieces, including figure pieces. Cardboard box, 10¼″ × 8¼″.

Fig. 15-43. *Checkmate.* Viking Mfg. Co., Cambridge, Mass. Circa 1933. 14″ × 20″, approx. 300 die-cut cardboard pieces. Cardboard box, 10¼″ × 8¼″.

Fig. 15-44. *Retreat in Autumn.* Built-Rite Diamond-Lock series. Warren Paper Products Co., Lafayette, Ind. 1960s. 21¼″ × 13¾″, 504 die-cut cardboard pieces. Cardboard box, 9¼″ × 10¼″, with guide picture.

Fig. 15-45. *Old Ironsides.* Masterpiece series. Whitman Publishing Co., Racine, Wisc. Circa 1950. 10½″ × 15″, over 275 die-cut cardboard pieces. Cardboard box, 5¼″ × 8¼″, with guide picture.

Fig. 15-46. *The Rim of Tonto.* Zane Grey series. Whitman Publishing Co., Racine, Wisc. 1940s. 13″ × 9½″, 252 die-cut cardboard pieces. Cardboard box, 8¾″ × 5½″, with small guide picture.

Fig. 15-47. *Golden West.* Guild series. Whitman Publishing Co., Racine, Wisc. 1960s. 14″ × 18″, 304 die-cut cardboard pieces. Cardboard box, 7″ × 9¼″, with guide picture.

Fig. 15-48. *The Last Elm.* Tekwood series. Whitman Publishing Co., Racine, Wisc. 1950s. 16″ × 20″, over 300 die-cut composition board pieces, including figure pieces. Cardboard box, 9¾″ × 7¼″.

16 MORE THAN A PUZZLE

GAME PUZZLES, message puzzles, book puzzles, edible puzzles—all of these have appeared over the years, as manufacturers have sought to embellish the standard jigsaw puzzle. This chapter explores some of these variations on the puzzle theme. Puzzle-making kits and production ephemera also are described. Sections include postcard and correspondence puzzles (greeting card puzzles for special days like Christmas, Valentine's Day, and birthdays are in Chapter 12); puzzle books (including mystery puzzles); puzzle games; other dual purpose puzzles; and puzzle making supplies and ephemera.

The color section includes the following items in addition to those described in this chapter:

- *Looking for You*
- *Jungle Killers* poster

▪ Postcard and Correspondence Puzzles

Fig. 16-1. *Head House and Beach City Point, South Boston, Mass.* Latest Novelty Picture Puzzle Post Card. Unknown maker. Circa 1909. 3½″ × 5½″, 18 perforated paper pieces. Mailing envelope, 3½″ × 6″. Serial no. U.S. 600.

Fig. 16-2. *The Emerald Isle.* Picture Puzzle Postcard set 3A. Raphael Tuck & Sons, London, England. Set of six die-cut cardboard postcard puzzles, each 3½″ × 5½″, 29 pieces, in 4½″ × 6¼″ mailing packet with matching postcard. Cardboard box, 4½″ × 6½″. Contains scorecard for use in puzzle contests.

Fig. 16-3. *The Lebauoy Airship.* Raphael Tuck & Sons, London, England. Circa 1909. 3½″ × 5½″, 30 die-cut cardboard pieces. Cardboard mailing packet, 4½″ × 6¼″, contains matching postcard. This was one of six puzzle postcards in set 20, Airships and Lighthouses.

Fig. 16-4. *Custom House, Boston, Mass.* Rogers Novelty Card Co., Boston, Mass. Circa 1933. 5½″ × 3½″, 39 die-cut cardboard pieces. Sealed in cellophane, with postcard back for mailing.

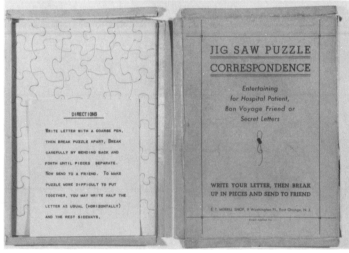

Fig. 16-5. *Jig Saw Puzzle Correspondence*. E. T. Merrill Shop, East Orange, N.J. 1930s. 7″ × 5″, 48 die-cut cardboard pieces. Cardboard box, 7¼″ × 5¼″. Contains directions for writing letter on blank pieces.

Fig. 16-6. *Jig Saw Greetings*. Hallmark Cards, Kansas City, Mo. Circa 1940. 6¾″ × 5″, 48 die-cut cardboard pieces. Cardboard mailing box, 4¼″ × 6¼″. Serial no. 58.

Fig. 16-7. *Puzzle Gram*. F. A. O. Schwarz, New York, N.Y. (Manufactured by J. K. Straus, Brooklyn, N.Y.) 1940s. 3½″ × 5½″, 28 hand-cut plywood pieces, with small space for message from sender. Cardboard mailing box, 3¾″ × 5¾″.

▪ Puzzle Books

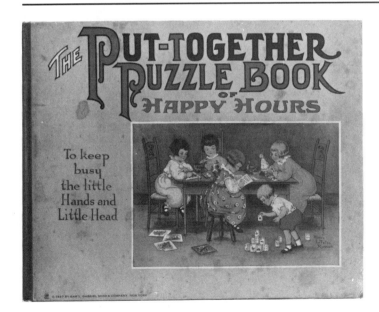

Fig. 16-8. *Put-Together Puzzle Book of Happy Hours*. Samuel Gabriel Sons & Co., New York, N.Y. Copyright 1927. 8½″ × 11″ book with 12 pages of uncolored pictures, and 12 gummed pages of colored pieces to be cut out and glued to the pictures.

297

Fig. 16-9. *Little Golden ABC.* Little Golden Book no. 101. Simon & Schuster, New York, N.Y. Copyright 1951. 8″ × 6½″ book, with 28 pages. Inside back cover has frame puzzle, 8″ × 6″, 12 die-cut cardboard pieces, with one figure piece.

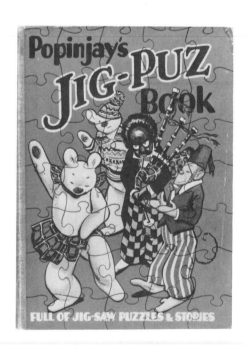

Fig. 16-10. *Popinjay's Jig-Puz Book.* John Leng & Co., Ltd., London, England. 1930s. 10″ × 7½″ book, with 10 pages. Five pages hold die-cut cardboard frame tray puzzles, each 8″ × 6¼″, 48 pieces. Puzzles include: 1) *The Clockwork Fury,* 2) *Order of the Bath* (illustrated in color section), 3) *Mister Whiskery Rabbit,* 4) *What a Picnic!,* and 5) *Wogga's Own Island.*

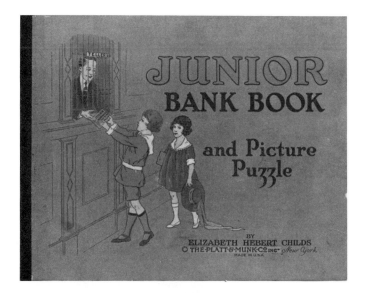

Fig. 16-11. *Junior Bank Book and Picture Puzzle*. Platt & Munk Co., Inc., New York, N.Y. 1920s. 6½″ × 8¼″ book, with six pages. Four pages have slots for coins, to be covered by gummed paper pieces that form 5¼″ × 6½″ puzzles. (One page is illustrated in Chapter 1.) Cardboard box, 7″ × 8¾″. Author is Elizabeth Hebert Childs. Books with intact puzzles are rare, as the puzzles were usually torn when the coins were removed.

Fig. 16-12. *Murder By the Stars*. Mystery-Jig series. Einson-Freeman Co., Inc., Long Island City, N.Y. 1933. 14″ × 20″, 300 die-cut pieces, including figure pieces. Puzzle is illustrated in color section. Cardboard box, 9¼″ × 7″. Contains 8-page booklet with story by Arthur Houston, and solution in invisible ink that appears when exposed to heat.

Fig. 16-13. *Cross Examination*. Mystic Jig no. 1. World Syndicate Publishing Co., Cleveland, Ohio, and New York, N.Y. Copyright 1933. 11¾″ × 14¾″, 204 die-cut cardboard pieces. Cardboard box, 8½″ × 5¾″. Contains 30-page book with story by John Varley.

Fig. 16-14. *Case of the Duplicate Door*. Mystery Puzzle of the Month no. 2. Pearl Publishing Co., Brooklyn, N.Y. 1940s. 10½″ × 13½″, 208 die-cut cardboard pieces. Cardboard box, 10¼″ × 5¼″. Contains 16-page booklet with story by Helen McCloy and solution in mirror printing.

Fig. 16-15. *Man from U.N.C.L.E. Mystery Jigsaw Puzzle.* Milton Bradley Co., Springfield, Mass. Copyright 1965. 14″ × 24″, 612 die-cut cardboard pieces. Cardboard box, 10″ × 11¼″. Contains 8-page story booklet, with solution concealed in uncut pages.

▪ Puzzle Games

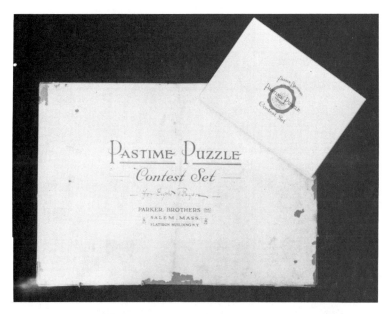

Fig. 16-16. *Contest Set for Eight Players.* Pastime series. Parker Brothers, Inc., Salem, Mass. 1932. Set of eight hand-cut wood puzzles, each 3½″ × 5½″, 30 pieces, including figure pieces, with 3½″ × 5¼″ cardboard box. All contained in cardboard box, 7¾″ × 11″. Set includes: 1) *Return from Hunt,* 2) *Just in Time,* 3) *On the Run,* 4) *Well Over,* 5) *Arrival of the Hounds,* 6) *In Full Cry,* 7) *Three Jolly Huntsmen,* 8) *Hacking Home.* Parker Brothers also made contest sets for four or twelve players.

Fig. 16-17. *Contest Set.* L. Bamberger & Co., Newark, N.J. 1932. Set of four hand-cut plywood puzzles, each 5½″ × 7¾″, approx. 75 pieces, including figure pieces, with 4″ × 5″ cardboard box. All contained in wood box, 8½″ × 10½″. Untitled puzzles all show coaching scenes by Arthur Birch.

Fig. 16-18. *Budge: Ships.* Oxford Specialty Co., Boston, Mass. Copyright 1933. 17″ × 17″, 288 die-cut cardboard pieces. Cardboard box, 5″ × 17½″. Contains instructions for four players to race to assemble their quarters first.

Fig. 16-19. *Eureko!* Graphicut Corp., New York, N.Y. Copyright 1942. Set of four die-cut cardboard frame-tray puzzles, each 13″ × 10″, 36 pieces. Cardboard box, 10¼″ × 13½″. Contains dice, markers, and rules for playing several bingo-type games with puzzle pieces.

Fig. 16-20. *Jig Chase.* Game Makers, Inc., Long Island City, N.Y. 1930s. Set of four die-cut cardboard puzzles, each 2½″ × 23¼″, approx. 30 pieces. Cardboard box, 7¾″ × 10½″. Contains instructions for speed contest for four players.

Fig. 16-21. *Jolly Faces Game.* Ideal Book Builders, Chicago, Ill. Patented 1912. Set of four die-cut cardboard form board puzzles, each 8″ × 5¼″, 4 pieces. Pieces are interchangeable between puzzles, to make metamorphic characters. Cardboard box, 8½″ × 8″, with one guide picture. Set includes: 1) Clown, 2) Grandpa, 3) Boy, 4) Cry baby.

Fig. 16-22. *Situation 7.* Parker Brothers, Inc., Salem, Mass. Copyright 1969. Set of two round die-cut cardboard puzzles, each 19″ diameter, 90 pieces. Cardboard box, 10″ × 20″. Contains playing board and implements for game where each player races to complete puzzle without having pieces claimed by opposing players.

Fig. 16-23. *Party Bridge Play.* Ely Culbertson. Copyright 1933. 6″ × 8″, 50 hand-cut plywood pieces. Cardboard box, 6½″ × 8½″. Was used in conjunction with bridge game.

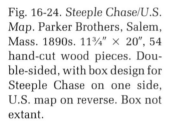

Fig. 16-24. *Steeple Chase/U.S. Map.* Parker Brothers, Salem, Mass. 1890s. 11¾″ × 20″, 54 hand-cut wood pieces. Double-sided, with box design for Steeple Chase on one side, U.S. map on reverse. Box not extant.

Fig. 16-25. *$500.00 Jig Saw Contest.* Fawcett Publications Inc., Minneapolis, Minn. 1933. 11½″ × 17½″, 205 die-cut cardboard pieces, including figure pieces. Cardboard box, 10″ × 5½″. Contest was to select a title for the picture on the puzzle.

▪ Other Dual-Purpose Puzzles

Fig. 16-26. *Cross-Word Jumbles.* Hall Brothers, Inc., Kansas City, Mo. 1930s. 9″ × 9″, 73 die-cut rectangular cardboard pieces. Reversible with Corot painting on one side, completed crossword puzzle on the other. Cardboard box, 9¼″ × 9¼″. Contains clues for crossword puzzle.

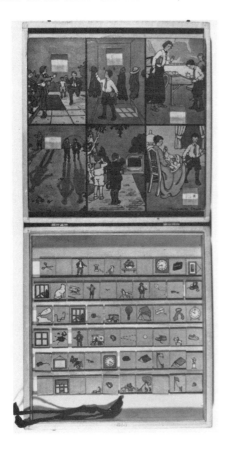

Fig. 16-27. Picture boards for educational testing. C. H. Stoelting Co., Chicago, Ill. Copyright 1918. Set of two hand-cut plywood form boards, each 10″ × 10½″, 5 and 6 pieces. Wood box, 11¾″ × 11¼″. Contains 60 square pieces that can be fitted to make appropriate or inappropriate pictures.

Fig. 16-28. Travel set of Interlox puzzles. Madmar Quality Co., Utica, N.Y. 1930s. Set of hand-cut plywood puzzles, each 5″ × 6½″, 50 pieces, with 4″ × 7¾″ cardboard box. All contained in trunk-like pressboard box, 5½″ × 8¼″. Set includes: 1) *Back from Trenton*, 2) *Mr. Turtle*, 3) *Raggedy Ann*, 4) *Nevada Falls, Yosemite*.

Fig. 16-29. *Jigolette Jig Saw Puzzle for Travel and Home.* Emery Products Co., New York, N.Y. Circa 1933. Set of two hand-cut plywood puzzles, each 4″ × 5½″, approx. 75 pieces. Book-like cardboard box, 8″ × 5¼″. Contains tray to hold an assembled puzzle.

Fig. 16-32. *Photographic Jig-Saw Puzzle.* Eastman Kodak Stores. 1930s. 12″ × 10″, 260 hand-cut plywood pieces, made from photo enlargement. Cardboard box, 8¼″ × 8¼″.

Fig. 16-30. *Comic Jig-Saw Puzzle with Candy.* R. L. Albert & Son, New York, N.Y. 1950s. 3¾″ × 5¾″, 15 die-cut cardboard pieces. Glassine envelope, 4″ × 6″. Contains plastic container of candy beads.

Fig. 16-33. *Jigsaw Puzzle Standees.* Capitol Publishing Co., Inc., New York, N.Y. 1950s. Set of four die-cut cardboard form board puzzles, each 10″ × 10″, 8 pieces. Cardboard box, 10½″ × 10½″, with four guide pictures. Pieces are figures with cardboard stands so they can be used as play figures.

Fig. 16-31. *Jig Saw Puzzle Enlargement.* E. J. Curtis, Inc., Pittsfield, Mass. 1930s. Original puzzle not extant. Cardboard box, 6¾″ × 5½″. (Courtesy of the Siegels)

Fig. 16-34. *Mary Had a Little Lamb*. Kiddie Puzzle Plaques series. Mayfair Games, New York, N.Y. Copyright 1936. Frame tray puzzle 6½″ × 8″, 8 hand-cut plywood pieces. Can be hung as a plaque on the wall.

▪ Puzzle Making Supplies and Ephemera

Fig. 16-35. *Stick-On Without Paste Picture Puzzles*. Built-Rite series. Warren Paper Products, Lafayette, Ind. Circa 1961. Set of four gummed paper pictures and four cardboard backs, all die-cut to matching patterns, so user can create own puzzles. Each puzzle is 6¾″ × 5½″, 12 pieces. Cardboard box, 7½″ × 11½″. Set includes: 1) Boy surfing, 2) Hula girl, 3) Eskimo boy fishing, 4) Girl and totem pole. Serial no. 1149:44.

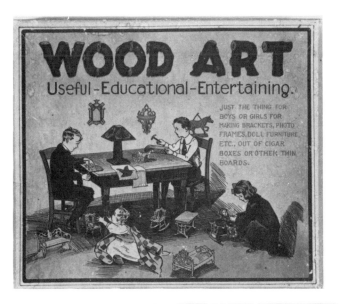

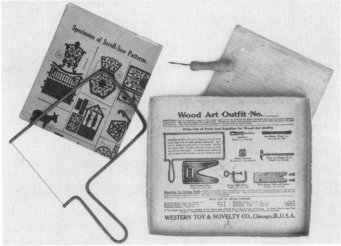

Fig. 16-36. *Wood Art Outfit*. Western Toy & Novelty Co., Chicago, Ill. Circa 1900. Cardboard box, 7½″ × 9″. Contains fret saw, awl, wood, patterns.

Fig. 16-37. *Table Top Workshop*. Parker Brothers, Inc., Salem, Mass. Copyright 1962. Cardboard box, 12¾″ × 16¾″. Contains fret saw, blades, bird's mouth and clamp, blank uncut cardboard, box of crayons, instructions.

309

Fig. 16-39. *Victory Catalog No. 805.* G. J. Hayter & Co. Ltd. Bournemouth, England. 1958. 11¼″ × 8¾″, 36-page booklet. Describes children's and adults' puzzles, and other games.

Fig. 16-38. *Catalog of Pastime Picture Puzzles.* Parker Brothers, Inc., Salem, Mass. Circa 1950. 8½″ × 5½″, 28-page booklet. Describes over 400 puzzle subjects, ranging in size from 65 to 1200 pieces.

Fig. 16-40. Nu-Friend Puzzles Sign. Nu-Friend Puzzle Co., Andover, Mass. 1930s. 8″ × 9¾″ partially cut plywood puzzle, mounted on masonite board, 13¾″ × 16″.

Fig. 16-41. Duo-Jig Poster. R. M. Sales Corp., New York, N.Y. Circa 1933. 11″ × 14½″ cardboard poster, advertising the week's double puzzle.

Fig. 16-42. August 1933 issue of *Woman's Home Companion*. Crowell Publishing Co., Springfield, Ohio. 13¾″ × 10¾″. Cover illustration by Diana Thorne.

17 PUZZLES FOR THE FUTURE

ALTHOUGH THIS GUIDE focuses on puzzles produced before 1970, new puzzles continue to appear by the thousands every year. This offers quite an opportunity for the forward-looking collector. You don't have to decide on the spot at an antique show whether or not to buy a puzzle that might turn up only once in a few years. Instead, you can browse retail shops that have dozens of each item and buy at your own pace. If you are lucky you'll pick puzzles that will be in great demand by the time you retire. And even if you don't want to wait that long, you can still enjoy your puzzles in the meantime.

The puzzles in this chapter represent a personal and idiosyncratic selection of puzzles that will be valued for years to come. The principal criteria for selection are visual appeal, craftsmanship, and potential future value. And, of course, a few are here just because the author thinks they are "neat." This last category includes a few puzzles where the pictorial character is achieved through the use of several different types of woods, rather than from a print.

All the puzzles in this chapter have been produced in the 1980s, and most are still available for purchase through normal retail outlets. For this chapter, the Price Guide gives retail price rather than current value on the antique market. The puzzles in this chapter are divided into the following categories:

- Wood puzzles, for both adults and children. Some of these are sold in stores, but the custom-cut puzzles for adults must be ordered directly from the makers.

- Die-cut puzzles, for both adults and children, all available in stores.

- Unusual puzzles, including some whose purpose is almost entirely decorative.

Within each category, puzzles are listed alphabetically by manufacturer.

▪ Wood Puzzles

Fig. 17-1. *Coughing Bear.* J. C. Ayer & Co., Salem, Mass. 14½″ × 10½″, 375 plywood pieces, including figure pieces, cut by water jet. Cardboard box, 9½″ × 7½″.

Fig. 17-2. *Mount Katahdin.* L. L. Bean, Inc., Freeport, Me. (Manufactured by Aptus, Rochester, N.Y.) 8″ × 10″, 120 plywood pieces, cut by water jet. Wood box, 4¾″ × 6½″.

Fig. 17-3. *A Rare Beauty.* F. A. Bourke, Inc., Middlebury, Vt. 15″ × 12″, 365 hand-cut cherry plywood pieces, including figure pieces and irregular edge. Wood box. Artist is Sandra Stevens. (Photo by Tad Merrick)

Fig. 17-4. [*Fishing*]. John Deere, Moline, Ill. (Manufactured by Aptus, Rochester, N.Y.) 8″ × 10″, 120 plywood pieces, cut by water jet. Wood box, 4¾″ × 6½″.

Fig. 17-5. *Mickey Mouse Picture Cubes.* Hermann Eichhorn, Egglham, West Germany. 4½″ × 6″, 12 wood cubes that make six different pictures. Wood and cardboard suitcase-type box, 5½″ × 7″. Contains six guide pictures showing: 1) Mickey in the jungle, 2) Mickey and Donald Duck in dirigible, 3) Donald and family at beach, 4) Mickey and Donald playing cowboys and Indians, 5) Three little pigs, 6) Dumbo, Huey, Dewey, and Louie.

Fig. 17-6. *Tyger Tyger.* Elms, Inc., Harrison, Me. 16″ × 30″, approx. 625 hand-cut okoume plywood pieces, including figure pieces, irregular edge. Cardboard box, 11¼″ × 11¼″. Artist is Barbara Wallace. (Courtesy of Elms, Inc.)

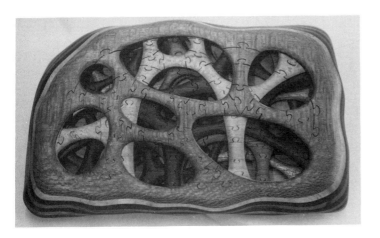

Fig. 17-7. *Bones Matrix.* FryeWeaver Puzzles, Albuquerque, N.M. Frame puzzle, 7″ × 11″, approx. 640 hand-cut wood pieces, irregular edge. Six layers use (from top down): lacewood, birdseye maple, padauk, teak, lauan, and imbuia. (Photo by FryeWeaver Puzzles)

Fig. 17-8. *Homesteaders.*
Glendex Shape-Cut series. J.
S. Guiles, Sarasota, Fla. 11″ ×
13″, 360 hand-cut plywood
pieces. Cardboard box, 6¾″
× 8¾″. (Photo by J. S. Guiles)

Fig. 17-9. *Lighthouse Point.*
Capt. G. G. Ely Kirk, Arlington, Va. Approx. 18″ × 24″,
750 hand-cut plywood pieces,
including figure pieces. Wood
box. (Photo by Capt. Kirk)

Fig. 17-10. [*Giraffes*]. George Luck, Martock,
Somerset, England. Frame tray puzzle 10″ ×
8″, 20 hand-cut plywood pieces. Cardboard box
with plastic lid, 10¼″ × 8¼″.

Fig. 17-11. *Timepiece or Piece of Time.* Steve Malavolta, Albuquerque, N.M. Three-layer puzzle, 9″ × 12″, approx. 350 hand-cut wood pieces. Three layers and base use: wenge, maple, imbuia, padauk. Glass cover. (Photo by Steve Malavolta)

Fig. 17-12. [*Train*]. Nashco Products Inc., Scranton, Pa. Frame tray puzzle 8¾″ × 11¾″, 10 hand-cut and hand-painted plywood pieces.

Fig. 17-13. [*Hen on Nest*]. Helen Seymour, Plainsboro, N.J. Layered frame tray puzzle 10″ × 12″, 43 hand-cut hardwood pieces (cherry, oak, walnut, poplar, teak). Three layers show hen, eggs, and chicks.

Fig. 17-14. [*Ice Cream Stand*]. Victory Series. G. J. Hayter & Co., Ltd., subsidiary of J. W. Spear & Sons, Ltd., Bournemouth, England. 8¾″ × 6¾″, 30 hand-cut plywood pieces. Cardboard box, 10″ × 8″, with guide picture.

Fig. 17-15. *A Midsummer Night's Dream*. Stave Puzzles, Inc., Norwich, Vt. 14″ × 15¾″, 550 hand-colored and hand-cut mahogany plywood pieces, including figure pieces, in two layers, irregular edge. Cardboard box, 7″ × 10″. Limited edition print by Henri Lousteau. (Courtesy of Stave Puzzles, Inc.)

▪ Die-Cut Puzzles

Fig. 17-16. *The Blue Boat*, by Winslow Homer. Battle Road Press, Lexington, Mass. 18″ × 24″, 500 die-cut cardboard pieces. Cardboard box, 14″ × 14″, with guide picture.

Fig. 17-17. *Return of the Jedi: Darth Vader.* Fundimensions, Division of CPG Products Corp., Mt. Clemens, Mich. Frame tray puzzle 11″ × 8″, 15 die-cut cardboard pieces.

Fig. 17-18. *Mickey Mouse.* Jaymar Specialty Co., Rochester, N.Y. Frame tray puzzle, 11½″ × 9¼″, 8 die-cut pressboard pieces. (Courtesy of Jaymar Specialty Co.)

Fig. 17-19. *Choo Choo.* Lauri, Inc., Phillips-Avon, Me. Frame puzzle, 8¼″ × 11½″, 13 die-cut crepe rubber pieces. Cardboard box, 8½″ × 12″.

Fig. 17-20. *Going Away for the Weekend*. Dr. Seuss series. Happy House Group, Random House, Lafayette, Ind. 11½″ × 16¼″, 60 die-cut cardboard pieces. Cardboard box, 7¼″ × 10¼″, with guide picture. (Courtesy of Random House)

Fig. 17-21. *Barbie*. Golden series. Western Publishing Co. Inc., Racine, Wisc. Frame tray puzzle 11″ × 8″, 11 die-cut cardboard pieces.

▪ Unusual Puzzles

Fig. 17-22. *Mickey Mouse.* Apollo-Sha Co., Japan. 2½″ × 2¼″, 143 plywood pieces, cut by water jet. Plastic case, 4″ × 4¼″, containing small tweezers, is enclosed in cardboard box, 4¼″ × 4½″.

Fig. 17-23. [*Cat with Kittens*]. Atelier BSB, Paris, France. 6″ × 15½″, 15 hand-cut and hand-painted wood pieces. Cardboard box, 6½″ × 15½″.

Fig. 17-24. *Christmas Jigsaw Puzzle.* Karl Bissinger French Confections, St. Louis, Mo. 10″ × 8″, 19 die-cut chocolate pieces. Cardboard box, 5″ × 15¼″.

Fig. 17-25. *Circus Day*. Boo Chee Toys, Athens, Ohio. Frame tray puzzle, 4¼″ × 3″, 17 hand-cut pieces of three species of hardwood.

Fig. 17-26. [*Space Shuttle*]. Karnan, Sweden. 2½″ × 2¼″, 99 plywood pieces, cut by water jet. Plastic packet, 4¼″ × 4″.

Fig. 17-27. *Stan Musial*. Diamond King series. Leaf, Inc., Bannockburn, Ill. 11″ × 8″, 63 die-cut cardboard pieces. Pieces are printed in sets of three on 2½″ × 3½″ cards, which are inserts in baseball card packages. Slight differences in registration make it difficult to construct a perfect puzzle.

Fig. 17-28. *Mental Blocks: The Block Party.* Perigee Books, Putnam Publishing Group, New York, N.Y. 7¼″ × 7¼″, 16 hollow cardboard cubes whose six sides form a single continuous picture. Artists are Jacklyn Lambert and Jeffrey Samborski.

Fig. 17-29. *Murder Can Be Comic.* BePuzzled Mystery Puzzle Series. Lombard Marketing, Inc., Bloomfield, Conn. 20″ × 20″, 506 die-cut cardboard pieces. Cardboard box, 11″ × 8¾″. Contains 8-page booklet with story by Mike W. Barr, solution in mirror printing.

Fig. 17-30. *Can Can!* Monkey Puzzle, Norfolk, England. 8½″ × 28″, 52 hand-cut and hand-painted plywood pieces. Cardboard box with plastic top, 10½″ × 14″. Artist is Carol Leith.

Fig. 17-31. *Desk Catty.* Richard Rothbard, Sugarloaf, N.Y. 5½″ × 9½″, 3 hand-cut mahogany pieces, with holes for paper clips, pencils, and stamps.

Fig. 17-32. *Schmuzzle Puzzle for Kids*. Schmuzzles, Inc., Chicago, Ill. 11″ × 14″, 58 die-cut cardboard pieces. Except at the edges, all pieces have identical shape with salamander design on reverse. Cardboard box, 8½″ × 10″. Contains 16-page instruction book on tesselated figures.

Fig. 17-33. *Pieces in Place*. Woodkrafter Kits, Yarmouth, Me. 6″ × 4″, 15 die-cut cardboard pieces, shrink wrapped to postcard backing, 6½″ × 4½″

Price Guide

THIS GUIDE contains prices for the puzzles that are described in detail in Chapters 6 through 17. All prices refer to puzzles that are *guaranteed complete and in very good condition*. This means that the puzzle has *all* the pieces, the original box (or envelope) and label, and any original inserts, and that none of these show any significant damage. If these criteria are not met, the price should be *substantially lower*; consult Chapter 4 for details on how defects affect value. (Even though a few puzzles pictured in this book are not complete and in very good condition, the prices listed below are for examples that meet these criteria.)

Price ranges are used to reflect factors like geographical variation in the market. Prices reflect market conditions in early 1990. They should be used only as a guide. They do not represent an offer to buy or sell. Neither the author nor the publisher assumes any liability for losses related to the use of this book, or to any errors contained in it.

CHAPTER 6

Fig. 6-1. $350–450
Fig. 6-2. $7–9
Fig. 6-3. $250–300
Fig. 6-4. $325–375
Fig. 6-5. $200–250
Fig. 6-6. $40–50
Fig. 6-7. $25–30
Fig. 6-8. $15–20
Fig. 6-9. $200–250
Fig. 6-10. $400–500
Fig. 6-11. $35–45
Fig. 6-12. $70–90
Fig. 6-13. $35–40
Fig. 6-14. $400–500
Fig. 6-15. $125–150
Fig. 6-16. $400–500
Fig. 6-17. $20–25
Fig. 6-18. $75–100
Fig. 6-19. $50–65
Fig. 6-20. $30–40
Fig. 6-21. $8–10
Fig. 6-22. $275–325

Fig. 6-23. $150–200
Fig. 6-24. $200–250
Fig. 6-25. $75–100
Fig. 6-26. $75–100
Fig. 6-27. $200–250
Fig. 6-28. $30–40
Fig. 6-29. $15–25
Fig. 6-30. $8–12
Fig. 6-31. $5–7
Fig. 6-32. $75–100
Fig. 6-33. $60–80
Fig. 6-34. $50–60
Fig. 6-35. $6–8
Fig. 6-36. $125–150
Fig. 6-37. $250–300
Fig. 6-38. $400–500
Fig. 6-39. $100–125
Fig. 6-40. $250–300
Fig. 6-41. $35–45
Fig. 6-42. $100–125
Fig. 6-43. $10–14
Fig. 6-44. $14–18
Fig. 6-45. $14–18

Fig. 6-46. $25–35
Fig. 6-47. $14–18
Fig. 6-48. $175–225
Fig. 6-49. $100–150
Fig. 6-50. $100–125
Fig. 6-51. $100–150
Fig. 6-52. $80–100
Fig. 6-53. $40–50
Fig. 6-54. $30–40
Fig. 6-55. $10–14
Fig. 6-56. $14–18
Fig. 6-57. $8–10

CHAPTER 7

Fig. 7-1. $200–250
Fig. 7-2. $400–500
Fig. 7-3. $200–250
Fig. 7-4. $50–75
Fig. 7-5. $175–225
Fig. 7-6. $65–85
Fig. 7-7. $6–8
Fig. 7-8. $3–5
Fig. 7-9. $10–14

Fig. 7-10. $175−225
Fig. 7-11. $8−12
Fig. 7-12. $12−15
Fig. 7-13. $15−20
Fig. 7-14. $125−150
Fig. 7-15. $10−12
Fig. 7-16. $200−250
Fig. 7-17. $45−60
Fig. 7-18. $75−90
Fig. 7-19. $50−60
Fig. 7-20. $12−16
Fig. 7-21. $20−25
Fig. 7-22. $70−85
Fig. 7-23. $8−10
Fig. 7-24. $75−90
Fig. 7-25. $14−18
Fig. 7-26. $6−8
Fig. 7-27. $100−125
Fig. 7-28. $35−45
Fig. 7-29. $20−25
Fig. 7-30. $8−10
Fig. 7-31. $25−30
Fig. 7-32. $18−24
Fig. 7-33. $18−24
Fig. 7-34. $15−20
Fig. 7-35. $300−350

CHAPTER 8

Fig. 8-1. $75−90
Fig. 8-2. $100−125
Fig. 8-3. $90−110
Fig. 8-4. $125−150
Fig. 8-5. $18−24
Fig. 8-6. $35−45
Fig. 8-7. $20−25
Fig. 8-8. $7−9
Fig. 8-9. $12−16
Fig. 8-10. $60−75
Fig. 8-11. $16−20
Fig. 8-12. $8−10
Fig. 8-13. $5−7
Fig. 8-14. $25−35
Fig. 8-15. $35−45
Fig. 8-16. $30−35
Fig. 8-17. $10−15
Fig. 8-18. $20−25
Fig. 8-19. $70−85
Fig. 8-20. $16−20
Fig. 8-21. $25−30
Fig. 8-22. $16−20
Fig. 8-23. $12−16
Fig. 8-24. $12−16
Fig. 8-25. $40−50
Fig. 8-26. $250−300

Fig. 8-27. $100−125
Fig. 8-28. $60−75
Fig. 8-29. $30−40
Fig. 8-30. $30−40
Fig. 8-31. $8−12
Fig. 8-32. $16−20
Fig. 8-33. $100−120
Fig. 8-34. $75−90
Fig. 8-35. $12−16
Fig. 8-36. $70−90
Fig. 8-37. $80−100
Fig. 8-38. $14−18
Fig. 8-39. $18−24
Fig. 8-40. $35−45
Fig. 8-41. $70−90
Fig. 8-42. $20−25
Fig. 8-43. $25−30

CHAPTER 9

Fig. 9-1. $25−30
Fig. 9-2. $12−16
Fig. 9-3. $30−35
Fig. 9-4. $20−25
Fig. 9-5. $20−25
Fig. 9-6. $30−35
Fig. 9-7. $60−80
Fig. 9-8. $90−110
Fig. 9-9. $18−24
Fig. 9-10. $8−10
Fig. 9-11. $14−18
Fig. 9-12. $25−30
Fig. 9-13. $20−25
Fig. 9-14. $8−10
Fig. 9-15. $8−10
Fig. 9-16. $16−20
Fig. 9-17. $80−100
Fig. 9-18. $25−30
Fig. 9-19. $35−40
Fig. 9-20. $35−40
Fig. 9-21. $12−16
Fig. 9-22. $18−24
Fig. 9-23. $16−20
Fig. 9-24. $10−14
Fig. 9-25. $10−14
Fig. 9-26. $5−7
Fig. 9-27. $10−14
Fig. 9-28. $14−18
Fig. 9-29. $100−125
Fig. 9-30. $35−45
Fig. 9-31. $16−20
Fig. 9-32. $12−16
Fig. 9-33. $100−125
Fig. 9-34. $12−16
Fig. 9-35. $35−40

Fig. 9-36. $14−18
Fig. 9-37. $25−30
Fig. 9-38. $4−6
Fig. 9-39. $20−25
Fig. 9-40. $25−30
Fig. 9-41. $3−5
Fig. 9-42. $30−35
Fig. 9-43. $30−35
Fig. 9-44. $100−125
Fig. 9-45. $30−35
Fig. 9-46. $30−35
Fig. 9-47. $30−35
Fig. 9-48. $100−125
Fig. 9-49. $350−450
Fig. 9-50. $100−125
Fig. 9-51. $200−250
Fig. 9-52. $20−25
Fig. 9-53. $4−6
Fig. 9-54. $35−40
Fig. 9-55. $3−5
Fig. 9-56. $8−10
Fig. 9-57. $14−18
Fig. 9-58. $14−18
Fig. 9-59. $100−125
Fig. 9-60. $35−45
Fig. 9-61. $35−40
Fig. 9-62. $150−200
Fig. 9-63. $25−30
Fig. 9-64. $18−24
Fig. 9-65. $7−9
Fig. 9-66. $25−30
Fig. 9-67. $4−6
Fig. 9-68. $16−20
Fig. 9-69. $40−50
Fig. 9-70. $16−20
Fig. 9-71. $35−45
Fig. 9-72. $30−35
Fig. 9-73. $35−40
Fig. 9-74. $6−8
Fig. 9-75. $2−4
Fig. 9-76. $35−40

CHAPTER 10

Fig. 10-1. $20−25
Fig. 10-2. $20−25
Fig. 10-3. $14−18
Fig. 10-4. $12−16
Fig. 10-5. $16−20
Fig. 10-6. $18−24
Fig. 10-7. $40−50
Fig. 10-8. $20−25
Fig. 10-9. $20−25
Fig. 10-10. $10−14
Fig. 10-11. $25−30

Fig. 10-12. $20−25
Fig. 10-13. $40−50
Fig. 10-14. $10−12
Fig. 10-15. $30−35
Fig. 10-16. $75−100
Fig. 10-17. $25−30
Fig. 10-18. $30−35
Fig. 10-19. $40−50
Fig. 10-20. $25−30
Fig. 10-21. $35−45
Fig. 10-22. $20−25
Fig. 10-23. $6−8
Fig. 10-24. $100−125
Fig. 10-25. $10−14
Fig. 10-26. $40−50
Fig. 10-27. $40−50
Fig. 10-28. $5−7
Fig. 10-29. $75−90
Fig. 10-30. $90−110
Fig. 10-31. $20−25
Fig. 10-32. $35−45
Fig. 10-33. $18−24
Fig. 10-34. $12−16

CHAPTER 11

Fig. 11-1. $160−200
Fig. 11-2. $275−325
Fig. 11-3. $225−275
Fig. 11-4. $125−175
Fig. 11-5. $18−24
Fig. 11-6. $25−30
Fig. 11-7. $125−150
Fig. 11-8. $200−250
Fig. 11-9. $45−60
Fig. 11-10. $60−75
Fig. 11-11. $60−75
Fig. 11-12. $60−75
Fig. 11-13. $35−45
Fig. 11-14. $125−150
Fig. 11-15. $45−55
Fig. 11-16. $16−20
Fig. 11-17. $16−20
Fig. 11-18. $12−16
Fig. 11-19. $125−175
Fig. 11-20. $150−175
Fig. 11-21. $8−10
Fig. 11-22. $250−300
Fig. 11-23. $40−50
Fig. 11-24. $15−18
Fig. 11-25. $100−125
Fig. 11-26. $14−18
Fig. 11-27. $30−35
Fig. 11-28. $20−25

CHAPTER 12

Fig. 12-1. $12−16
Fig. 12-2. $14−18
Fig. 12-3. $12−16
Fig. 12-4. $35−40
Fig. 12-5. $10−14
Fig. 12-6. $3−5
Fig. 12-7. $300−350
Fig. 12-8. $30−35
Fig. 12-9. $125−150
Fig. 12-10. $125−150
Fig. 12-11. $40−50
Fig. 12-12. $250−300
Fig. 12-13. $150−200
Fig. 12-14. $90−110
Fig. 12-15. $30−40
Fig. 12-16. $25−35
Fig. 12-17. $12−16
Fig. 12-18. $10−14
Fig. 12-19. $14−18
Fig. 12-20. $35−40
Fig. 12-21. $8−10
Fig. 12-22. $8−10
Fig. 12-23. $35−40
Fig. 12-24. $25−30
Fig. 12-25. $8−10
Fig. 12-26. $45−60
Fig. 12-27. $125−150
Fig. 12-28. $40−50
Fig. 12-29. $25−30
Fig. 12-30. $12−15

CHAPTER 13

Fig. 13-1. $80−100
Fig. 13-2. $60−80
Fig. 13-3. $7−9
Fig. 13-4. $10−12
Fig. 13-5. $5−7
Fig. 13-6. $4−6
Fig. 13-7. $16−20
Fig. 13-8. $18−24
Fig. 13-9. $7−9
Fig. 13-10. $10−12
Fig. 13-11. $30−40
Fig. 13-12. $40−50
Fig. 13-13. $14−18
Fig. 13-14. $20−25
Fig. 13-15. $20−25
Fig. 13-16. $14−18
Fig. 13-17. $60−80
Fig. 13-18. $10−12
Fig. 13-19. $16−20
Fig. 13-20. $35−45
Fig. 13-21. $16−20

Fig. 13-22. $35−40
Fig. 13-23. $18−24
Fig. 13-24. $16−20
Fig. 13-25. $20−25
Fig. 13-26. $30−35
Fig. 13-27. $3−5
Fig. 13-28. $35−40
Fig. 13-29. $16−20
Fig. 13-30. $12−16
Fig. 13-31. $40−55
Fig. 13-32. $35−45
Fig. 13-33. $500−600
Fig. 13-34. $10−12
Fig. 13-35. $25−35
Fig. 13-36. $18−24
Fig. 13-37. $35−45
Fig. 13-38. $12−16
Fig. 13-39. $35−45
Fig. 13-40. $10−12
Fig. 13-41. $45−55
Fig. 13-42. $20−25
Fig. 13-43. $50−60
Fig. 13-44. $35−40
Fig. 13-45. $16−20
Fig. 13-46. $12−16
Fig. 13-47. $25−35
Fig. 13-48. $20−25
Fig. 13-49. $16−20
Fig. 13-50. $20−25
Fig. 13-51. $250−350
Fig. 13-52. $8−10
Fig. 13-53. $25−35
Fig. 13-54. $45−60
Fig. 13-55. $18−24
Fig. 13-56. $16−20
Fig. 13-57. $35−45
Fig. 13-58. $16−20
Fig. 13-59. $16−20
Fig. 13-60. $70−85
Fig. 13-61. $16−20
Fig. 13-62. $12−16
Fig. 13-63. $12−16
Fig. 13-64. $18−24
Fig. 13-65. $16−20
Fig. 13-66. $35−45
Fig. 13-67. $14−18
Fig. 13-68. $20−25
Fig. 13-69. $18−24

CHAPTER 14

Fig. 14-1. $18−24
Fig. 14-2. $14−18
Fig. 14-3. $25−30
Fig. 14-4. $18−24

Fig. 14-5. $8−10
Fig. 14-6. $10−12
Fig. 14-7. $16−20
Fig. 14-8. $50−60
Fig. 14-9. $12−16
Fig. 14-10. $18−24
Fig. 14-11. $16−20
Fig. 14-12. $16−20
Fig. 14-13. $30−40
Fig. 14-14. $10−12
Fig. 14-15. $35−45
Fig. 14-16. $20−25
Fig. 14-17. $10−12
Fig. 14-18. $3−5
Fig. 14-19. $20−25
Fig. 14-20. $18−24
Fig. 14-21. $12−16
Fig. 14-22. $12−16
Fig. 14-23. $60−75
Fig. 14-24. $10−12
Fig. 14-25. $12−16
Fig. 14-26. $5−7
Fig. 14-27. $20−25
Fig. 14-28. $4−6
Fig. 14-29. $25−30
Fig. 14-30. $30−40
Fig. 14-31. $50−60
Fig. 14-32. $50−60
Fig. 14-33. $45−55
Fig. 14-34. $14−18
Fig. 14-35. $16−20
Fig. 14-36. $20−25
Fig. 14-37. $160−180
Fig. 14-38. $10−14
Fig. 14-39. $10−14
Fig. 14-40. $20−25
Fig. 14-41. $50−60
Fig. 14-42. $12−16
Fig. 14-43. $30−35
Fig. 14-44. $25−35
Fig. 14-45. $25−30
Fig. 14-46. $12−16
Fig. 14-47. $10−12
Fig. 14-48. $10−12
Fig. 14-49. $25−35
Fig. 14-50. $12−16
Fig. 14-51. $45−60
Fig. 14-52. $18−24
Fig. 14-53. $30−35
Fig. 14-54. $12−16
Fig. 14-55. $12−16
Fig. 14-56. $10−12
Fig. 14-57. $25−35
Fig. 14-58. $20−25

Fig. 14-59. $12−16
Fig. 14-60. $16−20
Fig. 14-61. $10−12
Fig. 14-62. $14−18
Fig. 14-63. $10−14
Fig. 14-64. $25−30
Fig. 14-65. $12−16
Fig. 14-66. $12−16
Fig. 14-67. $16−20
Fig. 14-68. $14−18
Fig. 14-69. $2−4 each
Fig. 14-70. $8−10
Fig. 14-71. $10−14
Fig. 14-72. $10−14

CHAPTER 15

Fig. 15-1. $2−4
Fig. 15-2. $2−4
Fig. 15-3. $2−4
Fig. 15-4. $4−6
Fig. 15-5. $2−3
Fig. 15-6. $6−8
Fig. 15-7. $7−9
Fig. 15-8. $3−5
Fig. 15-9. $2−3
Fig. 15-10. $2−4
Fig. 15-11. $2−4
Fig. 15-12. $5−7
Fig. 15-13. $4−6
Fig. 15-14. $5−7
Fig. 15-15. $10−14
Fig. 15-16. $14−18
Fig. 15-17. $5−7
Fig. 15-18. $4−6
Fig. 15-19. $2−4
Fig. 15-20. $35−45
Fig. 15-21. $4−6
Fig. 15-22. $2−4
Fig. 15-23. $3−5
Fig. 15-24. $4−5
Fig. 15-25. $5−7
Fig. 15-26. $10−12
Fig. 15-27. $14−18
Fig. 15-28. $12−16
Fig. 15-29. $4−6
Fig. 15-30. $25−30
Fig. 15-31. $4−6
Fig. 15-32. $12−16
Fig. 15-33. $30−35
Fig. 15-34. $4−6
Fig. 15-35. $6−8
Fig. 15-36. $5−7
Fig. 15-37. $5−7
Fig. 15-38. $2−4

Fig. 15-39. $16−20
Fig. 15-40. #1−12, $8−15
        #13−24, $6−10
        #25−31, $8−15
Fig. 15-41. $16−20
Fig. 15-42. $4−6
Fig. 15-43. $10−12
Fig. 15-44. $2−4
Fig. 15-45. $2−4
Fig. 15-46. $6−8
Fig. 15-47. $2−4
Fig. 15-48. $3−5

CHAPTER 16

Fig. 16-1. $8−10
Fig. 16-2. $55−70
Fig. 16-3. $30−35
Fig. 16-4. $6−8
Fig. 16-5. $4−6
Fig. 16-6. $8−10
Fig. 16-7. $10−12
Fig. 16-8. $12−16
Fig. 16-9. $10−14
Fig. 16-10. $100−125
Fig. 16-11. $60−75
Fig. 16-12. $14−18
Fig. 16-13. $14−18
Fig. 16-14. $10−14
Fig. 16-15. $20−25
Fig. 16-16. $50−65
Fig. 16-17. $45−55
Fig. 16-18. $12−16
Fig. 16-19. $16−20
Fig. 16-20. $8−10
Fig. 16-21. $16−20
Fig. 16-22. $10−14
Fig. 16-23. $20−25
Fig. 16-24. $35−45
Fig. 16-25. $5−7
Fig. 16-26. $8−10
Fig. 16-27. $45−60
Fig. 16-28. $50−65
Fig. 16-29. $25−30
Fig. 16-30. $5−7
Fig. 16-31. $16−20
Fig. 16-32. $25−30
Fig. 16-33. $12−16
Fig. 16-34. $12−16
Fig. 16-35. $4−6
Fig. 16-36. $12−16
Fig. 16-37. $18−22
Fig. 16-38. $30−35
Fig. 16-39. $20−25

Fig. 16-40. $16−20
Fig. 16-41. $14−18
Fig. 16-42. $12−16

CHAPTER 17

Fig. 17-1. $220
Fig. 17-2. $16
Fig. 17-3. $786
Fig. 17-4. $22
Fig. 17-5. $12
Fig. 17-6. $700
Fig. 17-7. $610
Fig. 17-8. $275
Fig. 17-9. $375
Fig. 17-10. $14
Fig. 17-11. $750
Fig. 17-12. $10
Fig. 17-13. $45
Fig. 17-14. $14
Fig. 17-15. $2195
Fig. 17-16. $10
Fig. 17-17. $2
Fig. 17-18. $3
Fig. 17-19. $8
Fig. 17-20. $4
Fig. 17-21. $1
Fig. 17-22. $10
Fig. 17-23. $65
Fig. 17-24. $25
Fig. 17-25. $26
Fig. 17-26. $4
Fig. 17-27. $2
Fig. 17-28. $20
Fig. 17-29. $14
Fig. 17-30. $60
Fig. 17-31. $25
Fig. 17-32. $8
Fig. 17-33. $1

COLOR SECTION

Fig. C-1. $400−500
Fig. C-2. $75−100
Fig. C-3. $200−250
Fig. C-4. $50−60

Fig. C-5. $400−500
Fig. C-6. $15−25
Fig. C-7. $14−18
Fig. C-8. $16−20

Fig. C-9. $25−30
Fig. C-10. $45−55
Fig. C-11. $15−20
Fig. C-12. $175−225

Fig. C-13. $30−40
Fig. C-14. $40−50
Fig. C-15. $40−55
Fig. C-16. $75−90

Fig. C-17. $55−65
Fig. C-18. $45−55
Fig. C-19. $14−18
Fig. C-20. $25−30

Fig. C-21. $30−35
Fig. C-22. $50−60
Fig. C-23. $25−30
Fig. C-24. $45−55

Fig. C-25. $10−14
Fig. C-26. $200−250
Fig. C-27. $4−6
Fig. C-28. $100−125

Fig. C-29. $35−45
Fig. C-30. $60−70
Fig. C-31. $40−50
Fig. C-32. $90−110

Fig. C-33. $275−325
Fig. C-34. $325−400
Fig. C-35. $8−10
Fig. C-36. $250−300

Fig. C-37. $550−700
Fig. C-38. $300−350
Fig. C-39. $25−30
Fig. C-40. $6−8

Fig. C-41. $25−30
Fig. C-42. $35−45
Fig. C-43. $30−35
Fig. C-44. $45−60

Fig. C-45. $80−100
Fig. C-46. $300−350
Fig. C-47. $35−45
Fig. C-48. $45−55

Fig. C-49. $80−100
Fig. C-50. $75−90
Fig. C-51. $125−150
Fig. C-52. $16−20

Fig. C-53. $30−35
Fig. C-54. $20−25
Fig. C-55. $25−30
Fig. C-56. $30−40

Fig. C-57. $25−30
Fig. C-58. $16−20
Fig. C-59. $4−6
Fig. C-60. $30−35

Fig. C-61. $100−125
Fig. C-62. $14−18
Fig. C-63. $18−24
Fig. C-64. $10−14

SELECTED BIBLIOGRAPHY

Accorsi, William. *Accorsi Puzzles.* New York: Simon & Schuster, 1978.

Aronson v. White, Vol 13, F. Supp., 913 (1936).

"Art for Puzzles' Sake," *Newsweek*, December 14, 1964, p. 94.

Bekkering, Betsy & Geert. *Stukje Voor Stukje: Geschiedenis van de Legpuzzle in Nederland.* (Piece by Piece: A History of the Jigsaw Puzzle in the Netherlands.) Amsterdam: Van Soeren & Co., 1988.

Berger, Meyer. "Jig Saw," *Good Housekeeping*, August 1944, pp. 24, 161–163.

Bradley, Milton Co. Springfield, MA. Various annual catalogs, circa 1870–1989.

Carver, Sally S. *The American Postcard Guide To Tuck.* Brookline, MA: Carves Cards, 1976.

Clark, Edie. "Passion for Puzzles," *Yankee*, November 1988, pp. 86–93, 156.

Copeland, George, "The Country is Off on a Jig-Saw Jag," *New York Times Magazine*, February 12, 1933, pp. 8, 16.

Dennis, Lee. *Warman's Antique American Games: 1840–1940.* Willow Grove, PA: Warman Publishing Co., 1986.

Falk, Peter H., editor. *Who Was Who in American Art.* Madison, CT: Sound View Press, 1985.

Faurot, W. L. "Jig-Saw Short Cuts," *Popular Science Monthly,* June 1933, pp. 61, 85–87.

Fishbeck, Linda Ellis, "Illustrated Blocks: Art of Child's Play," *Country Home*, December 1986, pp. 12, 14, 42.

Fitch, George, "Picture Puzzles," *Collier's National Weekly*, November 20, 1909, p. 23.

"Fitting It All Together," *The Gazette*, (Bournemouth?) England, May 6, 1972.

Fox, John J. "Parker Pride: Memories of Working Days at Parker Brothers," *Essex Institute Historical Collections*, Vol. 123, No. 2, April 1987, pp. 150–181.

Grismer, Karl H. *Akron and Summit County.* Akron, Ohio: Summit County Historical Society, n.d.

Hannas, Linda. *The English Jigsaw Puzzle: 1760 to 1890.* London: Wayland Publishers, 1972.

————. *The Jigsaw Book.* London: Bellew & Higdon, 1981. Distributed in the U.S. by Dial Press, New York.

————. "When Maps Were Cut Into Pieces," *The Map Collector*, September 1980, pp. 18–20.

Hayter, G. J. & Co., Ltd. Bournemouth, England. Various catalogs, circa 1935–1958.

Hearn, Michael Patrick. *McLoughlin Brothers, Publishers.* New York: Justin G. Schiller, Ltd., 1980.

Hertz, Louis H. *The Toy Collector.* New York: Thomas Y. Crowell Co., 1969; reprinted 1976 by Hawthorn Books, New York.

Hewitt, Karen and Louise Roomet. *Educational Toys in America: 1800 to the Present.* Burlington, VT: University of Vermont, 1979.

"How Jig-Saw Puzzles Are Made by the Million," *Popular Science Monthly*, April 1933, p. 29.

"Jig Saws," *Playthings*, February 1933, pp. 39–40, 96–97.

"Jig-Saw Jag," *Business Week*, January 18, 1933, p. 8.

"Jigsaw Puzzles Go Full Circle," *Business Week*, July 10, 1965, pp. 68, 70.

Jones, David. *Toy With the Idea*. Norfolk, England: Norfolk Museums Service, 1980.

Kaonis, Donna C. "Hood's Sarsaparilla," *Collectors' Showcase*, Vol. 9, No. 4, June 1989, pp. 41–46.

King, Constance Eileen. *The Encyclopedia of Toys*. New York, Crown Publishers, Inc. 1978.

Kleinfeld, Sonny. "A Par Puzzle Isn't Easy to Assemble—Or Easy to Pay For," *Wall Street Journal*, July 27, 1972, p. 1.

Laffin, Pat. "Peter G. Thomson," *Game Researchers' Notes*, February 1988, pp. 5015–5017.

"The Lure of Puzzle Inventing," *Popular Mechanics*, January 1935, pp. 20–23, 128A, 130A.

Madmar Quality Co., Utica, NY. Various annual catalogs, circa 1929–1956.

McCann, Chris. "Building Your Own Miniature Art Gallery with Depression Jigsaw Puzzles," *The Antique Trader*, January 3, 1990, pp. 50–53.

McLoughlin Brothers. New York, NY. Various annual catalogs, 1867–1920.

Nemy, Enid. "Boom in Jigsaw Puzzles: Three Pieces or Enough to Fill A Billiard Table," *New York Times*, December 24, 1966, p. 22.

"New Jag in Jigsaws," *Time*, March 26, 1965, p. 67.

Parker Brothers, Inc. *75 Years of Fun: The Story of Parker Brothers, Inc*. Salem, MA: Parker Brothers, Inc., 1958.

———. *90 Years of Fun*. Salem, MA: Parker Brothers, Inc., 1973.

———. Salem, MA. Various catalogs, 1883–1957.

Perry, L. Day and T. K. Webster, Jr. *Jigsaw Puzzles—And How to Make 'Em*. Chicago: Mack Publications, 1933.

Petrik, Paula. "The House That Parcheesi Built: Selchow & Righter Company," *Business History Review*, vol. 60, Autumn 1986, pp. 410–437.

"Picture Puzzles," *Playthings*, November 1908, p. 34.

Pinsky, Maxine A. *Greenberg's Guide to Marx Toys, Volume I: 1923–1950*, Sykesville, MD: Greenberg Publishing, 1988.

Reed, Walt and Roger. *The Illustrator in America, 1880–1980*. New York: Society of Illustrators, 1984.

"Reports Indicate Extent of Jigsaw Craze," *Toy World*, April 1933, p. 60.

Rinker, Harry L. "Pieces of Yesterday," *Allentown* (PA) *Morning Call*, February 5, 1989, pp. G1-2.

Robertshaw, Ursula. "Playing for a Century," *Illustrated London News*, January 1979, p. 77.

Sabin, Francene and Louis. *The One, The Only, The Original Jigsaw Puzzle Book*. Chicago: Henry Regnery Company, 1977.

Sass, Jeff. "Diversity: A Key to the Strength and Success of Western Publishing Company During 75 Years of Printing and Publishing," *The Westerner* (magazine of Western Publishing), Vol. 3, No. 2, Winter 1982, pp. 2–17.

Schroeder, Joseph T. Jr. *The Wonderful World of Toys, Games, & Dolls 1860–1930*. Northfield, IL: DBI Books, Inc., 1971.

Shea, James J. *It's All in the Game*. New York: G. P. Putnam's Sons, 1960.

Slocum, Jerry and Jack Botermans. *Puzzles Old & New*. Seattle: University of Washington Press, 1986.

Smith, Linda Joan. "Playful Pieces," *Country Home*, December 1988, pp. 114–119, 142.

Smith, Viola A. *A History of the Saalfield Publishing Company*. Unpublished M.A. thesis, Kent State University, 1951.

"Some Facts on Jigsawcracy," *Playthings*, April 1933, p. 170.

"Speaking of Pictures," *Life*, July 10, 1944, pp. 12–14.

"The Spectator," *The Outlook*, Vol. 89, No. 1, May 2, 1908, pp. 17–18.

"Stick To It, and You May Solve a Puzzle Picture," *New York Times*, July 26, 1908, pt. 5, p. 11.

"Three Million Puzzles Weekly," *Queensborough* (published by the Chamber of Commerce of Queens, NY), Vol 19, No. 2, February 1933, p. 51.

Tuck, Raphael & Sons, Ltd. London, England. Various catalogs, circa 1915–1935.

"Tuco Puzzles Sparked Fad," *Blue Center News* (magazine of the Upson Company), December 1954, pp. 12–14.

Tumbusch, Tom. *Illustrated Radio Premium Catalog and Price Guide*. Dayton, OH: Tomart Publications, 1989.

Vandivert, William and Rita, "Past Teaching Aids in Jigsaw Puzzles," *Smithsonian*, August 1974, pp. 66–73.

Wallerstein, Edward, "Alphabet Block Collecting," *Collectibles Illustrated*, January/February 1984, pp. 44–47.

Warren Paper Box Co. Lafayette, IN. Various annual catalogs, circa 1945–1975.

Whitehill, Bruce. "Selchow & Righter: 1867–1986," *Antique Toy World*, Vol. 16, No. 7, July 1986, pp. 98–101.

Wilcox, Julius. "Fret-Sawing and Wood-Carving," *Harper's New Monthly Magazine*, Vol. 56, No. 334, March 1878, pp. 533–540.

Williams, Anne D. "Jigsaw Puzzles," *Antiques and Auction News*, Vol. 19, No. 5, February 5, 1988, pp. 1, 4–6.

———. "Par Puzzles—When Par Meant Excellence," *Puzzle Connection*, Summer 1984, pp. 8–9.

———. "Parker Brothers' Puzzling History," *Game Times*, Vol. 3, No. 2, Summer 1987, pp. 122–123.

———. *Pieces in Place: Two Hundred Years of Jigsaw Puzzles*. Exhibition catalog. Lewiston, ME: Bates College Museum of Art, 1988.

———. "Puzzle? Or Game? Or Both?" *Game Times*, Vol. 4, No 2, August 1988, pp. 190–192

———. "Puzzles," in *Warman's Americana & Collectibles*, 4th edition, edited by Harry L. Rinker. Radnor, PA: Wallace-Homestead Book Co., 1990.

INDEXES

• Index of American Puzzle Manufacturers, 1850–1970

THIS INDEX lists American puzzle manufacturers who were in business before 1970 (whether or not they are mentioned in this book), along with cross references for the brand names of their puzzles. (Amateur cutters who did not sell commercially are generally not included in this list.) The index also gives location and dates of the company's operation if these facts are known. In cases where the exact dates are unknown, the approximate decade is specified.

The next item is a code for the type of puzzles that the company produced: **A** for adult puzzles, **C** for children's puzzles, **S** for advertising puzzles, **N** for novelty puzzles (postcard puzzles, book puzzles, etc.). The production method is indicated by: **D** for die-cut (virtually all cardboard), **H** for hand-cut (mostly wood), and **X** for sliced (all cardboard). For example, the notation **AH, CD** would indicate that the company made both hand-cut adult puzzles, and die-cut children's puzzles. **L** indicates a puzzle lending library; many of these libraries were operated by or commissioned puzzles from local cutters.

This index also includes the companies and brands mentioned in Chapters 1 through 17. For that reason, it includes a few amateur cutters, foreign manufacturers, and post-1970 American manufacturers whose work is described in this book. The index is not intended to be a comprehensive list of amateur, foreign, or contemporary puzzle companies, however. Figure and page references are included for both companies and brands. For example, to find references to Parker's Pastime puzzles, check the listings for either Parker Brothers or Pastime. Page references for company histories in Chapter 2 are printed in boldface. Puzzle titles and subject matter are included in separate indexes.

I appreciate the help of many collectors who have generously contributed information for this list. However, I have not personally seen all the puzzles listed, and may have made some errors in transcribing the information. I welcome corrections and any additional data for this listing. They should be sent to: Anne D. Williams, Department of Economics, Bates College, Lewiston, Maine 04240.

A & P Coffee. New York, N.Y. 1930s. SD. Fig. 14-1
Abbott, W. C. 1930s. AH
Abercrombie & Fitch. New York, N.Y. 1930s. AH. Fig. 9-39
Abraham & Straus. New York, N.Y. Circa 1909. AH
Academy: made by J. Salmon. Fig. 9-72
Academy Award: made by Jaymar
Accounting Supply Mfg. Boston, Mass. 1930s. AD
Acme Puzzle Co. Altoona, Pa. 1930s. AH
Adco Novelty Co. Buffalo, N.Y. 1930s. AD
Adler-Jones Co. Chicago, Ill. 1930s. AH
Adult Jig Picture Puzzle: made by Whitman
Adult Leisure Products Corp. Locust Valley, N.Y. 1960s. AD. Figs. 13-14, 13-15
Advertising Novelty Mfg. Co. Philadelphia, Pa. 1930s. AD. P. 47
After Dinner Puzzle: made by Novelty Game Co.
Agate Mfg. Co. Brocton, Mass. 1930s. AD
Aitkins & Aitkins. Wilkes-Barre, Pa. 1930s.
Akron Paper Products, Akron, Ohio. 1930s. SD. Fig. 14-50
Albany Chamber of Commerce. Albany, N.Y. 1930s. SD
Albert, R. L. & Son. New York, N.Y. 1930s. ND. Fig. 16-30
Alderman, Albert D. Holyoke, Mass. 1930s. AD
Alderman-Fairchild. Rochester, N.Y. 1920s. CD. Pp. 26–27
Alkire, D.D. New York, N.Y. Circa 1970. AD
All-American: made by Dell, 1940s
Allen & Adams. North Stoughton, Mass. Circa 1909. AH.
Allen, Harry N. Livermore Falls, Me. AH
Allen, P. J. Medford, Mass. 1930s. AH. Fig. 9-64
Allentown Dairy Co. Inc. Allentown, Pa. 1930s. SD
All-Fair: made by All-Fair Inc.; E. E. Fairchild. P. 26
All-Fair Inc. Churchville, N.Y. 1930s. CD. Fig. 11-24; p. **26**
Allied Radio Corp. Chicago, Ill. 1930s. SD. Fig. 13-16
Alox Mfg. Co. St. Louis, Mo. 1930s.
ALPSCO: see Adult Leisure Products Corp.
Altadena Puzzle Library: see Kimberly
Amend, Adolph. 1930s. AH

A-Adult   C-Child   S-Advertising   N-Novelty   D-Die-cut   H-Handcut   X-Sliced   L-Lending Library

America in Action: made by Leo Hart Co., 1940s
American: made by Reynolds & Reynolds
American Colortype Co. Chicago, Ill. 1930s.
American Greetings Co. Cleveland, Ohio. 1960s. AD
American Heritage Jigsaw Puzzle: made by Straus. Fig. 2-15; p. 42
American Jigsaw Puzzle: made by Parker Brothers
American Map Co. Boston, Mass. Circa 1900. CH
American News Co., distributed: Every Week, Happy Hour, Jig-Crossword, Jig of Jigs, Masterpiece, Miss America, Silent Teacher, Viking Picture Puzzle Weekly. Pp. 26, 47
American Publishing Co. Waltham, and Watertown, Mass. Circa 1960–1985. AD, SD. Fig. 9-28
American Stores Co. 1930s. AD
American Super: made by Dayton Publishing Co.
American Tobacco Co. Circa 1909. SD. Fig. 14-69
Amos & Andy: made by Pepsodent
Amusingtoy. Circa 1870. CX
Anchor Brand Puz. Co. Portland, Me. 1930s. AH
Andover Novelty Shop. Andover, Mass. 1930s. AH. Fig. 9-63
Andrews, Herbert. South Essex, Mass. 1930s. AH
Andrews, O. B. Co. Chattanooga, Tenn. 1930s. AD
Angel Food Marshmallows: made by E. H. Edwards & Co.
Angelus Marshmallows: see Campfire Marshmallows. Fig. 14-6
Angle-Play: made by L.H. Nelson
Animal Shapes. Circa 1909. AH
Apollo: made by Vera
Apollo-Sha. Japan. 1980s. NH. Fig. 17-22
Aptus. Rochester, N.Y. 1980s. AH. Figs. 17-2, 17-4
Arabian Nights Puzzle Picture. Circa 1920. CD. Fig. 7-9
Arend, F. Spencer. Newtonville, Mass. 1930s. AH
Arens, J. T. Philadelphia, Pa. 1930s. AH
Arlington Products. Chicago, Ill. 1930s. AD
Armstrong Cork Co. Lancaster, Pa. 1930s. SD. Fig. 14-2
Armstrong, Harriet B. Racine, Wisc. Circa 1909. AH
Arnold, Helen L. Braintree, Mass. Circa 1909. AH
Art Craft: made by Wire
Art in Puzzles. 1930s. AH. Fig. 9-68
Art Picture Puzzle. Circa 1909. AH
Art Picture Puzzle: made by K. R. Lunn; Tru-Art; Tuco. Fig. 10-25; p. 45
Art Puzzle, The. Circa 1909. AH
Art Study Jig Saw Puzzle: distributed by E. J. Brach & Sons
Artcraft: made by Boden; Saalfield; Wire
Arteno: made by R. T. Novelties; Mary Roberts
Arteno Co. Boston, Mass. 1930s. AH. Fig. 8-40
Artinet: made by Arteno Co. Fig. 8-40
Artistic: made by Hayter. P. 29
Arts & Crafts Studio. Washington, D.C. 1930s. AH
Art-Shape: made by Ullman
At Random: made by Capt. Kirk
Atelier BSB. Paris, France. 1980s. NH. Fig. 17-23
Aunt Hannah's Bread: made by Baur
Aunt Louisa's Cube Puzzle: made by McLoughlin Bros. Fig. 12-7
Austen, J. I. Co. Chicago, Ill. Circa 1909. AH
Austin, G. M. 1930s. AH
Autograph: made by Goldsmith
Avery, Ed. 1930s. AH
Avon: made by Bradley
Ayer, James C. & Co. Salem, Mass. 1987–present. AH. Fig. 17-1; p. 18
Ayer, M. Isabel. Boston, Mass. 1908–40. AH, L. Fig. 12-11; pp. 13, **36–37**

B Witching Weekly: made by J. F. Friedel. P. 14
Babcock, C. W. & Son, Somerville, Mass.: predecessor of Consolidated Paper Box Co. P. 25

Baby Ruth: made by Curtiss Candy
Baker & Taylor. New York, N.Y. 1930s. AH, AD
Ballou, C. N. S. Fort Lincoln, N.D. 1930s. AH
Ballyhoo: made by Dell Publishing Co., 1933. Fig. 9-27
Bamberger, L. & Co. Newark, N.J. 1930s. AH. Fig. 16-17; pp. 15, 35
Bandwagon Mfg. Inc. Boston, Mass. 1960s. AD
Banks, Cecil R. New York, N.Y. Circa 1945. CH
Bantam Pocket Picture Puzzle: made by Jaymar
Barbour, Florence A. Portland, Augusta, Me. 1930s. AH
Barfoot, J. W. London, England. 1831–65. CH. Fig. 7-16
Barnard, Louise. Montclair, N.J. and Woodstock, Vt. Circa 1960–present. AH
Barnard-Clogston & Co. Melrose, Mass. 1930s. AH
Barnes, Herbert H. Newton Lower Falls, Mass. 1930s. AH
Bar-Zim Mfg. Co. Inc. New York, N.Y. 1930s.
Bates & Paine. Newport, Vt. 1930s. AH
Bates, Harriet. W. Medford, Mass. 1930s. AH. Fig. 9-18
Batterson, Emily L. Hartford, Conn. Circa 1909. AH
Battle Creek Food Co. Battle Creek, Mich. 1930s. SD
Battle Road Press. Lexington, Mass. 1980s. AH, AD. Fig. 17-16
Baur. 1950s. SD
Bay State Puzzles. Lawrence, Mass. 1930s. AH
Beach: made by Bradley, circa 1933. P. 24
Beach, Frederick H. New York, N.Y. 1930s. AD
Beachcraft: almost certainly made by Frederick H. Beach
Beacon Hill. Boston, Mass. Circa 1909. AH. Fig. 9-5
Beacon Jig: almost certainly made by Bradley
Beacon Lending Library. New Britain, Conn. AH
Bean, L. L.: made by Aptus. Fig. 17-2
Beaudry, G. F. Cortland, N.Y. 1890s. CH
Beautiful 125 Piece. 1930s. AD
Beck, A. E. Mfg. Co. Herrick, Ill. 1930s.
Bedford: made by Hockliffe
Bee Brand. New Bedford. Circa 1909. AH
Bee-Cee Puzzle Co. Clifton Heights, Pa. 1930s. AH
Beech-Nut Packing Co. Canajoharie, N.Y. 1930s. SD
Belding's Laundry. Northampton, Mass. 1930s. SD
Bell City Puzzles. 1930s. AH
Bellevue Stratford. Circa 1909. AH
Bell's: made by H. Holdan
Bendel, Henri. New York, N.Y. 1960s. AH
BePuzzled: made by Lombard Marketing. Fig. 17-29
Berkshire Jig-Saw Puz. 1930s. AH
Best, E. P. New Haven, Conn. 1880s. CH
Best Garage. Herkimer, N.Y. 1930s. SD
Best O'Luck: made by Fred L. Foster
Best-Made: made by W. N. De Sherbinin
Betts, John. London, England. 1827–74. CH. Fig. 6-4
Big Ben: made by Bradley, 1942–present. Fig. 15-3; p. 24
Big Jig: made by La France Workshop
Big Star: almost certainly made by Consolidated Paper Box. Figs. 12-6, 15-1; p. 25
Big 10: almost certainly made by Consolidated Paper Box. Figs. 10-14, 15-2; p. 25
Bisbee Brothers. Rockland, Me. 1930s. AH
Bishop, Isaac C. New London, Conn. Circa 1909. AH
Bissinger, Karl. St. Louis, Mo. 1980s. ND. Fig. 17-24
Black and White: made by Schlicher
Black Cat Hosiery. Circa 1909. SD. Fig. 14-3
Blanchard, Annie Rea. Melrose, Mass. 1930s. AH
Blatz Brewing Co. Milwaukee, Wisc. 1930s. SD
Bliss, R. W. Wollaston, Mass. 1930s. AH. Fig. 8-11
Bloomingdale's. New York, N.Y. 1930s. AH
Blue Ribbon. 1930s. AD
Blue Ribbon: made by Madmar; Whitman. Pp. 32, 48
Blue Star Publishing Co. New York, N.Y. 1930s. AD
Blum, Stanley W. 1930s. AH
Blunden, J. W. 1800s. CH
Bo-Bo: made by Albert D. Alderman
Boden Mfg. Co. Detroit, Mich. 1930s. AH

A-Adult C-Child S-Advertising N-Novelty D-Die-cut H-Handcut X-Sliced L-Lending Library

A-Adult   C-Child   S-Advertising   N-Novelty   D-Die-cut   H-Handcut   X-Sliced   L-Lending Library

Columbian Offset Co. Chicago, Ill. 1930s. AD
Commanday-Roth. New York, N.Y. 1930s. AD
Coming Attraction: made by Esquire, Inc.
Commission Picture Puzzle Exchange. New York, N.Y.
    Circa 1909. L
Complex: made by MacLachlan
Condé Nast Publications. New York, N.Y. 1930s. AD. Fig.
    6-28
Confuseyu: made by Horsman
Consolidated Box Co.: see Consolidated Paper Box Co.
Consolidated Lithographing Corp. Brooklyn, N.Y. 1930s.
    AD, SD Figs. 15-7, C-42
Consolidated Paper Box. Somerville, Mass. Circa
    1932–1960. AD, CD. Figs. 2-2, 8-31, 8-35, 9-32, 9-41,
    9-53, 9-74, 13-49, 15-21, 15-22, 15-23, C-25, C-59; pp. 8,
    9, 22, **25**
Contempo: made by Bradley, 1960s
Continental Fire Insurance. New York, N.Y. Circa 1909.
    Fig. 14-14
Cooke, Frances A. Weston, Mass. Circa 1909. AH. Fig.
    C-21
Cooper & Warner. York, Pa. 1930s. AH
Cooper Paper Box Corp. Buffalo, N.Y. 1930s. AD
Copley Jig. 1930s. AD
Corey, Donald C. Springfield, Mass. 1930s. AH, L
Cork-Jig: made by Gray Litho Inc.
Cosmos Art & Novelty. New York, N.Y. Circa 1920. AD
Costa, Louis. Circa 1909. AH
Covens & Mortier. Amsterdam, Netherlands. 1700s. CH.
    P. 21
Coventry: made by Bradley
Cowperthwait, DeSilver & Butler. Philadelphia, Pa.: dis-
    tributor for S. A. Mitchell
CPG Products Corp: parent of Fundimensions
Cracker Jack Co. Chicago, Ill. 1930s. SD
Craft Shop Puzzle: made by Benjamin Hinchman
Craftsman: made by Playtime House
Crafty Art Puzzle. Boston, Mass. Circa 1909. AH
Cram, George F. Chicago, Ill. Circa 1880–1920. CH
Crandall, Charles M. Montrose, Pa. 1870s. CH. Fig. 9-49
Cream of Wheat. Circa 1909. SH. Fig. 14-15; p. 245
Creative Playthings. Hightstown, N.J. Circa 1950–70. CH
Crime Club: made by Einson-Freeman, 1933. P. 26
Crippen, A. J. Batavia, N.Y. 1930s. AH. Fig. 9-70
Criterion Jig. 1930s. AD
Crocker, Charles I. Stockton Springs, Me. 1920s. AH
Cromat Novelty Co. Berlin, N.H. 1930s. AH
Crosby, A. T. Attleboro, Mass. 1930s. AH
Cross, S. R. Worcester, Mass. 1930s. AH
Cross Jig: made by Commanday-Roth
Cross-Word Jumbles: made by Hall Brothers. P. 28
Crowell Publishing Co. Springfield, Ohio. Fig. 16-42
Crown: made by Whitman
Crown Guild: made by Whitman
Crown Puzzle. Chicago, Ill. AH
Croxley: made by Bradley. Fig. 15-5
Croyden: made by Bradley
Cruikshank Brothers Co. Pittsburgh, Pa. 1930s. SD. Fig.
    14-16
Culbertson, Ely. 1930s. AH. Fig. 16-23
Curley Cue: made by Warner
Curative Work Shop and Sales Room. Colorado Springs,
    Colo. 1930s. AH
Curley Cue Cut series: made by A. H. Warner. Fig. 9-34
Currier & Ives: made by Blum; Einson-Freeman; Metric;
    Morris & Bendien; Straus; Whitman. Fig. 10-9; p. 26
Curt, Teich & Co. Chicago, Ill. 1930s. AD
Curtis Art Co, Waterbury, Conn.: sold and perhaps made
    Zeitvertreib puzzles
Curtis, E. J. Pittsfield, Mass. 1930s. AH. Fig. 16-31
Curtiss Candy. Chicago, Ill. 1930s. SD. Fig. 14-17
Cushman, Brother. Montclair, N.J. Circa 1909. AH. Fig.
    14-71

Cushman, S. W. Decatur, Mich. 1930s. AH
Cut-Out Picture Puzzle. 1930s. AD
Cutwood. Circa 1909. AH

D. C. Puzzling Puzzle Co. Circa 1909. AH
Daintee Toys, Inc. Brooklyn, N.Y. Circa 1940. CH. Fig.
    11-27
Dake's Ice Cream. Saratoga, N.Y. SD
Danforth, H. W. New Bedford, Mass. Circa 1909. AH
Daniels, H.T. Providence, R.I. 1930s. AH
Dank, M. Carlton. Brooklyn, N.Y. 1930s. AD
Daring, Dick: made by Quaker Oats
Dart, S. T. N. London, Conn. Circa 1920. AH
Darton, William Jun. London, England. 1804–1830. CH.
    Fig. 6-1
Davidson Brothers. New York, N.Y. Circa 1909. AH
Davis, D. Mills, Mass. AH
Davis, George. Annapolis, Md. Circa 1909. AH
Davis, Porter & Co. Philadelphia, Pa. Circa 1860. CH. Fig.
    11-7
Davis, R. B. Co. Hoboken, N.J. 1930s. SD. Figs. 14-11,
    14-12
Davis, Robert S. Plymouth, Mass. and Lady Lake, Fla.
    1930s–present. AH
Dawley, W. J. Newport, R.I. AH
Dayton Publishing Co. Dayton, Ohio. 1930s. AD
Dayton Tires. 1950s. SD. Fig. 14-18
Daze Jig: made by C. F. Hatch
Daze Work: made by Weldon Wood Novelty Co.
De Sherbinin, W. N. Mt. Kisco, N.Y. 1930s. AD
Dearborn Truck Co. Chicago, Ill. 1930s. SD. Fig. 14-19
Dee-Gee: made by Detroit Gasket & Mfg Co. Fig. 10-13
Deere, John: made by Aptus. Fig. 17-4
Degen, Estes & Co. Boston, Mass. 1870s. CH. Fig. 7-4
DeHaven, James I. Lancaster, Pa. 1930s. AH. Fig. 12-19
Deisroth, W. H. Co. Philadelphia, Pa. 1930s. AD
DeLacy, W. L. Chicago, Ill. 1890s. CX. Fig. 6-15
Delft: made by Rawson
Delhaye Freres. Paris, France. Circa 1900. CH. Figs. 6-16,
    C-5
Dell Publishing Co. Inc. New York, N.Y. 1930s and 1940s.
    AD. Figs. 9-27, 13-19
Delta Series: made by A. V. N. Jones & Co. Ltd. Fig. 7-34
Deluxe: made by Deisroth; Regent Specialties; Schreiner;
    Tuco. Figs. 9-26, 10-23, 11-18, 15-37; p. 45
Deluxe Edition. 1930s. AD
Deluxe Edition Brain Storm: made by International Wood-
    working
Deluxe Guild: made by Whitman
Deluxe Pastime: made by Parker Brothers in 1930s
DeMartini Macaroni Co. Brooklyn, N.Y. 1930s. SD
Demorest's Young America. New York, N.Y. 1860s. CX
Dempsey Puzzle: made by Gold Medal Foods Inc.
Denholm & McKay Co. Worcester, Mass. 1930s. AH
Dennis, Ruth. Shaker Heights, Ohio. Circa 1960. AH
De-Pend-On: made by C. T. Sawyer. Fig. 9-69
Derby Jig: made by Bradley 1938–41
Dermac Studios. Portland, Me. 1930s. AH
DeRolf & Pridham. Flushing, N.Y. 1930s. L
Detective Jig Saw Puzzle: made by Independent News Co.
Detective Mystery Puzzle: made by Jaymar 1944
Detroit Gasket & Mfg. Co. Detroit, Mich. 1930s. AH. Fig.
    10-13
Detroit Publishing Co. Detroit, Mich. Circa 1909. AH. Fig.
    7-33
Devon: made by Bradley, 1960s
Diamond King series: made by Donruss; Leaf, Inc. Fig.
    17-27
Diamond-Lock: made by Warren (Built-Rite). Fig. 15-44
Dick Daring: made by Quaker Oats
Dickens: made by Emerson
Dif Corp. Garwood, N.J. 1930s. SD. Fig. 14-20;
    p. 26

A-Adult C-Child S-Advertising N-Novelty D-Die-cut H-Handcut X-Sliced L-Lending Library

INDEX OF AMERICAN PUZZLE MANUFACTURERS, 1850–1970

Dif-I-Cut: made by Walker Fogg
Dilks, Albert W. Philadelphia, Pa. Circa 1909. AH
Dime Jig Saw Puzzle. 1930s. AD. Fig. 1-14; p. 14
Dissected Maps: made by J. H. Colton
Dittmar, Louis. Williamsport, Pa. 1930s. AH
Dixie. 1930s. SD
Dixie's Jig-Saw Puzzle. 1930s. AD
Do-A-Jig. 1930s. AD
Dodge Brothers. 1930s. SD
Dodge Scroll Saw Puzzle: made by Albert D. Proudfit
Dolly Folding Kite & Toy Co. Dayton, Ohio. 1930s. AD
Donruss. 1980s. ND. Later made by Leaf, Inc.
Doo Dad: made by University Feature & Specialty
Dorothy Dainty puzzle: made by Parker Brothers. Fig. 10-26
Dorr, Wallie. New York, N.Y. Circa 1885–1935. CH, AH. Fig. 1-5
Dorset: made by Bradley, 1960s
Dorworth, H. M. Franklin, Pa. 1960s. AH
Doty, H. Newark and Morristown, N.J. Circa 1930.
Double: made by Consolidated Paper Box (Perfect). Figs. 15-21, C-25
Double Jigolette: made by Emery
Double L: made by Katharine Lord Studio
Double Set: made by Louis B. Marx. Fig. 13-44
Dover Jig: made by Bradley 1937–38
Dow, Louis F. St. Paul, Minn. 1930s. AD
Dower, Ernest G. Newbury, Mass. 1930s. AH
Draving Brothers. Philadelphia, Pa. 1930s. AD
Dresden. 1930s. AH
Drueke. Grand Rapids, Mich. 1930s. AH
Dual: made by Straus
Dubl-Thik: made by Tuco, 1940s. Fig. 15-8; p. 45
Duke Picture Puzzles. 1930s. AH
Duo-Jig: made by R-M Sales Corp. Fig. 16-41
Durcote: parent company of Chilcote
Durrel Co. Gardner, Mass. 1930s. AD
Dutton, E. P. New York, N.Y.: see Ernest Nister. Figs. 9-8, 11-22, C-36
Dutton Noble. 1930s. AH
Dwyer Brothers Stationers. Trenton, N.J. 1930s. AD

E.-F. Lith. Co., N.Y.: abbreviation for Einson-Freeman
E. L. M. Circa 1909. AH
E. M. B. Circa 1909. AH. Fig. 10-32
Eagle Indemnity Co. 1930s. SD
Eagleson, Harriet T. Watertown, Arlington, Mass. Circa 1909. AH, L
Earlville Novelty Co. Earlville, N.Y. 1930s. AD
Eastman Kodak Stores. 1930s. AH. Fig. 16-32
Ed Wynn Picture Puzzle: made by Viking Mfg Co.
Edgar, Paul. Titusville, Pa. 1930s. AH
Edmond, A. B. Brookline, Mass. Circa 1909. AH
Edsel: made by Ford Motor Co.
Ed-U-Cards Mfg. Corp. New York, N.Y. 1960s. AD
Educational Dissected Map: made by American Map Co.
Educational Playthings. New York, N.Y. 1930s. CH. Fig. 11-26
Educational Puzzle Co. 1950s. CD
Edwards, E. H. Co. Chicago, Ill. Circa 1920. SD
Effanbee: made by Fleischaker & Baum
Eichhorn, Hermann. Egglham, West Germany. 1980s. CH. Fig. 17-5
Einson-Freeman Co. Inc. Long Island City, N.Y. 1930s. AD, SD. Figs. 2-3, 6-2, 9-56, 13-20, 14-20, 14-35, 16-12, C-62, C-63; pp. 14, **26**, 245
El Capitan Coffee: made by R. L. Gerhart. Fig. 14-22
Elder Craftsmen. New York, N.Y. 1960s. AH
Elite: made by Tuco; S. Ward
Elliott, E. E. Springfield, Mass. 1930s. AH
Elms, Inc. Towson, Md. 1988–present. AH, CH. Fig. 17-6; p. 18
Embossing Co. Albany, N.Y. Circa 1909. AH

Emerson Jig Saw Puzzle. Brooklyn, N.Y. 1930s. AH
Emerson, William A. Fitchburg, Mass. 1880s. CX. Fig. 7-28
Emery Products Co. New York, N.Y. 1930s. AH. Fig. 16-29
Emmerts: Philadelphia, Pa. distributor for Jumble Jig
Empire: made by Brundage; Empire Greeting Card
Empire Greeting Card Co. New York, N.Y. 1930s. AD
Encore: made by New York News Co.
England, Robert. Hingham, Mass. 1930s. AH. Figs. 6-41, 9-42
Entertainer Puzzle Co. Old Town, Me. 1930s. AH
Epco Puzzle Mfrs. Norristown, Pa. 1930s. AD
Esanbe: trademark of Schranz & Bieber
Esky: made by Esquire
Esquire Inc. New York, N.Y. 1940s. AD. Fig. 13-17
Essell Co.: owned by George P. Schlicher & Son. Fig. 15-29
Essex: made by Andrews; Bradley
Esso. 1930s. SD. Fig. C-56
Etonian: made by Bradley, circa 1936. P. 24
Eureka Jig-Saw Puzzle Co. Philadelphia, Pa. 1930s. AH, AD
Eureko!: made by Graphicut Corp.
Eustis, Mrs. James B. New York, N.Y. Circa 1909. L
Evans, Robert. Los Angeles, Calif. 1950s. AH, L
Eveready Flashlight & Batteries. 1930s. SD. Fig. C-54
Eveready Specialties. New York, N.Y. 1930s. AH. Fig. 10-22
Everett Piano Co. Boston, Mass. Circa 1890. SD. Fig. 14-23
Every Week: made by Einson-Freeman. Figs. 6-2, 9-56, C-63; pp. 14, 26
Everybody's: made by Wilkie Picture & Puzzle Co. Also distributed by Middletown Distributing Co. Fig. 9-67
Everyman's Bible Class. Newark, N.J. 1930s. SD
Excelsior: made by Allen & Adams
Expression Blocks: made by Crandall
Eye Witness: possibly made by Einson-Freeman
E-Z-2-Du: made by National Scroll Novelty Co.

F & P Novelties. Burlington, N.J. 1930s. AH
Face Corp., Philadelphia, Pa.: distributed Schoenhut's Ole Million Face
Fairchild, E. E. Rochester, N.Y. Circa 1926–1978. AD, CD. Figs. 15-9, 15-10; pp. **26–27**, 68
Fairco: made by E. E. Fairchild. P. 27
Fairdurst, Francie Ltd. 1930s. AH
Fairy Tales Picture Puzzle. Circa 1920. CD
Falls Puzzle: made by Jones (Chagrin Falls, Ohio)
Falmun Puzzle Co. 1930s. AH
Family Circle Jig Puzzle: made by Draving Brothers
Famous Artists: made by Gabriel
Famous Biscuits. 1910s. SD. Fig. 14-24
Famous Comics: made by Stephens Kindred. Figs. 13-37, 13-41, C-48
Famous Picture Puzzle Co. Cincinnati, Ohio. 1930s. AD
Faris Mfg. Co. Portland, Ore. 1930s.
Farrar, John. 1930s. AH
Fascination: made by Paramount Puzzle Co.
Faurot, W. L. 1930s. AH
Favorite: made by Madmar
Favorite Pictorial Puzzle: made by Reynolds & Reynolds
Fawcett Publications. Minneapolis, Minn. 1930s. AD, CD. Figs. 13-65, 16-25
Fayle, W. H. Boston, Mass. 1930s
Fenn's Interlocking. New Britain, Conn. 1930s. AH
Fessenden's Library. Portland, Me. 1930s. L
Festetics, Countess Eila. New York, N.Y. Circa 1909. AH
Field's Stationery Shop. Boston, Mass. 1930s. AH
Fifield family cutter. Swampscott, Mass. 1910s. AH. Figs. 9-45, 12-16, 12-29
Fighters for Freedom: made by Whitman, 1940s. Fig. C-7; p. 48
Fighters for Victory Series: made by Jaymar, 1940s. Figs. 2-7, 15-16; p. 31

A-Adult   C-Child   S-Advertising   N-Novelty   D-Die-cut   H-Handcut   X-Sliced   L-Lending Library

Figure-It-Out: made by Holtzapffel & Co. Fig. C-18
Filene's. Boston, Mass. Circa 1960. AH
Fine Art Picture Puzzle: made by Transogram
Fine Arts Picture Puzzle: made by Fairchild; Playtime House; Saalfield. Fig. 15-11
Finesse: made by E. E. Fairchild
Finn, W. R. New Britain, Conn. AH
Fireside Games Corp. Chicago, Ill. 1930s. AH
Fireside Jig Saw Puzzle. Wormleysburg, Pa. 1930s. AH
Firestone Tire Co. 1930s. SD
Fischer's Vitamin-D Bread. 1930s. SD. Fig. 14-25
Fisher-Price. East Aurora, N.Y. 1931–present. CH. P. 27
Fisk Tire. 1930s. SD
Fitrite: made by Swanton
Fitting Reminder: made by American Greetings Corp.
Five Star Adult Jig: made by Whitman
Five Star Interlocking Picture Puzzle. 1940s. AD
Five Star Picture Puzzle: made by Warren 1947–56; Whitman
Fleischaker & Baum. New York, N.Y. 1940s. CD
Flood, Josephine. New York, N.Y. Circa 1930–1950. AH, L. Fig. C-24; pp. 35, 36
Florence Mfg. Co. Florence, Mass. Circa 1909. SD. Fig. 14-51. See also Prophylactic Brush Co.
Flying Family: made by Cocomalt
Flying Goose: made by Kimberly
Fogg, Walter. Lansdowne, Pa. 1930s. AH
Foley, Tip. Marblehead and East Orleans, Mass. Circa 1950–85. AH
Folger's Coffee. San Mateo, Calif. Circa 1965. SD. Fig. 14-26
For Young and Old: almost certainly made by Tru-Art
Ford, Helen Parker. 1930s. AH
Ford Motor Co. Detroit, Mich. 1959. SD. Fig. 14-21
Fort Wayne Paper Box. Fort Wayne, Ind. 1930s. AD
Foss, H. E. Springfield, Mass. 1930s. AH. Figs. C-22, C-29
Foster, Fred L. Lynn, Mass. 1930s. AH
Foster Paper Co., Utica, N.Y.: parent of Madmar circa 1955–67
4 Way Jig. 1930s. AD
Fox, G. Hartford, Conn.: sold Straus Currier & Ives puzzles in Fox box
Fox, George. Columbus, Ohio. 1950s. AH
Framed Puzzler: made by Adco Novelty Co.
Franklin Mfg. Co. Philadelphia, Pa. 1930s. AH
Franklin Novelty Co. New York, N.Y. Circa 1909. AH
Franklin Studio. Covington, Ga. 1930s.
Freihofer. SD
Fresno Art Novelty Co. Fresno, Calif. 1940s. ND
Fretts, Alden L. Pittsfield and West Springfield, Mass. 1930s. AH. Figs. 2-4, 6-34, 9-76; pp. **27–28**
Friedel, J. F. Co. Syracuse, N.Y. 1930s. AD
Frontiers, Inc. 1950s. CD
FryeWeaver Puzzles. Albuquerque, N.M. 1980s. AH. Fig. 17-7; p. 18
Full O'Cheer. Boston, Mass. 1930s. AH
Fuller's Magnesia Dental Cream. 1930s. SD. Fig. 14-27
Ful-Lock: made by Fairchild. P. 27
Fun Craft: made by Edward Smith
Fundimensions. Mt. Clemens, Mich. 1980s. CD. Fig. 17-17
Funny Page Jig-Saw Puzzle: made by Transogram

G. M. C.: made by Gebhard Manufacturing Co.
G. W. R: made by Chad Valley
Gabriel, Samuel & Sons. New York, N.Y. 1930s. AH, AD, CD, ND. Figs. 7-32, 15-12, 16-8
Gaffney, Walter M. Hyannis, Mass. 1930s. AH
Galles, Andrew L. Buffalo, N.Y. 1930s. AH. Fig. 12-26
Gambling's Gang, WOR: made by Thom McAn
Game Jig Weekly. 1930s. AD
Game Makers, Inc. Long Island City, N.Y. 1930s. ND. Fig. 16-20

Gameophiles Unlimited. Berkeley Heights, Morristown, N.J. AD. Fig. 6-30
Garbo: made by Allied Radio; Midwest Distributors
Gaston Mfg. Co. Cincinnati, Ohio. 1950s. CH. Figs. 9-52, 13-31
Gebhard Mfg. Co. Inc. Newark, N.J. 1930s. AD
Gebhart Folding Box. Dayton, Ohio. 1930s. AD
Gelco Interlocking. Chicago, Ill. 1930s. AD. Fig. 15-13
Gem: made by Bradley
Gendell, Paul Jr. Wenonah, N.J. 1930s. AH
Gene & Glenn & Jake & Lena: made by Sohio; Olman Music
General Electric. Schenectady, N.Y. Circa 1960. SD. Fig. 14-28
General Foods. Battle Creek, Mich. 1930s. SD. Fig. 14-47
Genesee: made by E. E. Fairchild. P. 27
Genuine Jig Saw Puzzle: made by Louis Marx
Geo-Jig: made by G. I. Spatcher
Gerhart, R. L. Lancaster and Johnstown, Pa. 1930s. SD. Fig. 14-22
Germantown Woodcrafter. Philadelphia, Pa. 1930s. AH
Gerstenlauer, Mrs. Karl. Milton, Pa. 1930s. AH
Get-To-Gether: made by T. S. Griswold
Giant Guild: made by Whitman
Giant Jig: made by Chilcote
Gibson Art Co. Cincinnati, Ohio. 1930s. AD
Gibson, C. R. New York, N.Y. 1930s. AD
Gibson Refrigerator. SD
Gilbert, A. C. New Haven, Conn. 1930s. AD
Gilchrist, W. L. Fall River, Mass. 1930s. AH
Gilman, Myron A. Westfield, Mass. 1910s. NH. Fig. 1-9
Gilmour, B. R. & Co. New York, N.Y. 1910s. CH
Gimbel Brothers. New York, N.Y. and Philadelphia, Pa. 1930s. AH. P. 15
Glamour Girl: made by Saalfield
Gleason, H. A. Arlington, Mass. 1930s. AH
Glen Echo: made by Arens
Glendex: made by J. S. Guiles. Fig. 17-8
Glengarry. Belmont, Mass. 1930s. AH
Glenville Unemployed Association. Scotia, N.Y. 1930s. AD
Globe Indemnity Co. 1930s. SD
Globe Puzzle Co. Boston, Mass. Circa 1909. AH. Fig. 10-2
Gold Box: made by Hayter Division of J. W. Spear. Pp. 18, 29, 41
Gold Medal Foods, Inc. Minneapolis, Minn. 1930s. SD
Gold Medal Picture Puzzles: made by Transogram. Fig. 15-31
Gold Seal: made by Parker Brothers in 1930s; Whitman. P. 48
Gold Seal Toy Co. Dundee, Ill. 1930s. AH. Fig. 10-21
Goldbergs: made by Pepsodent
Golden: made by Western Publishing. Fig. 17-21; p. 48
Golden Eagle: made by Parker Brothers in 1930s
Golden Hour: made by Gabriel in 1930s
Goldsmith, E. H. Glencoe, Ill. 1960s. AH.
Gong Bell Mfg. Co. East Hampton, Conn. 1950s. CH
Good Old Days: made by Bradley; Gabriel
Goodall, Leonard. Warrensburg, Mo. 1930s. AH
Goodenough & Woglom. New York, N.Y. Circa 1890. C
Goodnight Distributing Co, Oklahoma City, Okla.: distributed Jigee-Sawee
Goodrich Tire. 1930s. SD. Figs. 14-29, 14-30
Goofy Golf Puzzle: made by Richfield Gasoline. Figs. 14-54, 14-55
Gousha, H. M. Chicago, Ill. 1940s. CD
Graham, Charles S. Newark, N.J. 1930s. AH
Grant, W. T. Co. 1930s. AD
Graphicut Corp. New York, N.Y. 1940s. ND. Fig. 16-19
Gray Brothers. West Chester, Pa. 1930s. AH
Gray Litho Inc. New York, N.Y. 1930s. AD
Great Atlantic & Pacific Tea Co.: see A & P. Fig. 14-1
Great Western Railway: made by Chad Valley. Fig. 11-12

A-Adult C-Child S-Advertising N-Novelty D-Die-cut H-Handcut X-Sliced L-Lending Library

Green, Dorothy. Salmon Falls, N.H. 1950s. AH

Green, Peter. Wiscasset, Me. Circa 1970. AH

Green Bungalow: made by Leonard Goodall

Grimmons, Katie M. A. Circa 1909. AH

Grinnell, Arthur G. New Bedford, Mass. Circa 1909. AH. Fig. 12-8

Griswold, T. S. Wethersfield, Conn. 1930s. AH

Grose, Mrs. E. F. Ballston Spa, N.Y. Circa 1909. AH

Grosset & Dunlap. New York. 1930s–present. AD, CD, ND. Fig. 11-28

Gruener Hardware Store. Fitchburg, Mass. 1930s. AH

Grumette, Murray. Brooklyn, N.Y. 1930s. N3

GUA: made by Glenville Unemployed Association

Guarantee: made by Edgar

Guild: made by Whitman. Fig. 15-47; p. 48

Guild, W. R. Auburndale, Mass. 1930s. AH

Guiles, Jeremy S. N. Windham, Me. and Sarasota, Fla. 1970–present. AH. Fig. 17-8; p. 18

Haight, Adson: Scotia, N.Y. distributor for Eagle Indemnity Co.

Hale, Cushman & Flint. Boston, Mass. 1930s. AH

Half Way House: See Curative Work Shop and Sales Room

Hall, M. G. AH

Hall Brothers, Inc.: original name of Hallmark Cards, Inc. Fig. 16-26; p. 28

Hallmark Cards Inc. Kansas City, Mo. 1910–present. AD, CD, ND. Figs. 12-5, 16-6; pp. 28, 42

Halsam Products Co. Chicago, Ill. 1950s. CH

Hamblet Studios. Akron, Ohio. 1930s. AH, AD. Fig. 15-14

Hamlen, H. E. Chicopee, Mass. 1930s. AH. Fig. 10-4

Hammer, Valdemar. Branford, Conn. Circa 1909. AH. Fig. 1-12

Hammett, Emily. Newport, R.I. Circa 1909. AH

Hammond, C. S. New York, N.Y. 1930s. AH, CH, NH. Fig. 12-17

Hammond's Pleasure Time Picture Puzzles. 1930s. AD

Hanchett, Richard B. Springfield, Mass. 1930s. AH

Hancock, James and John. Minneapolis, Minn. 1930s. AH

Handicraft. 1930s. AH

Handicraft Supply Co. Springfield, Mass. 1930s. AH

Hank's Puzzle Shop. Conway, N.H. 1930s. L

Hanna Jig Saw Puzzle Co. Cleveland Heights, Ohio. 1930s. AH, L

Hap-E-Tyme: made by Smart

Happy Days: made by Ullman

Happy Days. 1930s. AD

Happy Hour Jig Puzzle Weekly: made by Epco Puzzle Mfrs.

Happy Hour Jigsaw Puzzle. 1930s. AH

Happy Hour Puzzle. Winsted, Conn. 1930s. AH

Happy Hour Puzzle. Circa 1909. AH

Happy Hour Puzzle. 1930s. AD. Fig. 15-15

Happy House Group: see Random House

Harett-Gilmar. Long Beach, Far Rockaway, and East Rockaway, N.Y. Circa 1960s–present. AD, CD. Fig. 7-8

Harmony Puzzles Co. Chicago, Ill. 1930s.

Hart, Leo. Rochester, N.Y. 1940s. AD, CD. Fig. 9-15

Harter Publishing Co. Cleveland, Ohio. 1930s. AD, CD. Fig. 10-31

Hartman, C. E. Utica, N.Y. Circa 1900. CH. Fig. C-51; p. **40**

Hasbro, Inc., Pawtucket, R.I. Parent of Bradley since 1984. Pp. 24, 39

Hassett, Waman S. 1930s. AH. Fig. 10-8

Hatch, C. F. Lowell, Mass. 1930s. AD

Hathaway Press, Inc. San Francisco, Calif. 1930s. AD

Hayter, G. J. Bournemouth, England. Circa 1920–1970. AH, CH. Figs. 2-5, 8-14, 11-6, 16-39, 17-14, C-8; pp. 10, 18, 22, **28–29**, 41, 42

Heavyweight: made by Playtime House

Heinz, H. J. Co. Pittsburgh, Pa. 1930s. SD

Heiser, Harry B. Lancaster, Pa. 1950s. NH. Fig. 8-15

Herendeen. Circa 1909. AH

H-G Toys: see Harett-Gilmar Inc.

Higgins Ice Cream. Exeter, N.H. SD

Hill, Samuel L. Williamsburgh, N.Y. Circa 1860–85. CH. Fig. 6-23; p. 6

Hills Brothers Coffee. San Francisco, Calif. 1930s. SD. Fig. C-53

Hillside: made by Blanchard

Hinchman, Benjamin. Boston, Mass. 1930s. AH

Hinds, Charles B. Portland, Me. 1930s. AH

Historic: made by Parker Brothers, 1960s

Historical: made by Famous Picture Puzzle Co.

HMH Publishing, Chicago, Ill.: see Playmate puzzle

Ho Ho Jig Saw Puzzle. 1930s. AH

Hoadley House. Bethany, Conn. 1930s. AH

Hobbey, Louise W. Boston, Mass. Circa 1909. AH

Hobby: made by Jaymar, circa 1945. Fig. 8-13

Hockliffe, F. R. Bedford. 1930s. AH

Hodges, William. Lexington, Mass. Circa 1965–75. AH

Holabird Co. Bryan, Ohio. Circa 1909. AH

Holdan, H. Roxbury, Mass. 1950s. AH

Holden, Stillman. Shirley, Mass. Circa 1880. AH

Holgate Brothers Co. Kane, Pa. Circa 1950. CH

Hollenbeck Press. Indianapolis, Ind. 1930s. AD

Hollister, Evan Jr. Kenmore, N.Y. 1930s. AH

Hollywood: made by Consolidated Lithographing Corp.

Holtzapffel & Co. Ltd. London, England. 1910s. AH. Fig. C-18

Home Craft Puzzle Co. Worcester, Mass. 1930s. AH

Honey Wood Krazy-Saw: made by House of Premiums

Hood, C. I. Lowell, Mass. 1870–1922. SD. Figs. 2-6, 3-3, 14-31, 14-32, 14-33, C-50; pp. 18, **29–30**, 61–62

Hoover Vacuum (Sears). SD

Hopper, A. H. Circa 1909. AH

Horsman, E. I. New York, N.Y. 1880s–present. CX, AH; pp. 11

House of Premiums. Cleveland, Ohio. 1930s. AH

Houser, Glad. Litchfield, Me. 1930s. AH. Fig. C-17

Howdy Doody: made by Bradley; Poll Parrot Shoes. Fig. 13-28

Howe, Charlie. West Roxbury, Mass. Circa 1909. AH

Howes, Ruth B. Augusta, Me. 1930s. AH

Howland, Paul Jr. New Bedford, Mass. Circa 1909. CD

Huld, Franz. New York, N.Y. Circa 1906. ND

Humble Great Moments: made by American Publishing Co.

Hutchinson, James. New Haven, Conn. 1930s. AH

Huvanco. Ilford, England. Circa 1920–1940. AH. Figs. 9-31, 10-1

Huylers. 1920s. SD

I. B. & Co.: abbreviation for Ives, Blakeslee & Co.

Ideal Book Builders. Chicago, Ill. 1910s. CD. Fig. 16-21

Ideal for Idlers: sold at Brentano's, Paris

Ideal Jigsaw Puzzle Co. Lynn, Mass. 1930s. AH

Ideal Picture Puzzles. Chattahoochee, Ga. 1930s. AH

Ideal Toy, Arcade, N.Y.: owner of Tuco, 1981–83

Idle Hour: made by Collier; Pulver Novelty Co.

Idle-Hour: made by Consolidated Paper Box. P. 25

Idle Hour Puzzle: made by Farrar; Fireside; Smith, Kline & French

Iliff, John W. & Co. Chicago, Ill. Circa 1900. CH

Imperial: made by Parker Brothers in 1930s

Independent News Co. New York, N.Y. 1930s. AD

Ingleside Co. Springfield, Mass. Circa 1909. AH. Fig. 8-22

Inner Sanctum Picture Puzzle: made by Simon & Schuster

Interlock: made by Ullman

Interlocked Picture Puzzle Co. Newton Lower Falls, Mass. 1930s. AH. Fig. 12-15

Interlocking: made by Russell

Interlocking Border Jig Saw Puzzle. 1930s. AD. Fig. 9-75

Inter-Locking Jig Saw Puzzle. 1930s. AH

Interlocking Puzzle Co. Cleveland, Ohio. 1930s. AD

Interlocko Novelty Co. Philadelphia, Pa. 1930s. AH

A-Adult   C-Child   S-Advertising   N-Novelty   D-Die-cut   H-Handcut   X-Sliced   L-Lending Library

Interlox: made by Madmar; Saalfield. Pp. 32, 38
Inter-Lox. 1930s. AD
International Shoe Co. SD
International Wood-Working. Jersey City, N.J. Circa 1909.
 AH. Fig. 11-16
Intracut: made by Paul Gendell Jr.
Ireland, L. 1800s. CH
Ironton Novelty Co. Ironton, Ohio. Circa 1890. CH
It's A Corker: made by Detroit Gasket & Mfg Co. Fig. 10-13
Ives, Blakeslee & Co. New York, N.Y. 1880s. CX. Figs.
 6-27, C-3
Ives, D. P. Boston, Mass. Successors to W. & S. B. Ives
Ives, W. & S. B. Salem, Mass. Circa 1855. CX. P. 6

J. D.: made by James DeHaven. Fig. 12-19
J. S. Publishing Co. New York, N.Y. 1940s. AD. Fig. 6-45
J. W. S. & S.: abbreviation for J. W. Spear & Son
Jacobs, Maurice. Appleton, Wisc. Circa 1930–present. AH
Jake & Lena Radio Jigsaw Puzzle: distributed by Olman
 Music; Sohio. Fig. 13-24
Jap Rose Soap: made by Kirk Co. Fig. 14-34
Jarvis, H. D. Boston, Mass. 1930s. AH
Jaymar Specialty Co. New York, N.Y. Circa 1925–present.
 CD, AD. Figs. 2-7, 8-13, 13-5, 13-6, 13-10, 13-34, 13-35,
 13-36, 13-40, 13-42, 13-45, 13-46, 13-50, 13-69, 14-5,
 15-16, 17-18, C-58; pp. 9, **30–31**
Je Jo Picture Puzzle: made by Jesse Jones Paper Box Co.
Jefferys, Charles. Philadelphia, Pa. 1890s. CH, AH. Figs.
 1-11, C-4; pp. 10–11
Jenks, H. A. Canton, Mass. Circa 1909. AH. Fig. 9-19
Jester: made by Bates & Paine
Jewel Puzzle Co. New Haven, Conn. 1930s. AH
Jewell, C. F. & Co. Brookline, Mass. Circa 1909. AH
Jiffy Jigsaws: made by Parker Brothers, 1960s
Jig Chase: made by Game Makers Inc.
Jig Craft: made by R. L. Turner
Jig De Luxe: made by University Distributing Co. P. 46
Jig 400: made by University Distributing Co. P. 46
Jig Foursome: made by Metric Game & Novelty
Jig Jag Jumbles: made by Hall Brothers
Jig Jam Picture Puzzle. 1930s. AD
Jig Joke: made by Riski-Raskal Co. Fig. 15-28
Jig of Jigs. 1930s. AD. Fig. C-32
Jig of the Week Puzzle: made by University Distributing
 Co. Figs. 2-18, 12-30, 15-40; pp. 14, 15, 16, 24, 46, 50
Jig Picture Puzzle: made by Cooper Paper Box; Whitman
Jig Play: made by Timken Silent Automatic Oil Burner Co.
Jig Puzzle For Young and Old: almost certainly made by
 Tru-Art
Jig Sau for Young and Old: made by Stratford Show Print
 Co.
Jig Saw Cross Cut: made by Adler-Jones
Jig Saw Greetings: made by Hallmark, circa 1940
Jig Saw Murder Case: made by Gabriel
Jig Saw Puzzle Correspondence: made by Kelloggs; Merrill
Jig Staff: made by Helen Parker Ford
Jig Time: made by Chilcote
Jig Wig Puzzle Co. White Plains, N.Y. 1930s. AH
Jig Wood: made by Parker Brothers; University Distribut-
 ing Co. Fig. 15-41; pp. 36, 46
Jig-A-Jig: made by Parker Brothers; Fort Wayne. Fig. 9-10;
 p. 36
Jig-A-While. 1930s. AH. Fig. 9-43
Jig-Crossword Puzzle: made by Pinkham Press
Jigee-Sawee: made by Pioneer Paper Box, distrib. by Good-
 night
Jigette: made by Hamblet Studios. Fig. 15-14
Jiggelogue Puzzle: made by Kenilworth Press
Jigger: made by Shut-In Society; Kindel & Graham. P. 47
Jigger Jig: made by Chilcote
Jiggers Weekly: made by Agate Mfg. Co. P. 14
Jiggerty Jumbles. Circa 1909. AH
Jiggety Jig: made by Harter Publishing Co.

Jiggity Jag: made by Murphy. Fig. 15-19
Jig-Jig. 1930s. AD
Jig-Kut Puzzle. 1930s. AD
Jigleo: made by Lee Olney. Fig. 8-5
Jig-Map. Buffalo, N.Y. 1930s. AD
Jigolette: made by Emery Products
Jig-O-Lox: made by Dolly Folding Kite and Toy Co.
Jig-O-ramA: made by Gold Seal Toy Co. Fig. 10-21
Jig-Saw Letter: made by Play Make Products
Jigsaw Picture Puzzle: made by Picture Prints Inc.
Jigsaw Puzzles on Wood. 1930s. AH
Jig-Saw Puzzle Co. St. Paul, Minn. 1930s. AH
Jigso Cut Out Puzzle: made by Blue Star Publishing Co.
Jig-Tite Puzzle Library. Evanston, Ill. 1930s. AH, L
Jig-Zag: made by Louis F. Dow
Jim's: made by J. M. McGregor
Jim-Jam Picture Puzzle: made by James Hutchinson
Johnson & Johnson. 1940s. CH
Johnson Toy Co. Chicago, Ill. 1890s. CH
Johnson Wax. SD
Jointite: made by Criterion Jig
Jo-Jig. Hyannis, Mass. 1930s. AH
Jolly: made by Simonds
Jolly Jigsaws. 1930s. AH
Jones. Chagrin Falls and Cleveland Heights, Ohio. 1930s.
 AH
Jones, A. V. N. London, England. 1930s. AH. Fig. 7-34
Jones, C. R. & J. L. West Pittston, Pa. 1930s. AH, L
Jones, Helen Foss: copyrighted R & J Specialty Patience
 puzzles
Jones, Jesse Paper Box Co. Philadelphia, Pa. AD
Jones, Paul. Mishawaka, Ind. 1930s.
Jouets Vera. Paris, France. 1950s. CH. Fig. 8-24
Jr. Jigsaw Puzzle: made by Bradley; Whitman. Fig. 13-61
Judy Company. Minneapolis, Minn. Circa 1940s–1970s.
 CH
Jumble Jig. Philadelphia, Pa. 1930s. AD. Fig. 15-17
Jumble Jig: made by Gibson Art
Jumble-Jig: made by Earlville Novelty
Junior: made by Saalfield; Warren (Built-Rite); Whitman
Just Plain Bill: made by Kolynos
Just-for-Fun Puzzle: made by H. E. Foss. Fig. C-29

K & H Puzzles. Wollaston, Mass. 1930s. AH
K. D. S. Newark, N.J. 1930s. AH
Kable News Co., Mount Morris, Ill.: distributor for Fort
 Wayne Paper Box
Kamman, Harold. Minneapolis, Minn. 1930s. AH
Karnan. Sweden. 1980s. NH. Fig. 17-26
Kaufman, Oscar & Bro. New York, N.Y. 1930s. SD
Kay Cee's Library. 1930s. AH
Kay's Kut-Ups. Bristol, Conn. 1930s. AH
Kellogg Co. Battle Creek, Mich. 1930s. SD
Kellogg, E. L. New York, N.Y. and Chicago, Ill. Circa 1910.
 CD
Kellogg, Robert W. Inc. Springfield, Mass. 1930s. AH
Kelloggs. 1930s. ND
Kelvinator. Grand Rapids, Mich. 1930s. SD
Kenilworth Press Inc. New York, N.Y. AD
Ken-Way. Greenwood, R.I. 1930s. AH. Fig. 6-6
Kerk Guild. Utica, N.Y. 1930s. AD
Kern, Alice E. Portland, Me. 1930s. AH
Keystone. Boston, Mass. Circa 1950. CD
Keystone Picture Frame Co. Pittsburgh, Pa. 1930s. AH
Kiddie Puzzle Placques: made by Mayfair Games. Fig.
 16-34
Kimberly, Silas R. Altadena, Calif. 1930s. AH
Kindel & Graham. San Francisco, Calif. 1930s. AD. P. 47
Kinem Art Studio. Hollywood, Calif. 1920s. CD
King, C. Pierson. Navesink, N.J. 1970s. AH
King Features Syndicate. New York, N.Y. 1930s. CD
Kirk, Capt. G. G. Ely. Arlington, Va. 1980s. AH. Fig. 17-9;
 p. 18

A-Adult C-Child S-Advertising N-Novelty D-Die-cut H-Handcut X-Sliced L-Lending Library

A-Adult C-Child S-Advertising N-Novelty D-Die-cut H-Handcut X-Sliced L-Lending Library

A-Adult C-Child S-Advertising N-Novelty D-Die-cut H-Handcut X-Sliced L-Lending Library

Norrish, Alfred H. St. Louis, Mo. 1930s. AH. Fig. 9-4
Northwoods Workshop. Minocqua, Wisc. 1950s. CH
Novelcraft Co. Framingham, Mass. 1930s. AD
Novel-T Mfg. Co. Long Island City, N.Y. 1930s. AD
Novelty: made by Richburg
Novelty Distributing Co, Newark, N.J.: distributed Famous Comics puzzles
Novelty Game Co. New York, N.Y. Circa 1870. CD. Fig. 8-33
Novelty Jig Saw Puzzle. East Hartford, Conn. 1930s. AH
Nowell, Bessie J. Bangor, Me. 1930s. AH
Noyes, Helen Haskell. New York, N.Y. Circa 1909. AH. Fig. 10-6
Noyes, Ray. Oneida, N.Y. 1950s. AH
Nu-Friend: made by Andover Novelty Shop. Figs. 9-63, 16-40
Nu-Art. 1930s. AD
Nufad. Rochester, N.Y. 1930s. AH
Nutter, Frank H. Portland, Me. 1930s. AH
NYCE Quality Line. 1930s. AD

O'Brien, Jack: made by Wheaties
Object Lesson Publishing Co.: see E. J. Clemens
OK Picture Puzzle: made by Oscar Kaufman
Old Colony: made by Edward L. Little
Old Colony Novelty Co., Hingham, Mass.: owned by Robert England
Old Gallery: made by Alfred H. Norrish. Fig. 9-4
Old Grist Mill Dog Bread: made by Potter Wrightington
Old Masterpiece: made by Regent Specialties
Ole Million Face: made by Schoenhut
Olive. 1930s. AH
Oliver & Mark. Elizabethtown, Pa. 1930s. AH
Olman Music Corp. New York, N.Y. 1930s. SD. Fig. 13-24
Olney, Lee. Bath, Me. and Pinehurst, N.C. Circa 1909. AH. Fig. 8-5
Once-A-Week: see Dime Jig Saw Puzzle
O'Neil Associates, Inc. Chicago, Ill. 1930s. AD
Original Picture Puzzle Exchange. New York, N.Y. Circa 1909. L
Original Thread & Needle Shop. Boston, Mass. Circa 1909. AH. P. 32
Osborne Manufacturing Co. Dorchester, Mass. Circa 1950. CD
Ottmann, J. New York, N.Y. Circa 1900. CX. Figs. 8-28, 12-14
Our Gang: made by McKesson & Robbins
Our Gang Gum Puzzle. 1930s. SD
Overman. Colorado Springs, Colo. 1930s. AH
Oxford: made by Bradley, 1960s
Oxford Picture Puzzle. Circa 1909. AH
Oxford Specialty Co. Boston, Mass. 1930s. AD. Fig. 16-18

Pacific Coast Borax Co. New York, N.Y. 1930s. SD. Fig. 14-44
"Painted Dreams" cast: made by Battle Creek Food Co.
Painted Picture Puzzle: made by Novelcraft
Palatial. 1930s. AD
Palmer Chase Co. Oakland, Calif. 1930s. AD
Palmer, K. V. Portland, Me. 1930s. AH
Palmolive. 1930s. SD. Fig. 13-21
Pan-Am Pete: made by Pan-American Products
Pan American: made by Jaymar
Pan-American Products. New York, N.Y. 1930s. SD. Fig. 14-45
Pandora: made by Selchow & Righter. Figs. 7-13, C-11; p. 39
→Par Company Ltd. New York, N.Y. and North Massapequa, N.Y. 1931–80. AH. Fig. 2-9, C-37; pp. 16–17, 18, **34–35**, 57, 65
Paramount: made by Salem Puzzle Co.
Paramount Novelty Mfg. Co. Minneapolis, Minn. 1930s. AD

Paramount Puzzle Co. Milwaukee, Wisc. 1930s. AH. Fig. 8-21
Paris Picture Puzzle. Circa 1909. AH
Park, William J. Madison, Wisc. 1880s. CH
Parker, Edna C. South Manchester, Conn. Circa 1909. AH
Parker, Frederick G. Springfield, Mass. 1930s. L
Parker Brothers, Inc. Salem, Mass. CH, CD, AH, AD, NH. Figs. 1-13, 2-10, 3-2, 3-4, 6-26, 6-56, 7-31, 8-6, 8-21, 8-29, 9-3, 9-6, 9-10, 9-11, 9-16, 9-44, 10-16, 10-18, 10-24, 10-26, 10-29, 10-30, 11-10, 12-1, 12-20, 13-43, 15-20, 16-16, 16-22, 16-24, 16-37, 16-38, C-2, C-9, C-10, C-13, C-24, C-28, C-33, C-57; pp. 7, 8, 9, 10, 12, 13, 15, 17, 18, 20, 22, 25, **35–36**, 46, 67, 73
Parkhurst, V. S. W. Providence, R.I. 1850s. CX. Fig. 9-50; p. 6
Parkway Jigsaw Puzzle Library. Boston, Mass. 1930s. L
Parrish, Maxfield Series: made by Jig of Jigs. Fig. C-32
Party Puzzles: made by Galles; Parker; Sawyer; Ullman. Fig. 12-26
→Pastime: made by Parker Brothers, 1908–1959. Figs. 2-10, 3-2, 3-4, 6-26, 7-31, 9-3, 9-6, 9-16, 9-44, 10-16, 10-18, 10-29, 10-30, 12-20, 12-28, 15-20, 16-16, 16-38, C-2, C-10; pp. 12, 15, 18, 25, **35–36**, 57, 65, 68, 73
Patchwork: made by Ryther
Patchwork Picture Puzzle. 1930s. AH
Patience: made by R & J Specialty Co.
Patriotic. England. 1910s. AH. Fig. 6-11
Patriotic Picture Puzzle: made by Franklin Mfg. Co.
Paul, Edward P. & Co.
Pearl Publishing Co. Brooklyn, N.Y. 1930s. AD. Fig. 16-14
Peerless Flour: made by Stott Flour Mills
Peerless Puzzle Co. Philadelphia, Pa. Circa 1909. AH
Pegasus Picture Puzzle. Jenkintown, Pa. 1930s. AH
Penelope Puzzles. Aigle & Leysin, Switzerland. Circa 1930–present. AH, CH. Fig. 6-8, 8-9
Penick & Ford Ltd. 1930s. SD
Pep Pretzels. SD
Pepsodent Co. Chicago, Ill. 1930s. SD. Fig. 13-23; p. 26
Perfect Double: made by Consolidated Paper Box Co. Figs. 15-21, C-25
Perfect Games Co. Fort Wayne, Ind. 1930s. AD
Perfect Jig Puzzle: made by Perfect Games
Perfect Picture Puzzle: made by Consolidated Paper Box; Sheahan. Figs. 6-47, 9-53, 9-74, 15-21, 15-22, 15-23, C-25; pp. 20, **25**
Perfect Puzzle Mfg. Co. Mount Morris, Ill. 1930s. AD
Perfection: made by Bradley, circa 1909. P. 24
Perigee Press: see Putnam Publishing Co.
Perin Gift Co. Brookline, Mass. 1930s. AH
Perin Manufacturing Co. Brookline, N.H. 1930s. NH
Per-Plex Puzzle Co. Boston, Mass. 1930s. AH. P. 65
Perplexing Puzzles: sold by Solle's Bookshop
Perplexity Puzzles. Circa 1909. AH
Perplexity: made by E. E. Lewis; M. Richardson. Figs. 2-11, 9-29, C-30; pp. 12, 37
Perplexyu: made by Horsman. P. 11
Perrin, M. Brookline, Mass. Circa 1909. AH
Personal Book Shop. Boston, Mass. 1930s. L
Personal Finance Co. Bangor, Me. 1930s. SD. Fig. 14-46
Peter Pan Puzzle. New York, N.Y. AH
Peters Woodcraft. Baltimore, Md. 1930s. AH
Philadelphia Branch of the Shut-In Society: see Shut-In Society
Philadelphia Sunday Inquirer: see Sunday Inquirer
Philbrooke, Augustus. Shelburne, N.H. 1930s. AH
Phillips 66. Bartlesville, Okla. SD
Phillips, H. J. Branford, Conn. Circa 1909. AH
Photo Picture Puzzle: made by Davidson Brothers
Photographic Jig-Saw Puzzle: made by Eastman Kodak Stores
Picadilly Jig: almost certainly made by Bradley. Fig. 15-24
Pick Wick Wood Crafters. Glenside, Pa. 1930s. AH
Pick Wick Zig Zag. AH

A-Adult C-Child S-Advertising N-Novelty D-Die-cut H-Handcut X-Sliced L-Lending Library

A-Adult C-Child S-Advertising N-Novelty D-Die-cut H-Handcut X-Sliced L-Lending Library

RCK Map Series: made by Ruth Collins
Read, Harwood E. Newport, R.I. Circa 1909. AH
Readmore Rental Library. York, Pa. 1932–45. L
Real Art: made by Spencer Novelty Co.
Real Art Puzzle. 1930s. AD
Real Engraved Card Co. New York, N.Y. 1930s. AD
Real Puzzle: made by Hollenbeck Press
Reane, W. A. Circa 1909. ND
Rebus: made by Accounting Supply Mfg Co.
Recco: made by Real Engraved Card Co.
Recreation Hour Puzzle: made by A. B. Pond
Recreation Puzzle: made by Isaac C. Bishop
Recreation Puzzle Co. Cincinnati, Ohio. Circa 1909. AH
Recreation Series: made by Madmar
Red & Black Jig-Saw Puzzle. 1930s. AD
Red Bank Book Store Puzzle Library. Red Bank, N.J. 1930s. AH, L
Red Box. 1930s. AH
Red Seal. 1930s. AD
Red Seal Jig. 1930s. AH
Regal: made by Straus. P. 42
Regent Specialties. Rochester, N.Y. 1930s. AD
Reg'lar Fellers: made by Selchow & Righter. Fig. 13-48
Relaxation: made by Raritan Valley Mfg. Co.
Remembrance. 1930s. AD
Rent-A-Jig. 1930s. AH
Rexall Drug Stores. 1930s. SD. Fig. 13-66
Reynolds & Reynolds. Dayton, Ohio. 1930s. AD
Rialto Mfg. Co. Los Angeles & San Francisco, Calif. 1930s. AH
Richardson, Margaret H. (Mrs. Hayden). New York, N.Y. and Dennis, Mass. Circa 1909. AH. Figs. 2-11, 9-17, 9-29; pp. 12, **37**
Richardson, Miss. Concord, Mass. Circa 1909. AH
Richburg, C. W. N. Andover, Mass. 1930s. AH
Richfield Gasoline. 1930s. SD. Figs. 14-54, 14-55
Richmond's Art Puzzles. La Grange, Ill. 1930s. AH
Riggledy: made by Stafford & Ryan
Riker Drug Stores: distributor for Putnam Dyes
Riley, Perry and Lorraine. Carthage, Mo. 1930s. AH
Rinso. 1930s. SD
Riski-Raskal Co. San Francisco, Calif. 1930s. AD. Fig. 15-28
Roberts, Mary. Holbrook, Mass. 1930s. AH
Rockingham Hotel. Portsmouth, N.H. 1930s. SH
Rockland Puzzle. Short Beach, Conn. 1930s. AH
Roemer, Bernard J. Colorado Springs, Colo. 1930s. AH
Rogers Novelty Card Co. Boston, Mass. 1930s. ND. Fig. 16-4
Root, L. B. Canaan, Conn. 1930s. AH
Rose, Bernard S. 1930s. AH
Rosemont Cash Grocery. Pa. 1930s. SD
Rosenberg, Melrich V.: publisher of Duo-Jig
Ross, Richard. 1930s. AH
Rotato Chips: made by Grumette
Rothbard, Richard. Sugarloaf, N.Y. 1980s. Fig. 17-31
Routledge, George & Sons. New York, N.Y. Circa 1900. CH
Rowe and Emery. Waterville, Me. 1930s. AH
Royal: made by Royal Puzzlemakers; Royton Paper Products
Royal. 1930s. AD
Royal Fairco: made by E. E. Fairchild
Royal Jig Puzzle: made by Royal Novelty Co.
Royal Novelty Co. New York, N.Y. 1930s. AD
Royal Puzzlemakers. Roslindale. 1930s. AH
Royal Scarlet Coffee. 1930s. SD
Royton Paper Products. Buffalo, N.Y. 1930s. AD
Rubens, Morris: copyrighted R & J Specialty Co. Jig Saw puzzles
Rusco: made by Russell Mfg. Co.
Russell, Charles W. Auburn, Mass. 1930s. AH. Fig. 1-15
Russell Jig-Saw Puzzle Rental Library: see Wehrly
Russell Mfg. Co. Middletown, Conn. 1930s. SD

Russell News Agency. Sarasota, Fla. Circa 1950. ND
Ryther, H. A. Millers Falls, Mass. 1930s. AH

S & H Novelty Co. Atlantic City, N.J. 1930s. AH
S & S Distributing Co. Rochester, N.Y. 1930s. AD
S. G. S.: see Samuel Gabriel & Sons
S.-M. News Co., New York, N.Y.: distributor of Jig of the Week puzzles. Pp. 14, 46
S. P. Co.: abbreviation for Saalfield Publishing Co.
Saalfield Publishing Co. Akron, Ohio. 1900–1974. CD, AD. Figs. 1-7, 2-12, 6-43, 8-12, 10-5, 13-32, 13-39, 13-56, 13-57, 15-11, C-35, C-47; pp. 8, 9, **38**, 214
Saint Clair, Ida G. Newport, R.I. 1930s. AH
Salem Chemical & Supply Co. Salem, Mass. 1930s. AD
Salem Puzzle Co. (Subsidiary of Parker Brothers). Salem, Mass. 1930s. AH, AD. Fig. 8-21; p. 36
Salmon, J. Ltd. Sevenoaks, England. 1930s. AH, NH. Fig. 9-72
Salom, M. Boston, Mass. 1860s. CX. Fig. 6-36
Sanford, Franklyn R. Ansonia, Conn. 1930s. AH.
Sanford Puzzles. 1930s. AH. Fig. 10-17
Sanguinetti, Percy A. 1870s. CH
Santway Photo-craft. 1930s. AD. Fig. 9-24
Sapolin. 1930s. SD. P. 26
Savage, Mrs. A. R. Auburn, Me. Circa 1909. AH
Savoy. 1930s. AD
Sawyer, C. T. Fitchburg, Mass. 1930s. AH. Fig. 9-69
Scenic Art. Richmond, Calif. 1950s. ND
Scenic USA: made by Warren (Built-Rite)
Scenic: made by Tuco. Fig. 15-38
Schaeffer Ross Co. Webster, N.Y. 1970s. AD. P. 27
Schisgall Enterprises Inc. New York, N.Y. 1960s. AD
Schlicher, Geo. & Son. Allentown, Pa. 1930s. AD. Fig. 15-29
Schmuzzles, Inc. Chicago, Ill. Circa 1975–85. AD, CD. Fig. 17-32
Schoenhut, A. Phila, Pa. Circa 1930. NH, AD
Schranz & Bieber. New York, N.Y. 1930s.
Schreiner, C. L. Pasadena, Calif. 1940s. AH
Schwarz, F. A. O. New York, N.Y. 1862–present. AH. Fig. 16-7; pp. 25, 42
Scotch Scenic Series: made by Reynolds & Reynolds
Scott & Bowne. New York, N.Y. Circa 1900. SD
Scott Paper Co. Chester, Pa. 1930s. SD. Fig. 14-56
Scottie "Fit-Tight" Puzzle: made by Youngstown Printing Co.
Scottie Puzzle Co., Youngstown, Ohio: distributed Scottie "Fit-Tight"
Scrambled Eggs. Chicago, Ill. 1930s. NH
Sculptured: made by Straus. Fig. 9-73
See America First Picture Puzzle: made by Tichnor Bros. Inc. Fig. C-27
See-Saw. Circa 1909. AH
Selchow, E. G.: original name of Selchow & Righter. Figs. 8-36, 8-41; p. 38
Selchow & Righter. New York, N.Y. 1870–1988. CH, CX, CD, AH, AD. Figs. 1-6, 6-39, 6-57, 7-13, 13-48, C-11; pp. 7, 8, 27, 38–39
Serfass, Jerry. Niagara Falls, N.Y. 1930s. AH.
Seuss, Dr.: made by Esso; Random House. Fig. 17-20, C-56; p. 20
Seymour, Helen. Plainsboro, N.J. 1980s. NH. Fig. 17-13
Shackman, B. New York, N.Y. 1930s–present. CH, NH, AD. Fig. 3-7
Shafer Puzzle. Newark, N.Y. 1930s. AH
Shaffer, Jacob. Philadelphia, Pa. Circa 1860. CH. Fig. 6-24; p. 6
Shape: made by E. E. Fairchild. P. 27
Shapiro Candy Co., Inc. Brooklyn, N.Y. 1930s. SD
Sheahan, M. T. Boston, Mass. Circa 1909. AD
Sheffield: made by Bradley, 1930s and 1940s
Shelfer: made by Springbok Editions

A-Adult C-Child S-Advertising N-Novelty D-Die-cut H-Handcut X-Sliced L-Lending Library

Shenandoah Community Workers. Shenandoah Alum
Springs, and Bird Haven, Va. 1930s. AH, CH
Shepherd, Charles C. Passaic, N.J. 1880s. CH. Fig. 7-14
Sherwin Williams: see Silent Teacher. Fig. 1-19; p. 18
Shop of Gifts: see Louise Turner
Shorey Studio. Gorham, N.H. 1930s. L
Short Line Bus Co. 1930s. SD
Shreve, Crump & Low: made by Hale, Cushman & Flint
Shut-In Society. Philadelphia, Pa. 1930s. AH
Sifo. St. Paul, Minn. Circa 1960. CD, CH. Figs. 7-15, 9-55
Silent Teacher: made by Clemens; Hartman; Tackabury;
Union Sectional Map Co. Figs. 1-19, 2-13, C-51; pp. 18,
39–40
Silhouette: made by Holabird Co.
Simco: made by Simkin Paper Box Mfg.
Simkin Paper Box Mfg. Philadelphia, Pa. 1930s. AD
Simon & Schuster. New York, N.Y. 1930s–1950s. AD, ND.
Fig. 16-9
Simonds, Don. Winchester, Mass. 1930s. AH
Singer, Jasper H. New York, N.Y. 1890s. CX. Fig. 8-38
Singer Sewing Machine. Circa 1909. SD. Fig. 4-4
Sliced Animals, Birds, etc: made by Selchow & Righter
Sloan's Liniment. New York, N.Y. 1930s. SD
S-M News Inc., New York, N.Y.: distributor for Jig of the
Week Puzzle
Smart, Harold B. Hartford, Conn. 1930s. AH
Smith, Edward. Highland Park, Ill. 1930s. AH
Smith, Kline & French. Philadelphia, Pa. Circa 1920. AH
Smith, L. S. Acushnet, Mass. Circa 1909. AH
Smith, R. E. Taunton, Mass. 1930s. AH
Snellenburg's. 1930s. Fig. 14-57
Society: made by Davis; Putts; Ullman. Fig. 15-39; p. 11
Society. Circa 1909. AH
Society, The. Circa 1909. AH. Fig. 9-37
Sohio: see Standard Oil Co. of Ohio. Figs. 13-24, 14-59,
14-60; p. 19
Solle's Bookshop. Omena, Mich. 1930s. AH
Solvet: made by Walter M. Gaffney
Solve-Me-Rite: made by Liggett's Drug Stores
Somerset: made by Bradley, circa 1970
Sorosis Shoe Co. New Haven, Conn. Circa 1909. AH. Fig.
14-58
Southard, F. L. Groton, Conn. 1930s. AH
Southgate, Walter. Marshfield, Mass. AH
Spare Time: made by Dutton Noble; S & H Novelty
Spare Time Jig Saw Puzzle. 1930s. AH
Sparetime: made by P. J. Allen. Fig. 9-64
Spatcher, George I. Attleboro, Mass. 1930s. AH
Spear, J. W. & Son. Enfield, England and Bavaria.
1878–present. CH, AH. Figs. 8-10, 11-9, 17-14; pp. 8,
18, 22, 29, **40–41**
Spear & Co. Department Store. Pittsburgh, Pa. 1930s. SD.
Fig. C-52
Special Cut: made by Straus for F. A. O. Schwarz. P. 42
Specialty Adv. Service, New York, N.Y.: made various ad-
vertising puzzles. Fig. C-55
Spectator Puzzle Library. Melrose, Mass. 1930s. L. See
also Barnard-Clogston
Spencer Novelty Co. Springfield, Mass. AH
Spilsbury, John. London, England. 1760s. CH. Fig. 1-1; pp.
4, 6, 10, 21, 65, 77
Spooner, William. London, England. 1831–1854. CH. Fig.
7-35
Springbok: after 1967, a division of Hallmark. P. 28
Springbok Editions. New York, N.Y. 1964–67. AH, AD.
Figs. 2-14, 10-10, 10-28, 11-17; pp. 17, 28, 29, **41–42**,
50, 65, 68
Springfield Coal Co., Springfield, Mass.: distributor of
New England Coke
Spurr, Mabel Stewart. York Harbor, Me. Circa 1909. AH
Squarecut Puzzle Co. New York, N.Y. 1930s. AD. Figs.
13-8, C-41
Squibb. 1930s. SD. P. 26

Squirlijig: made by Bouvé
St. Clair, Ida G. Newport, R.I. 1930s. AH
Stafford & Ryan. 1930s. AH
Sta-Lock: made by Fairchild. P. 27
Stamford Novelty Prod. Stamford, Conn. 1930s. AH
Standard Crayon Mfg Co. Danvers, Mass. 1930s.
Standard Oil Co. of Ohio. 1930s. SD. Figs. 14-59, 14-60;
p. 19
Standard Puzzle Co. Boston, Mass. Circa 1909. AH
Standard Toykraft Products Inc. New York, N.Y. 1930s.
CD
Standees: made by Capitol Publishing
Stanfield, Michael Ltd. Bicester, Oxon, England. AH. P. 41
Sta-N-Place: made by Warren (Built-Rite)
Star Publishing Co. Chicago, Ill. 1890s. NX
Star Puzzle: made by Adult Leisure Products Corp. Figs.
13-14, 13-15
Stave Puzzles, Inc. Norwich, Vt. 1974–present. AH. Fig.
17-15; p. 18
Stearns, R. H. Boston, Mass. 1930s. AH
Stedman, Clarke K. 1930s. AH
Stephens Kindred & Co. New York, N.Y. 1930s. AD. Figs.
13-37, 13-41, C-48
Stevens, C. C. Auburn, Me. 1930s. AH. Fig. 8-16
Stevens, Fred H. Silver Lake, N.H. 1930s. AH
Sthen, Grace. Portland, Me. 1930s. AH
Sticku: made by Allen & Adams
Stoelting, C. H. Chicago, Ill. 1910s. NH. Fig. 6-27
Stoll, H. Stewart. New York, N.Y. 1930s.
Stortz, Robert. Emmaus, Pa. Circa 1950. CH. Fig. 7-7
Storyland: made by Harett-Gilmar Inc., 1960s. Fig. 7-8
Stott Flour Mills. Portland, Me. 1930s. SD
Stoughton Studio Workshop. Stoughton, Mass. 1930s. AH
Straight Arrow: made by National Biscuit Co.
Strand: made by Bradley, 1930s. P. 24
Stratford Show Print. Philadelphia, Pa. 1930s. AD
Stratford: almost certainly made by Bradley
Straus, Joseph K. Brooklyn, N.Y. 1933–74. CH, AH. Figs.
2-15, 8-23, 9-54, 9-73, 10-9, 15-30, 16-7; pp. 10, 18,
42–43
Strauss Mfg. Co. New York, N.Y. Circa 1910. CH, CD
Strever, J. C. Hartford, Conn. 1930s. AH
Studebaker. Circa 1909. SD
Subscribers Puzzle Co. Peabody, Mass. 1930s. AD
Sunday Inquirer. Philadelphia, Pa. 1930s. SD. Figs. 13-30,
13-38
Sun-Drop Golden Cola. 1960s. SD
Sunshine Lone Star Sugar Wafers. Made by L.-W. B. Co.
Super 400: made by Novelcraft Co.
Superior. 1930s. AH
Superior: made by Arthur Grinnell. Fig. 12-8
Super-Jig: made by O. B. Andrews Co.
Supreme: made by Tichnor Bros.
Surprise: made by Novel-T Mfg. Co.
Surprise Bag: possibly made by Einson-Freeman
Sussex: made by Bradley, 1960s
Swanton, K. M. Attleboro, Mass. 1930s. AH
Swastika: made by H. Noyes. Fig. 10-6
Swift & Co. 1930s. SD

Tableau: made by Cadaco-Ellis
Tablet & Ticket Co.: made by E. L. Kellogg
Tackabury, G. N. Canastota, N.Y. 1870s. CH. Pp. **39–40**
Talisman: made by Shut-In Society
Tamblyn Novelty Corp. New York, N.Y. NH
Tantalizing Teaser: made by Hanchett
Tasty Cake. 1930s. SD
Taylor Atkins Paper Co. Burnside, Conn. 1930s.
Teaser: made by Harter
Technicrat: made by Puzzle Guild
Tekwood series: made by Whitman. Fig. 15-48
Temple of Knowledge: made by A. Chamberlain

A-Adult   C-Child   S-Advertising   N-Novelty   D-Die-cut   H-Handcut   X-Sliced   L-Lending Library

A-Adult C-Child S-Advertising N-Novelty D-Die-cut H-Handcut X-Sliced L-Lending Library

Warsaw Paper Box Co. Warsaw, N.Y. 1930s. AD
Wastetime: made by Imbrie Mfg Co.
Watts, Harry L. & Edith M. Virginia Beach, Va. Circa 1960. AH. Fig. 8-43
Wayne Jig-A-Jig: made by Fort Wayne Paper Box
Web: made by E. E. Fairchild, 1960s
Webb, C. B. New York, N.Y. 1930s.
Webber, Chester E. Lisbon Falls, Me. 1930s. AH, L
Weber, Helen. Magnolia, Mass. Circa 1909. AH
Weber Pullman Bread. 1930s. SD
Wee McGregor. Circa 1960. AH
Wee Saw Puzzle Co. E. Greenwich, R.I. Circa 1909. AH
Wee-Chee Interlocking. Hartford, Conn. 1930s. AH
Weekly: made by Gelco; Pollock Paper & Box. Fig. 15-13; p. 14
Weekly Picture Puzzle: see Picture Puzzle Weekly
Wehrly, H. A. & Sons. Russell, Mass. 1930s. AH, L
Weiler Mfg. Co. Dunkirk, N.Y. 1910s. CX
Weinberger's Drugs. 1930s. SD
Weldon Wood Novelty Co. Lowell, Mass. 1950s. AH
Well Made Toy Co. Hampton, N.H. 1930s. AH
West Side Woodworking Shop: see C. R. & J. L. Jones
West, W. Frank. Newport, R.I. Circa 1909. AH
Wester Printing & Lithographing Co.: original name of Western Publishing Co.
Western Publishing Co. Racine, Wisc. 1907–present. AD, CD, CH, ND. Fig. 17-21; pp. 8, **47–48**. See also Whitman.
Western Toy & Novelty Co. Chicago, Ill. Circa 1900. N. Fig. 16-36
Westinghouse. 1930s. SD
Westoner, Ernest. AH
Whatami Puzzle Co. Arlington, Mass. Circa 1909. AH. Fig. 8-30; pp. 11, 12
What-Fun Picture Puzzle. 1930s. AH
Wheatena: made by Brother Cushman
Wheaties. 1930s. SD. Fig. 14-72
White Baking Co. 1930s. SD
White Box Picture Puzzle. Circa 1909. AH
White Mountain Picture Puzzles. Woodsville, N.H. 1930s. AH
White Rose Tea. 1930s. SD
White Sewing Machine: see Silent Teacher. Fig. C-51; p. 18
Whiting, Susan A. New Bedford, Mass. Circa 1909. AH
Whitman Publishing Co.: subsidiary of Western Publishing Co. Figs. 2-19, 7-12, 7-23, 7-26, 7-30, 9-14, 11-21, 13-3, 13-4, 13-7, 13-9, 13-25, 13-52, 13-58, 13-59, 13-61, 13-64, 13-68, 15-45, 15-46, 15-47, 15-48, C-7, C-40; pp. 8, 20, **47–48**, 68
Wicker Toy Mfg. Co. Columbus, Ohio. 1930s.
Wiggly Jig Pict Puzzle. Oakland, Calif. 1930s. AD
Wig-Saw. Philadelphia, Pa. AD
Wilder, Margaret. Circa 1909. AH
Wilder Mfg. Co. St. Louis, Mo. 1930s. AH, CD, CH. Figs. 13-1, 13-12, C-14
Wilke's Laundry. 1930s. SD
Wilkie Picture & Puzzle Co. Dayton, Ohio. 1930s. AD. Fig. 9-67
Willard, L. M. Keene, N.H. 1930s. AH
Williams, Sherwin: see Silent Teacher
Williamson, Lydia H. West Chester, Pa. 1950s. AH. Fig. 11-13
Williamson-Haffner Co. Denver, Colo. Circa 1909. ND
Wilmarth, H. T. AH
Wilson, R. H. Thomasville, N.C. 1930s. CH

Windsor Jig: almost certainly made by Bradley
Wire, Robert J. York, Pa. 1930s. AH
Wisconsin Toy Co. Milwaukee, Wisc. 1930s.
Witch: made by Salem Chemical & Supply Co.
Wizard: made by Radin-Steffens and Co.
WLS Prairie Farmer. Chicago, Ill. 1930s. SD
Wolfe Brothers. Harrisburg, Pa. 1930s. AH
Wolverine Drug Products. Detroit, Mich. 1930s. AD
Women's Educational and Industrial Union. Boston, Mass. Circa 1909. AH. Fig. 7-20
Womrath's Library Shop. New York, N.Y. 1930s. L
Wonder: made by Gabriel; Gebhart Folding Box
Wood: made by Bradley, 1938–40. Fig. 15-6
Wood, Henry F. Boston, Mass. Circa 1909. AH
Wood, Herman. AH
Wood Masters: made by Trojan Sporting Goods
Woodcraft Studio. Middletown, Conn. 1930s. AH
Wooden Jigsaw Puzzle. 1930s. AH
Woodkrafter Kits. Yarmouth, Me. 1980s. ND, CH. Fig. 17-33
Woozy Jig: made by J. R. Brundage
WOR: made by Thom McAn
Worcester Salt Toothpaste. New York, N.Y. 1930s. SD
Worcester Woman's Exchange. Worcester, Mass. 1930s. AH
Worcester-Powers Coke Co., Worcester, Mass.: distributor of New England Coke
World in Color: made by Playtime House
World Syndicate Publishing Co. Cleveland, Ohio and New York, N.Y. 1930s. ND. Fig. 16-13
Wright, J. L. Chicago, Ill. 1930s.
Wrobel Brothers. Sprakers, N.Y. 1930s. AH
Wunderlich, R. New York, N.Y. 1930s
Wyvern Picture Puzzle. Chicago, Ill. 1930s. AH

X-L-ENT Jigsaw Puzzle. Waltham, Mass. 1930s. AH

Yale: made by Lederer
Yankee Cut-Ups: made by Alden L. Fretts. Figs. 6-34, 9-76; pp. 27–28
Ye Squirlijig: made by Bouvé. Figs. 9-47, 10-27, C-20; p. 23
Yeaton, Abbie. Conway, N.H. 1930s. AH
Yeaton, H. L. Conway, N.H. 1930s. AH. Fig. 9-66
Yells, Fred M. & Son. Geneva, N.Y. 1930s. SD
YLDR: trademark for Wilder Corp
Yogi Bear's Delicious Honey Fried Chicken. 1960s. SD
York: made by Bradley, 1960s
Youngstown Printing Co. Youngstown, Ohio. 1930s. AD
Your Favorite Funnies Jigsaw Puzzle: made by Jaymar. Fig. 13-35
YWCA Puzzle Exchange. New York, N.Y. Circa 1909. L

Zag-Zaw: made by Tuck. Figs. 2-16, 6-13, 15-33; p. 44
Zane Grey series: made by Whitman, 1940s. Fig. 15-46
Zeitvertreib Co. Waterbury, Conn. Circa 1909. AH. Figs. 10-33, 12-24
Zig Zag Puzzle Co. Chicago, Ill. 1930s. AH. Fig. 8-18
Zigzag Puzzle Co. London, England. 1910s. AH. Fig. 6-7
Zig-Zag: made by Hathaway Press; Parker Brothers; Transogram; Zigzag Puzzle Co. Figs. 6-7, 9-11
Zig-Zaw: made by Pleasent (sic) Pastime Co. Fig. 15-25
Zimmerman. Chicago. Circa 1909. ND
Zion Candy Industry. Zion, Ill. 1930s. SD
Zulu Mfg. Co. Battle Creek, Mich. 1930s

A-Adult   C-Child   S-Advertising   N-Novelty   D-Die-cut   H-Handcut   X-Sliced   L-Lending Library

▪ INDEX OF PUZZLE TITLES

THIS INDEX includes both figure numbers and text references to the titles of puzzles, games, and books that are illustrated or discussed in Chapters 1 through 17. The Subject Index and the Index of American Puzzle Manufacturers, 1850–1970 will also help you to find specific references of interest. For example, brand names and series titles are listed in the Index of Manufacturers.

▪ Subject Index

THIS INDEX includes both figure numbers and text references for subjects covered in Chapters 1 through 17. When puzzles depicting certain subject matter are concentrated in a single chapter, the index lists the chapter rather than specific references within it. Puzzle titles and manufacturers are contained in separate indexes.